Praise the Lord
and Pass
the Contribution

ALAN BESTIC

Praise the Lord and Pass the Contribution

TAPLINGER PUBLISHING COMPANY
New York

First published in the United States in 1971 by
Taplinger Publishing Company, New York, New York

Library of Congress Catalog Card Number: 77-155804

ISBN 0-8008-6460-3

To Geoff, who performs reasonable miracles at very competitive prices and sometimes for nothing.

CONTENTS

'Avoid as you would the plague a man of God
who is also a man of business.'

*St Jerome, through courtesy
of Dr Sheldon Hendler, who insists
that he found the quotation in a
scientific journal in the University
of California.*

PREFACE

IN the beginning, if I may plagiarize without being thumped by a thunderbolt, I thought it was a simple question. How do men of God acquire the coin of Mammon and how do they spend it? Yet, when I asked, I ran into barbed wire entanglements that would have ripped the hair shirt off a medieval monk.

Most religious leaders and evangelists, I found, will plunge fully mitred or mohaired, into the Old or New Testament and surface with a text to fit any subject from space travel for pregnant women to sex education for minority groups under seven. Given the measurements and a suitable love offering, some would provide, post-paid, money back if not satisfied, plastic reproductions of the tablets from the Mount, guaranteed indistinguishable from the first edition, now out of print or out of chisel.

When I mentioned financial statements, however, they began to twitch and with a rare unity of voice hinted that I should go and wash my tongue. Then, as if saddened by their own intolerance of the moment, they explained gently that there are no pennies in Paradise, that the entrance fee cannot be paid in cash, nor even with a credit card, golden for executives only.

That coyness about currency I encountered on a pilgrimage which took me zig-zagging from New York to New York, via Chicago, Minneapolis, San Francisco, Los Angeles, Del Mar, Modesto, Tucson, Miracle Valley (believe me or believe me not), Tulsa, the Mississippi Greenville, Atlanta and the South Carolina Greenville. Despite the barbed wire, I soon learned that it is easier to sell religion than most earthly goods, perhaps because there are no trial runs, no sample weekends in heaven as guests of the firm. Those who buy bits of Florida blind and find that they own swamps, can sue or set fire to the real estate office. Those who buy eternal life after reading glossy brochures, must wait until they die before checking the small print against the promised land.

Here, indeed, is a thriving business. Those who guide it with smooth reverence can whip up enough dollars for a moon-shot—which some fundamentalists might think would be a step in the right direction—despite the fact that they bewail their poverty perpetually or perhaps because they bewail brilliantly. A few use the money to help the under-privileged. Some buy their own, personal, earthly paradise. Most put it in stocks and shares and property and banks and watch it breed. Talk to them about hungry children or sagging slums and they will weep but seldom will they help. After a couple of millennia, they have begun timid chat about the Church's place in the social structure; but so far there has been little action.

I chose America for my mission because its people are interested in religion and like to shop around. Being a bastion of free enterprise, it nourishes many emporia, offering a wide variety of choice. England is so conservative about its churches that its people seldom visit them, though there are signs of change. Billy Graham's fine religious repertory company has packed English arenas. The Mormons and the Jehovah's Witnesses, both American bred and trained, are making dramatic headway on Saxon soil. One day the nation may be evangelized, American style, for many patterns cross the Atlantic; but at the moment it is an underdeveloped market, dominated by staid monopolies.

Should the scene change, the English will discover, as I discovered in America, that free enterprise in the religious field is no freer than it is in any other sphere. In fact it can be very expensive indeed.

ALAN BESTIC

Woking, Surrey
13 April 1970

1: HI-FI HEAVEN

I lay on my back, floating in a variety of heavens, pulverized by paradise, which was pouring in on me from all directions. Here was a celestial package deal, delivered absolutely free without even a tiny down payment of martyrdom.

There was the heaven of the Californian sun, a very special brand which, I suspect, is manufactured locally. It beamed down on me, braising me gently, firmly, but never burning, providing constant running hot air, its flow unsullied by cloud or wind.

There was the month—November. In New York they were freezing, scampering miserably from one centrally heated haven to another. In London the creeping damp was gnawing at a million bones, fogging windows and minds, freezing sullenly on the roads; and there was I in Del Mar, just north of San Diego, luxuriating in selfish thoughts of those poor people so far away.

There was the private swimming pool, which kept me afloat, cosseting me like an electric blanket. In California, of course, such luxuries are part of life, like food and clothes and income tax; but to me, poor, pallid creature from the wastelands of Europe, they were little miracles which mortals did not deserve, but should enjoy before the gods whipped them away.

All this and another heaven, too, oozing over the blue, blue waters from a transistor radio on the shore; for this was Sunday, the day when the revivalists of the air dismiss all frivolous, earthy, earthly programmes and flood the wavelengths with cosy promises of joy to the accompaniment of softly muted cash registers.

The words lapped over me, fascinating me by their sheer weight and persistence. The warm, kind water broke the sequence from time to time; but that did not matter, for the tone, the mood, the message never changed, no matter who was plugging what particular brand of faith. Love and peace came over by the bucketful, laced occasionally with sadness, but devil a mention—if I may be excused the phrase—of hell or hate.

I flipped my toes gently and listened to a strong, manly voice that reached me in snatches through the ripples: 'This is Brother Burble . . . I was a sick man last September . . . The doctors said I would never see another sun . . . Then God made me whole.'

Burble? Bubble? Marvel? What is in a name, when there is so much fleece-lined truth to be told? He faded, anyway, as the programme changed, and was replaced by another voice, anonymous this time, soft, persuasive, trusting, for here was the commercial:

'Help us send this beautiful message to more and more people. Help us with your love offering ... anything you can afford ... even just one dollar.'

A heavenly choir sang heavenly music, inspiring the love that inspires an offering. Then the dial above me spun again and a woman's voice, soft, gentle and sodden with purity, was telling a story that would have melted the purse strings of a Wall Street banker, provided he had downed enough martinis.

There was this poor woman who had saved and saved to send her son to college so he could be a doctor. But what did he do? He married this school teacher and they came home to live with Momma.

And then do you know what happened? That school teacher said that Momma would have to go—go from her very own home. She was a nuisance, said this wife. She spoke badly and taught the children bad grammar. So out she went.

She would be struggling on her own still, but for a miracle. One day she wrote to Brother Burble.* He prayed that those young people would have a change of heart. And you know what? The very next day they asked to have her back and now they're a happy, harmonious family.

A splendid choir played her out, voices soaring at the thought of those hard hearts melting. I submerged, torpedoed by this incredible performance that was so much like a marriage between *East Lynne* and the Red Army choir; and at the same time I marvelled at the men and women who made this unlikely union not only possible, but very nearly plausible.

I surfaced to be greeted by another voice with yet another message: 'Have you got money troubles? Job troubles? Mother Humble† is not God; but she has the gift of helping others. Ring her right now, if you are confused, depressed, disturbed, or even if you are just standing at the cross-roads of life, wondering what to do, where to go ...'

A new voice from yet another source, crooned, 'Send a dollar. Help her help others. These broadcasts, which have brought hope and happiness to thousands, cost so much, yet mean so much.'

The voices and the music rose and fell with the motion of the water, undulating, alluring, but never grating. They lulled me, but I listened and my wonder grew.

* Bubble, Marvel, Mangle, in the order of your choice.
† Bumble, perhaps, but certainly not Grumble.

'Do you want better relations with your loved ones . . .?'

'Has your wife taken herself a sweetheart . . .?'

'Is your family rejecting you just because you are old . . .?'

'Does your husband drink too much . . .? Is your son in the demon grip of narcotics . . .?'

'Do you want to meet Sister Salvation in person? Come to her church next Sunday at three p.m. Come and find comfort and joy. Hear her prayers that can wash away your money worries.

'Only a dollar to a dollar fifty at the door . . .'

A dollar to a dollar fifty. Eight to twelve shillings. I thought of the surreptitious sixpences sliding on to the collection plates in British churches; but my thoughts were soon drowned by the transistor, by the choirs, the spirituals, the voices, coaxing so casually and I climbed out of the pool, saturated by much more than those blue, blue waters.

My host switched off the radio. Deliberately he had been spinning the dial, spraying me with revival, soulful over-save. I said to him: 'Who listens to so much for so long? Who gives when so many are asking? Don't they feel like kids in a supermarket devoted entirely to sweets?'

'Who listens?' he said. 'Mostly the shut-ins, the old who have out-lived their friends and are ignored by their relatives. Then there are the simple and the unhappy, who are offered hope and comfort—and all for a dollar. They send away for their lucky charms and their prayer sheets, their booklets and their spiritual recordings at bargain prices and they are happy when they get them. If the bargains don't work mir-acles, they probably reckon that life would have become a damn sight worse without them.

'But don't think of it as a supermarket. There are many shops and they compete hard for customers, all quite convinced that their product is the best. It may be argued that they promise the impossible; but remember that the main commodity is hope, which can't be weighed or measured.'

'But surely they get some complaints,' I said. 'Surely some customers kick up because their dreams haven't come true?'

'Very seldom. And the few that do are told, presumably, that they didn't pray hard enough. Or that they hadn't enough faith. Or that they didn't give enough to God.'

He had posed very briefly the problem that I had faced since my arrival in America and would continue to face throughout my stay: is this high-pressure sale of hope ethical or unethical, a massive confidence trick or a service that helps the lonely and the needy?

The answer depends on the quality of the product and on the sales technique. Some salesmen may say that all is fair so long as souls are saved and that in an ultra-materialistic world this difficult job costs money. They will insist that the ethics become questionable only when the money becomes more important than salvation. Unfortunately some seem to find difficulty in gauging when this point has been reached. Even more regrettably, a few seem to have forgotten all about the souls, so engrossed have they become in the highly complex job of finding the money to save them.

One way or another, it has become a multi-million dollar business, as I discovered soon after I arrived in New York from London. There in Washington Heights, a crumbling, wall-peeling area, I had my baptism of hellfire and heavenly bliss, skilfully blended into a chocolate-coated pill that thousands were clamouring to swallow; and, appropriately perhaps, my initiation took place in a 10,000,000-dollar converted cinema, an ornate, pre-war, pre-television dream house, dating back to the days when the cinema was almost a social service, that swept away drabness for a few hours and a few cents.

Today it remains a dream house in an area that still needs magic. It is the headquarters of the Reverend Frederick J. Eikerenkoetter II, known to his followers as Rev. Ike. He is the magician now, a handsome black preacher,* who outshines the Gables and Garbos and Astaires of yesterday, the Presleys, the Brandos, the Streisands of today. Here is a spellbinder, dispensing jet-propelled religion, high-speed hallelujahs, a Message that throbs and overwhelms and makes the mild, almost apologetic manners of more orthodox clerics seem as exciting as watered milk.

When I attended Service at his church, which he has called the United Palace, he was not there, but in Cincinnati, Ohio, half-way through a tour that had taken him barnstorming from Atlanta to Philadelphia to Cleveland and ultimately delivered him unto Houston and Dallas before a triumphal reappearance in New York. Wherever he went he held what he called Miracle Deliverance Meetings, which were described as gatherings where 'many people who have been given up by doctors or were suffering with cancer, T.B., heart trouble, nerves,

---

* I refer to his colour merely because most of the clerics mentioned in this book are white. I do not wish to be either biased or racist.

arthritis, strokes, mental conditions and other disorders are being healed and helped through Rev. Ike's ministry'.

Though I was sorry to miss him, the performance I saw was far from dull. His stand-in—an entranced lady whispered to me that his name was Brother Love—was no great crowd-puller compared with Rev. Ike, but certainly he was a trier with alarming energy and panache, a man who fought all the way for the funds which, he said, would please the Lord so much.

My first impression, when I arrived, was that the old place had not changed a bit since the distant days of cine-variety. A cinema organ was fluting away and a fine blues singer was pouring his heart and his soul into a number that had his audience swaying in their seats.

First impressions, however, are usually deceptive. The song had a top-ten beat; but it was a hymn. The audience seemed scarcely swingers. They were neat, but not groovy, three or four hundred strong, mostly middle-aged women in shapeless, drab overcoats and hats like German helmets. Yet there they were, lapping up music that would have made many a British vicar barricade himself in his belfry.

That, however, was merely a warmer-upper, as they say in my native Dublin. The real performance began only when the star appeared, Brother Love in person, a tall, handsome figure in a shining, whiter-than-white suit, Gabriel in modern dress. The organ thrumped out a long, loud, welcoming chord, an electronic ta-rah, and immediately he swung into action with all the verve—if not the star quality—of Sammy Davis, Jnr.

Microphone in hand, he paced the stage, thundering out his message of joy and hope and heaven. The chandeliers may have shuddered; but the audience, far from wilting beneath the weight, the power of his words, flowered before him.

'Are you free from sin and free from pain?' The voice was commanding, yet intimate, embracing them rather than assaulting them. 'You can be. You can be. You can be orderly in your minds. Hallelujah!'

'Hallelujah!' they echoed. 'Praise the Lord!'

'You feel like shouting? You feel like singing?'

The questions were rhetorical, for they were his now after a few minutes. He had them on their feet, hands fluttering in the air, heads flung back, voices high with excitement. 'Yeah, yeah, yeah!' they shouted and sang. 'We love you, Jesus.' The organ matched the mood, growing louder and louder, urging them into something near to ecstasy.

For some it was too much—or perhaps just enough, for this could have been just what they were seeking that Sabbath and every Sabbath. A frail little old lady began dancing in the aisles, eyes closed, hands fluttering high, body swaying backwards and forwards from the waist, entranced by the mood that had been manufactured so quickly and with such expertise.

'Glorify your Father who is in heaven,' yelled Brother Love. 'But heaven is inside us all. Right now turn and tell your neighbour that. Heaven is inside us all. The Lord IS here right now.'

Somehow he managed to insinuate several syllables into the word 'is', transforming it into a firm caress. They turned to each other, clasped each other and chanted, convinced and content: 'The Lord IS here right now!'

I was clasped, too, by a large, plump lady in front of me. I did not reply when she intoned the message, but she did not notice. Nobody noticed and certainly not the little old dancer in the aisles. She had stopped her jiving. Now she simply stood, her body jerking spasmodically, seeing nothing, hearing nothing, not even Brother Love, whose handsome face was gleaming with sweat, whose voice was driving on and on and on.

'God is waiting for us. God is waiting for us.' The congregation took up the phrase, clapping to the rhythm of the words, a complete unit now, a million miles from the grey streets outside. Somewhere someone began to beat a tambourine. Out into the aisles they began to spill, matronly figures jiggling, voices raised in shrill moans of devotion. They were sent, spiritually and sensually and the sight of them would have filled many a minor pop group with envy and admiration. Here was the Beatle touch, the magic. Here, too, of course, was a tinge of the jungle, but they were happy, immensely happy and Brother Love, who knew it, who felt it, intended to keep them that way.

'Hallelujah!' he shouted. 'God moves. Can't you feel it? Sickness has to go. You've no reason getting sick when others are getting well. JEEESUS says it. He's our King, our hero. Isn't that so?'

'Jeeesus!' they chorused. 'He's our King, our hero. Jesus, we love you, we love you!'

'What did St John say? He said: "Wilt thou be made whole? The verdict is yours." He meant that spiritually, mentally, physically and financially.'

Financially. I wondered whether the moment had come, whether these people, captured completely now, were about to be asked to prove their love of Jesus with cash; but Brother Love was not quite ready yet.

'If you want to be made whole,' he said, 'we've a healer round here. While He's healing one, He's healing others. He never runs out of supplies. Wilt thou be made whole? The verdict is yours!'

Gradually he began to explain how that verdict could be reached. His talk now was of giving, not of receiving, of making sacrifices for the Lord; but inevitably it got to the point. In a voice that was tender, pleading, but heard clearly by every member of that congregation, he said: 'Help make His heart feel great. Help this work go on. Come forward all those who will give twenty dollars to the Lord.'

Suddenly I saw for the first time the white buckets in front of the stage behind a vast vase of gladioli. This theatre, its atmosphere charged with religious fervour verging on hysteria, was no place for discreet collection plates. It needed, it demanded money by the bucketful; and it was going to get it. I watched about fifteen people, far from rich, judging by their appearance, move forward. Each of them dropped what is about £8 in English money into the white buckets of Rev. Ike.

Brother Love, however, was only beginning. 'Come forward,' he pleaded, 'all who will give fifteen dollars to the Lord. He will bless your pocket book and your bank roll.'

About twenty moved forward and then we were down to the ten-dollar bracket with Brother Love exhorting, praising, sometimes chiding, but all the time using the techniques of a Petticoat Lane salesman, a small town auctioneer. Always he seemed on the verge of saying: 'Walk up, folks, you'll never get a bargain like this again.' Perhaps that was what he was thinking and sincerely, too.

The ten-dollar call brought about fifty forward and now it was time for a change in tactics. With the faintest tinge of disapproval in his voice, a 'this-hurts-me-more-than-it-hurts-you' tone, he said: 'All those who can give five or three or just one dollar, stand up. Believe in God to work a miracle—bless your hearts.'

The sheep were being separated from the goats. Slowly the poor ones stood. I watched them and I wondered whether they were believing that God would work that miracle for them; or were they feeling an inner shame because they had to stand in public and reveal themselves too mean to give the Lord more than a measly few bucks and this after they had just been told the obvious, pulsating Truth that He loved them and was among them to wash away their woes and, indeed, their debts? It is hard to say, but after Brother Love had asked them to stand up and be counted, there was a late trickle of contributors towards the ten, fifteen and twenty dollar buckets by the altar.

Certainly, walking, standing or sitting, everyone was embraced by this final act in the Service. I was a sitter, bemused still by the spectacle; but my musings were interrupted by a gentle pressure on my right elbow. I turned to find that I was being nudged by one of these buckets, held by a haughty and handsome girl, who obviously felt that she was not going to cop much from this patent interloper, but that there was no harm in trying.

I remained seated and smiled up at her, but made no move towards my pocket. She did not return my smile. Instead she waited in excruciating silence for about fifteen seconds before searing me with a look of blistering contempt and turning away from this field that incredibly had remained fallow after all that had been said and sung.

I felt that the moment had come for me to leave. As I walked up the aisle, I did some rough mental arithmetic and came to the conclusion that Rev. Ike's ministry had benefited to the extent of something short of two thousand dollars, or about £800, from a service that had lasted just over an hour; but obviously no such sordid thoughts were in the minds of the congregation. They floated out after me, still smiling, still savouring the fading, fragrant excitement of it all, clinging as long as possible to its magic.

I spoke to a few of them. Did they go every Sunday? Yessir . . . wouldn't miss it. Had it been a big meeting. No . . . not really, they told me. When Rev. Ike was there in person, the place was packed. Then it was really wonderful with every one of those 5,000 seats occupied and every single person there, praising the Lord. I nodded in agreement, but my mind was straying. I was wondering how many white plastic buckets would be needed to receive the donations of such a multitude. How many of them would go forward to give ten, fifteen, twenty dollars? How many would stand to give their love offerings in numbers from one to five? I abandoned the problem, not so much because it was hard, but because I found it a little unpalatable.

Nor, I learned, was he just a massive preacher, but a man of many facets, a pastor, I was told, whose prayers could bring about miraculous cures. One man was reported to have been cured after twenty-four years in a mental hospital. A woman claimed that she could walk again after a stroke had paralysed her legs. Another had been cured of diabetes and yet another of blindness.

The most intriguing story I heard, however, concerned a woman who had had chronic constipation for twenty years. While listening to one of Rev. Ike's radio programmes, she placed the transistor set on her stomach and from that moment on never a stroke of trouble did she have.

There seemed to be no end to the stories, no field to which this man's powerful prayers failed to reach. They brought relief not only where physical and mental ailments were concerned, but eased the pain of poverty, too. I was told, for instance, of a woman who needed money desperately. She asked Rev. Ike to pray for her and soon afterwards an aunt died, leaving her 70,000 dollars. Nobody could tell me what the aunt thought of that particular prayer, but at least somebody was happy about it.

Frequently he insists both in letters and otherwise that his prayers are absolutely free. He makes it clear, however, that the more people give to his ministry the more they will receive in return. Rev. Ike's prayers, in fact, are said to have brought new homes, cars, jobs, and farm equipment to the needy, to say nothing of the expenses that have been saved, when cures have obviated the need for expensive medical treatment.

Regular giving, he says, is the best way. 'Put God first, not last,' he urges. 'Put him ahead of your bills and your business. And don't give the smallest thing you can.'

Give, in fact, until it hurts, or you may slide off God's mailing list. In Rev. Ike, indeed, God has an efficient treasurer and an even more efficient estate manager. He can offer the faithful a product which comes in a variety of handy sizes and shapes, guaranteed to suit every need.

There is the Blessing Plan, for instance, which, I gathered, was aimed mainly at solving financial problems. Join hands with it and your dreams can come true. 'Write for it now,' says Rev. Ike, 'and you can stop being hard-up and beat down . . .'

Then there is the specially blessed Prayer Cloth, which is not only efficacious, but portable, too, a little piece of Rev. Ike, so to speak, that can be carried with you wherever you go and used whenever necessary. Like the Blessing Plan, it, too helps to heal mental, physical and financial illnesses and, of course, there is absolutely no charge, though the Rev. does suggest fairly strongly—and fairly frequently— that a little love offering will grease the wheels of heaven.

It certainly seems to pack a powerful punch. According to one report a man, dying because his throat had been cut, was healed when a thread from a Prayer Cloth fell accidentally on him. A woman who had had heart trouble for twenty-five years was cured by the Prayer Cloth; a husband who had left home returned three days after his wife had received the Cloth through the post.

My favourite story, however, concerns the woman who was having trouble with the Income Tax authorities. She claimed they owed her money and would not pay up. So she got herself a Prayer Cloth, put it in her mail box and the very next day found an envelope containing her Income Tax cheque, on top of it.

To move the Inland Revenue authorities on either side of the Atlantic is, in my view, a mighty miracle indeed.

Needless to say, I wrote for a Prayer Cloth—haven't we all got our tax problems?—but, being a poor foreigner travelling far in a foreign land, I enclosed no money. I asked also for a Blessing Plan because with the tax people, a double-barrelled gun is often necessary. In return I received a document entitled 'The Winning Combination by Rev. Frederick Eikerenkoetter II (Rev. Ike)'. The winning combination, I learned, was a phrase which read: 'I shall have this or something better.' There followed a stream of platitudes, urging me to have faith in God, and that was about it.

Was it a Prayer Cloth? Was it a Blessing Plan? I do not know and so far I have not woken up screaming in the night in a torment of doubt about that particular problem.

On one point, however, I have no doubt. The Rev. Ike's organization is making a lot of money. Not only does it own that 5,000-seat auditorium, but an office building seven floors high. It has been able to purchase the entire block, covering four streets; one side alone has retail stores, a restaurant, medical offices and other enterprises.

That is a substantial chunk of property. Obtaining it, however, does not seem to have overtaxed the financial resources of this remarkable outfit. It still has enough in the kitty—or should I say plastic bucket?— to buy time, often daily, on fifty-six radio stations which span not only the United States, but a fair slice of Canada, together with Bermuda and the West Indies.

On the other hand, Rev. Ike's followers, if the congregation I saw in the United Palace is a fair cross-section, are far from rich. They were mainly black and therefore their chances of getting any more than menial jobs were poor. Their opportunities for getting out of their dismal surroundings into more genteel areas would be, I would have thought, microscopic, for there would go the neighbourhood. Financial problems were part of their lives, but Rev. Ike with his Midas message, his stories of those whose worries wafted away at the flick of a Prayer Cloth, gave them hope. The majority present did not look as if they had been very heavily blessed financially and for a while I wondered whether they ever felt a twinge of disillusionment. The answer, of course, was no. For those who did not receive there was always the handy answer: 'You did not give enough to the Lord.' Or: 'You didn't obey the Blessing Plan.' How, after all, can a sick man get well, if he does not follow the instructions on the medicine bottle?

Does the Rev. Ike, therefore, prey on the very poverty of these people? It is true that he offers them riches which many, obviously, do not receive. It is equally true, of course, that he cheers them up every Sunday, brings a little colour into their grey lives.

Certainly his organization makes a lot of money by methods which I, personally, found both unsubtle and distasteful; but at least that is better than being subtle and distasteful and in my travels I was to meet quite a few in that category. They were, what is more, richer than Rev. Ike.

2: GOD'S JET SET

HENRY Ford revolutionized the motor car industry with his T Model, which brought a new excitement into millions of lives, even if it were only through courtesy of the back seat. Sister Aimee Semple McPherson did something similar for evangelism, giving it a happy, heady, emotional content that left the old-fashioned hell-raisers growling in half-empty tents. Today's religious jet-set preachers owe her a great deal, though I do not imagine that many of them would admit to that.

Whatever their views on her, however, she was a very remarkable woman of considerable vision. From 1921, when she founded the International Church of the Four Square Gospel, until her death at the age of fifty-four in 1944, she built an organization that was far-flung, spectacular and glamorous. Woven into its complex fabric were 420 churches in the United States and Canada; 36 mission centres throughout the world; a Bible training college; a network of Sunday Schools; a magazine with the intriguing title, the *Bridal Call Four Square;* and—away back in 1924, when radio was still in swaddling clothes—Station KFSG—Kall Four Square Gospel. It was only the third to be established in Los Angeles and its casually contrived call—or should I say 'kall' —sign reflected admirably her breezy, uninhibited attitude to a subject which too often in the past had been sombre and drenched with fear.

Whatever her methods, she certainly thrilled thousands, who saw her as a simple, inspired and very beautiful woman. They were oblivious to the golden touch of Madison Avenue ad-mass which tinged her mission. They responded readily and rapidly when she swept the dust from bare collection plates with her heart-warming, purse-splitting piece of plain-chant: 'Let's hear the rustle, not the jingle.'

There were thousands of others, of course, who failed to appreciate such brash, blatant appeals. Like her successors today, she was accused constantly of being no more than a publicity-seeking money-spinner. Always—again like most of her successors—she was buoyed up by a shrewd optimism that could turn seeming disaster to her advantage. Even when she was accused in court of staging her own kidnapping for propaganda purposes and the end of her church seemed nigh, she emerged unbowed and relatively unscathed.

So splendid, indeed, were her spiritual spectaculars, that she deserves a place in any book of this nature. I mention her, however, not so much for what she did, but because her star-spangled career marked the beginning of a new era of evangelism. She gave birth to a pattern, which forced its way rapidly from childhood, through adolescence until today it has reached plump, prosperous maturity. As the Model T Ford has been replaced by more powerful, more sophisticated machines, so Aimee, too, has been followed by evangelists who proclaim their faith with the aid of colour television, computers and all the latest toys of big business. Many times I saw these atrociously expensive scientific wonders at work; and occasionally I wondered what Sister would think of them, if she were to glance down from whatever blissful cloud she happens to be decorating.

What, for instance, would that rip-roaring, barnstorming preacher have to say about the Rev. Herbert W. Armstrong, Chairman of the World Wide Church of God, an organization with an annual budget of something in the region of 34,000,000 dollars,—over £14,000,000, twice that of the Billy Graham organization? Consider his record which, for my money, if I may be forgiven an ugly word, takes some beating, even in a land where sects grow so thick and so rich.

He is founder and Chancellor of Ambassador College, which has three campuses—one in Pasadena, California, one in Big Sandy, Texas and one in St Albans, England. He commutes between all three in his private executive jet, which is big enough to fly the Atlantic.

From the College in Pasadena flows an ocean of highly costly publications in superb colour, together with a weekly magazine, *The Plain Truth*, which is printed simultaneously in their own plants in Pasadena, Watford and Sydney, has a circulation of over two million and is published in English, Dutch, French, German and Spanish. Despite the fact that none of the publications carries any outside advertising, all are distributed free.

This monumental printed message is augmented by a radio network that covers, through 310 stations, not only the United States and parts of Canada, but Spain, Portugal, England (through Manx Radio), Guam, Okinawa, South America and the West Indies. Inevitably there is a television network, too, thirty-five stations strong, beaming the unique gospel of this unique organization to various parts of the North American continent.

Viewing such a spiritual complex from her celestial vantage point, Sister Aimee could not fail to be impressed. What would bewilder her, however, as it did me, is the fact that the annual budget of 34,000,000 dollars is raised without one appeal on sound radio or television, without a single request for alms in any of the publications which stream in such profusion from those highly professional editorial offices. No rustle is solicited, no jingle wheedled.

How does it happen? In an effort to unravel what was to me a financial mystery—or should I say miracle?—I telephoned the Pasadena headquarters and asked if I could speak to the Rev. Herbert W. Armstrong. I was told that he was visiting the English college, which in itself was an indication of his remarkable energy, for at that time he was seventy-seven years of age.

Instead they suggested that I might care to go along in the hope of meeting his son, the Rev. Dr Garner Ted Armstrong, who was, I learned, no mean substitute. The Rev. Herbert W. is Chairman of the Church. The Rev. Dr Garner Ted is First Vice-President. Father is founder, Chancellor and President of the colleges and Chairman of their Board of Trustees; Director of *The World Tomorrow* sound and television programmes; and editor and publisher of *The Plain Truth* and the Ambassador College Correspondence course. His son is Vice-Chancellor of the colleges; Vice-Chairman of the Board of Trustees; principal speaker on *The World Tomorrow* programmes; and Executive Editor of *The Plain Truth* and the Correspondence course. When first I learned of Garner Ted's eminence in the organization, I must admit that I toyed with the thought of nepotism; but when I met him, I found him shrewd, intelligent and self-assured, a sound man for all those jobs.

Before our meeting, however, I put in some extra homework on the Rev. Herbert. He was, I discovered, even more remarkable, perhaps, than Sister Aimee, though in a very different fashion. I doubt, indeed, if they would have got on very well together.

He was born into a Quaker family in Des Moines, Iowa, and began life as an advertising copy writer. Even in those early days he was a man of drive and initiative, to say nothing of faith.

The legend of his first, firm steps in his chosen career are well known to his followers. He went along to the *Daily Capital*, when he was eighteen, but did nothing so negative as to ask them for a job. Instead he told the manager of the 'want ad' department that he was entering the advertising profession and had decided to join his staff because he felt that there he could have the best chance to learn what it was all about.

He got the job—a tough one. He had to go from door to door, persuading citizens to insert small advertisements in the *Daily Capital*. Yet even to this dreary beat he brought a panache which Des Moines had seldom seen.

His first call, for instance, was to a woman who rented rooms. He did not ask her to advertise them in his newspaper. He asked whether he could see one. She let him in immediately, which meant that she could not slam the door in his face.

On the contrary, she welcomed him as a potential cash customer. When he saw the room, he praised it to the heavens, but explained that she had not been able to rent it because she had not advertised it properly. Before she had time to turf him out or call the cops, he had written a long, glowing piece of expensive prose on a blank advertising form. Dazzled, no doubt, by the sheer effrontery of the lad, she paid for the advertisement, which, incidentally, brought her all the customers she could handle.

Some time later he got himself a better job, not by asking for it, but by telling the advertising manager that he would report for work the following Monday. When the poor man tried to hold back the tide by muttering something about there being no vacancies, young Armstrong simply told him that he was talking nonsense, that his newspaper could not afford to do without him and that it was a crummy sheet, anyway. He reported for work the following Monday.

Later he was to tell his followers that the advertising business was fine training for his work in the ministry. 'God,' he said, 'was steering my formative years in a training I could never have obtained, had I gone through the customary universities and theological seminaries.'

Pushing and brash he may have been; but he also seems to have been successful. Certainly, apart from periods spent as one of the earlier public opinion pollsters, as a piano salesman and as a purveyor of mud packs, he continued his apprenticeship for the ministry through the medium of advertising. It was only after his marriage on his birthday in 1917 to Loma Millar, his third cousin, that God decided to edge his instrument closer to the action.

Loma, a Methodist, was a keen student of the Bible. One day she told her husband that her studies had revealed a startling truth. The Sabbath was not Sunday, but Saturday.

She could not have known then that she had just planted a seed which would bear exotic fruit in California, Texas, England, Canada, South Africa, France, Switzerland, Australia, the Philippines, South America and Germany, for Herbert's first reaction was fury. He told her straight that he was not going to have any religious fanatics cluttering up the house and that she was to stop that Saturday/Sunday nonsense right away. Loma, however, dug in her heels. To prove her wrong, Herbert dug deep in the Bible. When he emerged, he not only admitted that she was right, but came out with a few startling conclusions of his own.

He had discovered, he told her, that Christ was not crucified on Good Friday but on a Wednesday. He was not resurrected on Easter Sunday, but late on Saturday afternoon. Further probes into the Bible convinced him that what is known now fairly widely as the Christian Church was no more than Roman paganism; and since then he has preached some strong words about it and particularly about the Pentecostal Church, of which Sister Aimee was such a vital part.

He held, for instance, that some of its members were simply seeking physical and sensual pleasure, thrills and excitement under the deceptive illusion that they were pleasing God. It was, he said, plain lust of the flesh, a sublimated sex thrill.★

After that the Bible became Herbert's constant companion. Soon he came up with some even more startling revelations. He had found proof, he said, that the lost ten Tribes of Israel had migrated to north-western Europe, the British Isles and later to the United States; and, according to one admittedly hostile commentator, Walter R. Martin, he produced one mind-boggling theory to add weight to this argument. Martin quotes him as having explained it thus—and be careful how you tread because the words might confuse the simpler-minded, among whom I include myself:

The House of Israel is the covenant people. The Hebrew word for covenant is *beriyth* or *berith* . . . The Hebrew word for man is *iysh* or *ish*. In the original Hebrew language, vowels were never given in the spellings, so omitting the final *e* from *berith*, but retaining the *i* in its Anglicized form to preserve the *y* sound and you have the Anglicized Hebrew word for covenant, *brith*. The Hebrews, however, never pronounce their aitches. The Jew, even today, in pronouncing the name 'Shem', will call it 'Sem'. Incidentally this ancient Hebrew trait is also a modern British trait, so the Hebrew word for covenant would be pronounced in its Anglicized form as *Brit*.

Again the word for covenant man or covenant people would therefore be Brit-ish. So the true covenant people today are called the British. And they reside in the British Isles . . .

★ Similar thoughts darkened my mind when I attended Pentecostal services; and some of Sister Aimee's writings undoubtedly had a heavy sensual beat. I pass no judgement, however, for I am not a psychiatrist, an evangelist or a Kinsey.

They are descended from Isaac and therefore are Isaac's sons. Drop the *i* from Isaac—vowels are not used in Hebrew spelling—and we have the modern name, Saac's sons, or, as we have spelled it in shorter manner, Saxons.

As a keen if disenchanted, student of this remarkable theory, Walter R. Martin comments that Herbert Armstrong cannot read Hebrew, Aramaic or Greek. As a keen and enchanted Irish student of the English language, I must point out that they seldom drop their aitches from the middle of a word. Indeed, I can hear some of them muttering, Eliza Doolittle fashion: "Ave a 'eart, Dr Harmstrong—hespecially about Hisaac!'

Another Armstrong theory, quoted by Martin, will come as an even greater surprise to most British readers. It is that Queen Elizabeth II sits on the throne of King David of Israel, of whom she is a direct descendant. He is referring here to the Stone of Scone which, he holds, is really the stone which Jacob used for a pillow and which he took with him when he departed from Bethel. Later it came under the care of Jeremiah, the Prophet. Jeremiah took it with him to England, where it became the Coronation Stone for the British (Davidic) dynasty.

On that heady point of Biblical scholarship, Walter R. Martin commented: 'The disturbing scientific fact that the Stone of Scone has been examined and analysed and found to be a sandstone of a reddish or purplish colour with heterogeneous pebbles and of Scottish origin does not deaden the enthusiasm of Anglo-Israelites, who must make Jacob a native of Scotland and Bethel a suburb of London.'

As an Irishman, of course, I must remain neutral in this dynamic controversy. Apart from feeling disinclined to intrude in other people's arguments, I feel that we have troubles enough of our own. I must confess, however, that I would not mind at all hearing Buckingham Palace's views on this point.

From such small beginnings, anyway, are churches with annual budgets of 34,000,000 dollars built, though their construction, naturally, takes time. In search of a church which shared his beliefs, Herbert W. Armstrong studied first the Seventh Day Adventists and then the Seventh Day Baptists. Neither satisfied him and ultimately he joined with the Oregon Conference of the Church of God, under whose authority he was ordained in 1931. For a while he preached for a salary of only three dollars a week. A disagreement with the Conference, however, led him to refuse even that meagre sum and he might have slid back into the secularism of advertising for good . . . or, rather, bad . . . had it not been for a spectacular event in the late autumn of 1934.

KORE, the local radio station in Eugene, Oregon, devoted fifteen minutes every morning to a religious programme. Despite the fact that it was free time, offered by the station as a public service, few ministers applied for it.

One who did, however, was the Rev. Herbert W. Armstrong. He went on the air for the first time at 7.45 on the morning of 9 October 1934, and thus what was to become known internationally as the Radio Church of God was born. After no more than a few seconds of mike fright, he embraced this new medium lovingly and proved himself a superb radio preacher.

His popularity grew and grew. The professionals were baffled, but delighted with the magic of the man. Even Armstrong himself was surprised, though later he found in the Bible what seemed to him a logical explanation.

'God marks off time spaces, except for the week, by the movement of the earth, the moon and the sun in relation to one another,' he wrote in his autobiography. 'These mark the duration of the day, the month and the year. Also God divides time into nineteen-year time cycles—for every nineteen years these three bodies come into exact conjunction.'

One example he quoted was the way God 'opened a door for Paul' to preach the Gospel in Europe nineteen years after the apostle had begun proclaiming it. Another was the opening of the Radio Station KORE door in 1934, which Ambassador College researchers discovered was the end of yet another nineteen-year cycle; and then in 1953, again nineteen years later, the door to Europe was opened when Herbert W. Armstrong began broadcasting over Radio Luxembourg.

In other words God had anticipated using the radio in general and Herbert W. Armstrong in particular many aeons ago. With that imposing thought in my mind, I drove from Los Angeles to the heart of the matter, to Ambassador College in Pasadena, known as the City of Old Ladies because so many widows of millionaires have retired there.*
I entered the campus to be overwhelmed by vast modern buildings, magnificent, middle-aged mansions, undulating lawns and lofty trees and delicate, whispering fountains, the overall impression reminding me vaguely of the lush luxury of Forest Lawn, Hollywood's famous cemetery.

* It is called, also, the City of the Three Rs—Rich, Retired and Reactionary.

Suitably humbled by the grandiose surroundings, I went into what I took to be the administrative building and here again I found this atmosphere of costly, genteel dignity. Even the students seemed to glide along, as if they were on castors, protected from rude materialism by order and carefully restrained opulence.

One of them led me to the executive suite, disappeared discreetly and left me standing on a beige carpet so thick that its pile seemed to enfold my ankles. At a desk sat the secretary to whom I had spoken the previous day. Politely, softly, she told me that she was not quite sure whether I would be able to see Dr Garner Ted Armstrong that day, but suggested that I might like to wait a while.

I sat on a couch before an exquisitely elegant coffee table and gazed around at solid, sombre walls of dark, well-bred panelling. Here was no Forest Lawn mausoleum, but a carefully arranged marriage between a private museum and the offices of an extremely successful antique dealer with big business—very big business—lurking in the shadows, just waiting to create an eternal triangle.

That, certainly, was my first impression; and it was inspired in me, perhaps, by two aloof, impassive statues on my right-hand flank. They could have been richly clad Nubian slaves, but I am no expert. Thirsting for knowledge, however, and waving my ignorance around my head, I asked the secretary about their origin.

'Mr Armstrong got them from Harrods in London,' she said with a gracious smile. 'He knows them there. They always let him know when they have anything they think might interest him.'

It was a sobering thought, but it was interrupted brusquely. A door opened silently and an athletic figure in a mustard-coloured suit swept in, followed at a respectful, regulation distance by an entourage of underlings. His face bore a classic Californian tan. His crisply tailored hair was flecked impressively with grey and his movements, quick, decisive, were the accepted hall-marks of the five-star executive. The secretary rose and introduced me to the Rev. Dr Garner Ted Armstrong, at forty years of age First Mate of all I had been surveying.

Keen eyes dissected my face as I told him who I was and why I was there. When I had finished, he said swiftly: 'Have you seen our television shows, heard us on the radio?'

With some embarrassment I shook my head, but assured him that I had every intention of repairing that gap in my knowledge. Showing neither pleasure nor displeasure at this astounding confession and humble promise, he said: 'It's very difficult to find time for interviews. You must remember that I'm running a world-wide organization.'

Then, flicking a hand towards the aristocratic coffee table, he said: 'You'll find all the answers to all the questions you want to ask me there.'

I followed his finger. The table was strewn with copies of *The Plain Truth*. Resisting the temptation to suggest that he scarcely could know what questions I intended to ask, I said: 'I have travelled quite a long distance to learn about your church and your colleges. Naturally I would prefer to hear the story from you.'

He flicked a glance at his watch. Clipping his words economically, as if every second counted, he said: 'I'm flying to our Texas campus at nine o'clock tomorrow morning. If you want to see me, be here at eight.'

Then he was gone in a flurry of aides. I asked the secretary whether anyone else could talk with me about the college and immediately—for she was kindly as well as efficient—she picked up a telephone in an attempt to get me organized. A few minutes later I was being escorted to the faculty dining-room by a quiet, dark-suited member of the staff; and there in an atmosphere of velveteen calm, we sat down to a simple, but thoroughly appetizing lunch, served by thoroughly wholesome domestic economy students who, my host explained, were not only working their way through college, but learning the social graces, too.

After the meal I was handed over to yet another member of the staff, a tall, well-built, slightly breezy man, who with brisk efficiency took me on a tour of this fabulous campus. The rain poured down, putting California to shame, but my guide was undeterred. He sheltered me from the elements with an umbrella, while saturating me with facts, figures and vistas, leaving me convinced that here was a college the like of which I would never see anywhere else in the world, except, perhaps at Big Sandy in Texas or St Albans in England.

Dutifully I trotted after him around this glut of riches. Here, gleaming, almost arrogantly, was the new Hall of Administration, spacious lawns paying homage before it. There was the Loma D. Armstrong Academic Centre, facing on to sunken gardens and fountains, planned with mathematical precision in monumental tribute to she who began it all by needling Herbert into a deep study of the Bible. Round the corner was the cradle of the establishment—Ambassador Hall in South Orange Grove, now a science laboratory, library and classrooms, set amid palm trees and exotic flowering shrubs. Once it was the property of Hulett C. Merritt, the largest stock holder in United States Steel Corporation, and college rumour whispers that once he stored black-market sugar in the basement. My guide smiled at that story and went on quickly to explain that this proud building was the first property bought by Ambassador College. It was not, however, the last. The homes of four other multi-millionaires, built on this land that carries the highest tax rate in Pasadena, were bought later; and here the college had the advantage over the previous owners, for educational and religious organizations are beyond the clutches of the Revenue men.

I saw student lounges that many a five-star hotel would envy for their ponderously quiet elegance. I was shown the gymnasium with its three basket-ball courts and its tiers of seats that fold up into the wall, like spare beds. 'It holds 1,500,' murmured my guide. 'We have services and meetings here. It's part of the new Physical Education Faculty that cost a million dollars.'

Then, with scarcely a pause for breath, we moved on to another part of it—the Olympic-size swimming pool with its under-water viewing rooms, where spectators could get an eel's-eye view of the diving competitions. 'Our natatorium,' said my escort, 'is said to be one of the finest in Southern California.' I had not seen the others, but I was quite ready to agree with him.

Next came the recital hall that seats 266. 'There are student recitals here and combination recitals and faculty recitals,' I was told. 'We have a college orchestra and a college choir—a good deal of musical talent, indeed. Sometimes Dr Garner Ted Armstrong gets out his banjo and sits down with them for a sing-song.'

I brooded on that cosy thought for a second or two; but the sight of the Italian gardens washed it from my mind, and then that in its turn was obliterated by further wonders—the radio and television studios that beam their carefully polished messages to 45,000,000 on every continent; the publishing department with its massive, four-colour printing presses; the data processing centre; the $2,500,000 (more than £1,000,000) computer; the audio-visual aids; all cold in their efficiency, but cradled in the carefully planned warmth of the scene outside with its burbling streams, its fountains, its giant, bronze sculpture of swooping egrets, fashioned by David Wynne of London Town.

I summarize, of course. There are many more colourful petals to this enormous, full-blown flower of the educational world—so many, indeed, that the scent of it all becomes overpowering after a while. This report on my conducted tour, however, would be incomplete without a quotation from the college bulletin, which states blandly: 'On the original campus, forty-five magnificently landscaped acres in the heart of Pasadena's finest residential district, are the School of Liberal Arts and Sciences, the School of Education and the Graduate School of Theology. At present the campus is undergoing a $22,000,000 building expansion development.

'Ambassador College in Texas is, like its sister institutions, a co-educational college of liberal arts and theology. It was established in September, 1964, on a beautiful 2,500 acre campus 100 miles east of Dallas, near Big Sandy on U.S. Highway 80. It has its own paved 3,500-foot lighted air strip, equipped with unicom.*

'Ambassador College in England began operation in October, 1960. It is administered by the Chancellor and a Deputy Chancellor. It maintains identical standards with the same purpose and character as its sister colleges in the United States. It is, however, more international in student enrollment with students from the United Kingdom and other countries in Europe, from Australia, New Zealand, Canada, South Africa and India and from the United States . . . Some of the most beautiful gardens in England are enjoyed at the Ambassador campus and an expansion program of new buildings also is in progress there.'

Finally—with apologies to those with weak stomachs for such over-rich food—I feel that it is my duty to report that there is a $7,000,000 expansion programme under way at the Texas campus, to which, incidentally, is attached a 4,000-acre experimental farm which provides students both there and at Pasadena with meat, dairy products, eggs, poultry, vegetables and fruit. The wheat grown on the farm, I need hardly add, is ground into flour on the campus and turned into bread in the college bakeries.

I know that I was sated by the suave, smooth efficiency of it all by the time I returned with my escort to his office. The fresh memories of millionaires' mansions and antique furniture were being chased around my mind by statues of Nubian slaves from Harrods; and my host, as if he were reading my thoughts, said with a soft smile: 'Mr Herbert Armstrong likes fine quality and tries to inject this love into his students.' Weight was added to those words later, when I was shown the founder's office, where the carpets were even thicker than those in the

* Sorry, I don't know what 'unicom' is, either.

executive suite outside. A huge chair in dark leather stood empty behind a vast, magnificent desk. A brooding wooden elephant supported
an occasional table. A carved coffee table made that supporting *The
Plain Truth* outside seem almost tawdry; and surveying it all was a por-
trait of Loma, who died in 1967. On the desk to my surprise I saw two
leather-bound copies of *Don Quixote*. It is true that I had not met the
Rev. Herbert W. Armstrong, but from what I had heard and read of
him, I could not imagine him being interested in those who tilted at
windmills.

Back in the office of my guide, however, I was not concerned with
the problems of romantic Spanish knights of long ago. For the first time
since I had driven on to the campus that morning I was feeling a nip of
uneasiness in the air and frankly I was finding it refreshing after all the
balmy breezes.

The conversation had begun smoothly enough in keeping with the
surroundings. He had told me, for instance, that he was a Minister of
the World Wide Church of God as well as a member of the Faculty.

'I do public relations work and counselling work,' he had explained.
'I wear many hats. I don't have my own congregation, but I go out to
outlying congregations and speak to them.'

At that point I asked how he had become a member of the Church
and he told me: 'I was baptized and confirmed in the Lutheran Church.
Then I went to the Baptists. As a teenager I changed over to the Methodists, but I left them when a friend introduced me to the World Wide
Church of God. He had listened to one of their radio programmes.'

From there we moved easily to the immediate history of the Church
and the college. Formerly it had been called the Radio Church of God,
he told me, and had been incorporated under that name to avoid con-
fusion with other Churches of God. That seemed reasonable, for in the
Year Book of American Churches, a dozen of them are listed.

'Originally,' he went on, 'we were primarily a radio ministry. That,
however, is not entirely true now. So we are known as the World
Wide Church of God. We have full-time Ministers and we hire halls
for our meetings and so on. Our services, of course, are held on
Saturdays.

'We still do a great deal of radio and television work, mind you, *The
World Tomorrow* programmes. Our television productions, which are
sponsored by the college, are primarily educational. Radio is more on
religious lines, though you would not really classify it as a religious

programme. Dr Garner Ted Armstrong may bring God into it, but it
is more a news commentary type of programme. He may talk, for
instance, on water and air pollution; and there have been programmes
on marriage and students and the rise in crime.'

Intrigued by the catholic range of subjects and particularly by a programme on religious lines that was not a religious programme, I asked:
'Does Dr Armstrong speak as a minister of the Church or as a member
of the college faculty?'

'He doesn't bring the college into it,' he replied. 'He doesn't say: "I
am the Executive Vice-President", or anything like that.'

It was at that moment that I began to detect a slight turbulence in the
air, though the temperature had yet to drop. A little more firmly, I said:
'Does he speak as a minister or as a member of the faculty?'

Equally firmly he replied: 'He speaks as an individual, commenting
on the world situation and conditions, though at the end he might
mention one of the college booklets relating to his subject and tell
viewers or listeners that they could have one free, if they wanted to
know more about it.'

Calm returned for a while, as we discussed the colleges. I learned that
there were about 700 students at Pasadena, including maybe 150 graduate students. In Texas there were 400 and in England between 250 and
300. Then, rudely, perhaps, I introduced the subject of money, the
financing of the Church and the colleges; and all of a sudden the conversation seemed to be caught in a high wind, as the words flew like
autumn leaves.

'We're a tithe-paying Church,' he told me. 'Individuals who listen to
the broadcasts probably send in contributions, too, though they are
never requested to do so. These contributions are unsolicited, but they
send them in. We're not funded by a foundation. People thought we
were funded by the John Birch Society.* They've called Mr Armstrong
a Nazi, but that's not true. None of it is true.'

Just how we had managed to jump from church and college finances
to the subject of right-wing extremists I could not quite understand. In
an effort to untangle the web, I asked: 'Why would people suggest that
you are funded by the John Birch Society?'

'I don't know,' he said, 'but people do write about the Armstrong
cult.'

The web remained. For the moment I pushed it aside and substituted
_____
* An extreme right-wing organization in the USA.

what I thought was a safer subject—the rules of the Church. 'I gather that they are fairly strict,' I said, slipping into fine old Anglo-Saxon understatement. 'You don't eat pork, for instance, and smoking is strictly banned. Presumably you have strong views on alcohol, too.'

'We don't eat pork products,' he said, 'because there are dietary laws which the scientists are beginning to support. Drinking in moderation is permitted, though God condemned drunken people. We don't smoke because there are several scriptures in which God says that the body is the temple of His Spirit and that we should take care of it.'

That all sounded very reasonable to me and, had he left it there, it would have been fine; but suddenly he glanced off at a tangent again and said: 'People accuse us of all sorts of things—even of having animal sacrifices. We were going to have a barbecue here, but we abandoned it when we thought what the neighbours might say.'

I thought of the babbling brooks outside and the fountains and the tall, dignified trees. I tried to align them with sacrificial ritual, but abandoned the task quickly, preferring to return to the simple life and the simple interview. I said: 'How many members are there in the Church?'

'I don't know what the count is right now,' he told me. 'I don't know what's going on in the office in Germany and wherever.'

At least the reply was uncomplicated, if somewhat unsatisfactory. I was encouraged to continue and I asked: 'Is it easy to become a member of the Church?'

'It depends,' he said, 'what you mean by easy.'

'I mean can anyone join?'

'Not anyone. They have to meet a lot of requirements. As long as a person is interested in being taught and is receptive to the teachings of the Bible, we will teach them. We don't force them in any way, of course. We don't push religion down people's throats. We don't go round from door to door, saying: "Are you saved, brother?" A person may come to us and say: "I believe in what you are doing. Have you anyone who can visit me?" Sometimes, too, they come to the college. I had a woman recently who was in dire need of help, a woman who had tried to take her life. She may need psychiatric care.'

That was a rare, if sad moment. I was face to face with an unusual commodity—American understatement. A woman had attempted suicide and I had just been told that she might need psychiatric care! I asked: 'Who was head of the World Wide Church of God before Mr Herbert Armstrong?'

He hesitated for a moment. Then he said: 'I don't want to answer that question because I think Mr Armstrong would rather answer himself. In fact I don't want to be quoted at all.'

Now it was my turn to hesitate because I was somewhat bewildered by this strange switch. Twice I had telephoned the college and told them that I was writing a book and wanted to include a chapter about their activities, both religious and educational. I had repeated this to Dr Garner Ted Armstrong in front of his secretary and his aides. As gently as possible, I said: 'If you do not want to be quoted, why are you talking to me?'

'I thought you just wanted to see over the college,' he said. 'I didn't know you were going to interview me.'

Had the lines of communication in this streamlined college broken down? I had to presume so; and that is why I have not mentioned the name of my guide and escort.

After that, at any rate, any rapport which may have existed seemed to melt away. I asked: 'When was Mr Herbert Armstrong ordained?'

'He came on the scene in 1934,' he told me. 'That was when he began his ministry. He was ordained before that by the Church of God, the branch which had its headquarters in Missouri. There was no World Wide Church of God then, just a Church of God.'

'Who ordained him?'

'I don't know.'

'Who was the head of the Church before Mr Armstrong?'

'I don't know.'

'But you are a minister of the Church. Surely you have a knowledge of its history?'

'Sure. Mr Armstrong came on the scene in 1934, as head of the Church.'

I tired of that particular merry-go-round and asked: 'Who pays for the colleges?'

'The money comes from tithing.'

'But I thought the colleges and the Church were two separate entities.'

'That's true,' he said, 'but it doesn't mean that those who contribute cannot spend money on the college.'

'Why are the Church and the colleges separate?'

'I don't know. You must ask Mr Armstrong that.'

Obviously the interview was dwindling to a close, running out of gas. Nevertheless, I kept on trying and said: 'It has been reported that your annual budget is over 30,000,000 dollars. Is that true?'

'I cannot quote the exact figure.'

'Do you publish your accounts annually?'

'I have never seen them. Personally I am not concerned with where the money is going. I just see the effect it is having on a world-wide scale.'

I am not quite sure what prompted me to ask the last question, though maybe I was thinking back to that remark about the John Birch Society. I said, anyway: 'Are your colleges integrated? Do you have black as well as white students?'

'There is no discrimination here,' he said. 'We have Negro students and one Negro on the faculty. We have almost every race you can think of, including an Arab. There are about twenty-five Negro students.'

We shook hands and parted for obviously our lines of communication were about to snap. There were still gaps in my knowledge, of course, but I had decided to take his advice and ask Dr Armstrong the questions which he had seemed to find so embarrassing.

Accordingly I was sitting by the Nubian slaves again the following morning at eight o'clock. Soon afterwards the First Vice-President of the Church arrived. He was brisk still, but no longer brusque. Gone was the rather lofty attitude of the previous day. It had been replaced by a charming intensity, an urbane eagerness to complete my education so far as the Church and the colleges were concerned.

I asked him first how many members the World Wide Church of God had. With scrupulous fairness, he replied: 'I would say that we have about 55,000 to 60,000 in regular attendance in the United States alone. It's quite small compared with other churches.

'We are not, however, evangelists in the traditional sense. Dr Graham and so on are concerned with obtaining members, with growth, with counting heads, with getting people to attend church regularly. We, you might say, are disinterested in that. It is not our desire to start any large denominational movement. We are not engaged in an evangelistic campaign. Membership is only a secondary concern of ours. We are more interested in the educational aspect.'

I asked him how many ministers there were and he told me: 'About

350. They are supported as totally local entities. We have many Faculty members in our colleges who are members of the Church. On the other hand there are others who are not ordained, who have no intention of being ordained. Many are not even members of the Church.

'We don't own church buildings because we can't afford them. We've been so busy building colleges to provide a broad basis of education for the world. Right now, if it were a matter of choice for me to go on five additional radio stations in various parts of the world—India or China, for instance—or put up a local church building, I would choose the broadcasts.'

On the question of his father's ordination, he was a little more explicit than the anonymous member of his faculty. He told me: 'He was ordained at the Oregon Conference of the Church of God which had its headquarters in Stanberry, Missouri. Who was head of the Church before my father? I was only four years of age at the time, but I understand it was Andrew Dugger. About twenty or thirty ministers in areas such as Oregon formed the Oregon Conference of the Church of God, a separate body. It was among these people that my father began to learn and study and finally was ordained.'

'And your own ordination?'

With a smile he said: 'I rebelled against my father's Church and hit out on my own. I ran away from home and joined the navy. I said that I would never become a minister, but I returned eventually and was ordained by a group of ministers with my father participating. I studied at the college here and got a Doctorate in Child Psychology and Education. No, I haven't a Doctorate of Theology, though it is true that I am Professor of Theology here.'

'How does one become a member of the Church?' I asked. 'What would you say, for instance, if I told you now that I wanted to join?'

'I'd open the Bible at Romans VI and ask you if you believed it,' he told me. 'If I found that you truly did and believed everything in the Bible, including the Four Gospels and the writings of Paul, I would ask you about specific changes in your life, about your moral standards and whether you were prepared to try and live the life of Christ in the Bible.

'If I found you sincere, it would be fine. There is no period of education, no series of booklets or pamphlets to read. A person literally could have heard only one broadcast or read only one magazine and, if he wanted to live by what was there, that would be fine.

'If we thought your motives were right and that you wanted to make changes in your life, we would encourage you, or any person who wanted to make changes, to put one foot forward to see if the water was cold. If a man had an alcoholic problem or was a confirmed user of marijuana or had personal habits which were not in accordance with the life of Christ, we would want to see his willingness to try to make changes. We accept human frailty, but we believe that human beings must make some changes.'

He became really enthusiastic when we turned to radio and television. 'We began as a radio ministry,' he said. 'A few years ago I would take a text from the Bible for a series of radio programmes. Now we have programmes which are primarily educational. I am sure that the broad majority never see anything in our programmes except that they teach right contact and morality, something which any Rotary Club would do.'

'Why did you change?'

'For the same reason that the Apostle Paul said: "I am all things to all men",' he replied. 'There is a communications gap between the cloistered type of religion and younger people. We still say things we are morally responsible for, but we say them in the people's language, in a way people will find palatable. I can take words out of the Gospel and put them in modern businessmen's language. I don't have to sound like a theologian and, if I mention the Bible, it's only as any layman would in ordinary conversation.'

'Do you speak as a minister or as a member of the college faculty?'

'Neither. I speak as a member of the public, commenting in depth on social affairs. The background information is fed to me by our own World Wide News Bureau, which embraces many languages, and by the major wire services right here on the campus. I try to avoid the smaller, more localized problems. I have spoken on world issues, like air pollution or people rioting over higher incomes when their nations are starving.'

When I asked how this amazing organization was financed, he was more forthcoming than the gentleman I had interviewed the previous day. 'Our financial report is not for publication,' he said, 'but it is made public in the sense that our annual operating base is not secret. It is something in the nature of $34,000,000. It rose by twelve per cent in 1968 and by thirteen per cent the two previous years.

'The total activities of the Church and the college, involving three campuses—staff salaries in the college alone are $6,000,000 a year—a monthly magazine, a constant stream of booklets, ministers' salaries, the cost of mailing our publications and buying time on radio and television, add up to $33,200,000. A little more comes in than goes out, but not enough really for a corporation of this size. It is, however, a work of faith. If the postman doesn't arrive, we can't keep going; and there are many times when outgoings are bigger than income.'

'Where do you get the money?'

'Seventy per cent of our income comes from tithing, a doctrine of the Church. Members are expected to pay one-tenth of their income, but we have no file checking system to probe into whether they do or not. It is a matter between themselves and God.'

I presumed that the remaining thirty per cent came in contributions from those who watched the television programmes or heard him on the radio. I asked him, nevertheless, whether they had any large investments.

'We have bought Government bonds,' he told me. 'We may have a few thousand dollars bequeathed to us by some member in stocks and bonds. Other than that, however, we have no heavy investments and we have no income-producing property whatsoever.'

'Is the college supported mainly by the Church?'

'Yes and no. The college handles the publishing, broadcasting and television and the receipts from these are split on a sixty/forty basis between the college and the Church of God, Inc., so that the college can be self-supporting. You must remember, too, that the college produces the Ministry of the Church through its graduates in theology.'

As he spoke, I was thinking of the vast capital expenditure on the buildings outside. Perhaps he was sharing my thoughts, for he said: 'When I was ordained a minister, the college property consisted of only two buildings. It was a very tiny, struggling, little thing which could have gone under at any moment.'

He glanced at his watch. It was nearly time for him to catch his plane for Big Sandy, Texas. Quickly I asked: 'Why do you produce so much literature?'

'We feel we have a strong educational and research base here. We have not only a wealth of information, but the ability to acquire a tremendous amount of education unavailable to the average person. We believe it is our moral duty to get such knowledge to people for their own good.'

'Why do you think that some people have suggested you are funded by the John Birch Society?'

'I don't know. I'm not a member and I don't even know who they are. I don't know who John Birch is and I've never read any of their literature.'

'I was told yesterday that you have been called a Nazi? Why would anyone say that?'

'I don't know . . .'

He rose, shook hands with me and apologized for having to dash off. I thanked him for his courtesy, but was sorry that we had not had a little more time, for there was one more question which had arisen out of our talk.

It was reasonable enough that the 55,000 members of his Church should contribute seventy per cent of its income in tithing, for it worked out at something like 430 dollars a head, about £180. The remaining thirty per cent would be about $10,200,000, or £4,250,000. I would like to have asked him why he thought his radio and television audiences donated such a huge sum without even being asked to do so.

He was gone, however. Feeling that a clue might lie in his television programme, I watched it and filled that gap in my education. It began with an announcement that the opinions expressed on the programme did not necessarily reflect the views of the station. Then came pictures of the National Guard fighting floods and Garner Ted's voice saying: 'As a result of some of the wide-scale riots in the big cities, the National Guard has become known as an organization to be feared. We have seen the pictures of fixed bayonets on street corners . . . They play their part in emergencies, national disasters, but today they seem more frequently acting as military support to overwhelmed local law enforcement organizations.'

There followed an interview with Major General Ames, Commanding Officer of the Californian National Guard. First he touched on race riots, saying: 'The most frightening manifestation occurred after the assassination of Dr Martin Luther King, when cities in nineteen of our States needed the National Guard.'

Then, prompted by Armstrong, he moved smoothly to student demonstrations, saying: 'A good proportion of our student bodies are captives of hard-core revolutionaries. Some have been infiltrated by the Communist Party of the United States.'

Asked by Armstrong whether he found 'a new willingness of young people today to defy authority', he replied: 'There is lack of respect for law enforcement, parental authority, duty and country and a desire to avoid the draft. There is a willingness to take on constitutional authority.'

He agreed readily when Armstrong asked him whether concessions made to students had led them to believe that they could gain their ends by violent action; and a few minutes later he was going even further, stating that the revolutionaries were receiving financial support from outside the country.

Armstrong wound up the discussion by saying: 'We find ourselves facing an obnoxious situation with crime increasing, where young men are called out of their beds to confront other young people who think that violence is the only answer. It has been proved time and again that their objective is immense and that their ultimate desire is to overthrow the Government.'

Then, holding up one of his publications, he said: 'The Government need informing about the true facts. Any of you who want this booklet on crime, write to Ambassador College, P.O. Box 111, Pasadena . . .'

The programme closed with yet another announcement that the views expressed in it were not necessarily those of the station; and I picked up the booklet on crime to learn the facts that the Government did not know. The sombre words, linking student demonstrations and race riots with crime, still hung heavily in the air.

It was packed with statistics and graphs. The commentary, however, included a reference to what I thought was the understandable reaction of America's black population to the murder of Dr King. It went on to indict 'our criminal youth' and to warn against the 'dangerous hippie movement'. There were four small paragraphs about Cosa Nostra, the Mafia, but swathes about permissive parents and the permissive society.

I was beginning to understand why Dr Armstrong did not ask for money from his radio and television audiences. He did not have to ask. He had his headquarters in Pasadena which, as I mentioned earlier, is known as The City of Old Ladies, the widows of millionaires, and as the City of the Three Rs—Rich, Retired and Reactionary. Both those descriptions could be applied to the State of California, a bastion of conservatism. There were other States, particularly in the South and middle West, where strong views flourished on race and student rebellion—anything which threatened the comfortable *status quo*. There was President Nixon's 'silent majority'.

I glanced through a few more of his booklets—*Modern Dating*, for instance, which lashed out at beat groups, hippies and again, of course, at permissive parents. A double-page picture spread showed an innocent-looking boy smiling at a demure girl on a cinema screen, while in the back row of the cinema a boy watched, his arm over his girl's shoulder. To me it appeared natural behaviour, but not to Dr Garner Ted. The caption read: 'A DANGEROUS DATE! Seems innocent enough—sitting in a dark movie, only holding hands, or with arms around date. The movie may appear harmless. Perhaps two teenagers—away from parents—experiencing a romantic interlude. But such "innocent" dates all too often lead to increasing intimacy and even pre-marital pregnancy.'

Even more enthralling is *True Womanhood—Is It A 'Lost Cause'* by Dr Roderick C. Meredith, Second Vice-President of both Church and college. It is a classic piece of Victoriana.

'The truly feminine and happy wife is one who *wants to have a husband as the head of her home*,' he writes (the italics are his). 'She does not marry in order to have an "equal partnership" agreement.' He goes on: 'This tender, yielding state of mind *automatically* gives such a woman added beauty, a sparkle in her eyes and an unusual capacity for patience, love and compassion for others.'

Broadly speaking, Dr Meredith is opposed to wives taking jobs and violently opposed to career women. For the benefit of those who feel they should work, he writes: 'She should definitely choose the type of work which will enable her to *remain feminine*. Such job situations would include that of a secretary, a hostess or waitress in a *nice* restaurant, perhaps a saleswoman in a reputable establishment or other types of occupations or professions where she is *serving others*. In these job situations she is therefore *serving* and *responding* to her boss, perhaps her fellow employees and customers. She is NOT the "driving force" in the business, a high-pressure door-to-door or plant-to-plant saleswoman, a supervisor over men or anything of this sort . . .'

When he gets down to the wife's attitude to her husband in the home, however, Dr Meredith pulls out all plugs. Bolstering his words with quotations from I Peter 3: 1–11, he writes: 'The Christian woman is instructed to consider her husband as her "lord" or *boss* . . . With the attitude of deep *respect* for her husband, a truly feminine woman will NOT be arguing, bickering or NAGGING at her husband. She will anticipate his wishes and his directions. Because of its altered meaning in modern terminology, she may not literally call her husband "lord", but she can and should respond to him "Yes, *sir!*" when he is addressing her in an "official" capacity as her husband!'

Unfortunately, however, not all the writings which emerge from the Armstrong organization are so prim or so amusing. When I read 'This Is Ambassador College', for instance, an extremely expensive production, I began to understand why some people might think that Dr Garner Ted Armstrong was inclined towards the right.

It begins with a mention of the expensive buildings, gardens and equipment and carries on comfortably: 'Even more impressive are the students themselves. They appear to be actually happy! They radiate. They are animated. They give you a smiling, warm and cheery "Hi!" And, if you have visited other campuses, you are surprised by the noticeable absence of hippie-type students. No students or faculty revolt, no protest marches, no riots or violence. These students give evidence of having a purpose and knowing where they are going.'

There follows a diatribe about cesspool morals, soaring crime and the need for discipline in the home, a strong family system . . . comparatively routine stuff for this establishment. When, however, they begin to give examples of what happens when the family structure collapses, they scarcely make themselves lovable in the eyes of integrationists or those fighting for civil rights. They single out the black population in America, in which, they write 'family cohesion is lowest of all'. Ignoring the more obvious reasons for this—lack of education, lack of decent housing, lack of work, lack of hope—they proceed to quote figures which imply that young black American citizens are responsible for more crime—particularly crimes of violence—than their white brothers and sisters. In my view those figures seem unlikely to foster inter-racial amity or to curb the violence which Dr Armstrong and his colleagues deplore with so many words in so many pamphlets.

3: MAIL ORDER BLESSINGS

JOURNEYMEN, like myself, who spend a fair time bumbling, bewildered, around the world in pursuit of their trade, may anticipate one symbol of stability wherever they go. The scene may be strange and shifting; but usually a permanent feature of every hotel room, haughty or humble, is a Bible, placed there by the Gideon Society. Who its members are I do not know, but always I have admired their faith and perseverance.

When first I went to my room in the Alvin Plaza Hotel, Tulsa, Oklahoma, therefore, I was not surprised to find that once again they had done their duty. This time, however, their gentle offering, so often utterly alone, was cheek-by-jowl with another religious work, *Daily Blessing*, issued by the Oral Roberts Evangelistic Association, Inc., the organization which had led me to Tulsa in the first place.

My knowledge of Roberts at that stage was sketchy, having been derived entirely from newspaper and magazine cuttings. *Life* magazine had described him as 'the loudest and flashiest revivalist since Billy Graham', a man who yelled at his audience: 'Don't let a mother's son go to hell!' Other sources reported—and here I summarize drastically— that he claimed to have received audible messages from God many times; that miraculous healing took place at his services; that he encouraged members of his extensive television audience to hold their sick children up to the screen so that they might benefit from these curative powers by proxy and through courtesy, presumably, of the cathode tube; that, like the Rev. Herbert Armstrong, he had built a remarkable university; that in April 1968 he had caused a mild religious rumpus by leaving his Pentecostal Holiness Church to join the Methodists; and—sombre note—that one of his followers, who believed that she had been cured of diabetes, had died because she had thrown away her insulin.

All in all, it seemed a fairly provocative, though as yet unconfirmed, record. It was with interest, therefore, that I picked up *Daily Blessing* in the hope that I might find clues to the character of this obviously unusual man. My hopes were realized, though I regret to say that they did not encourage me to raise his banner high.

The bulk of the book was taken up with potted parables, interspersed with folksy tales of how various poor, deserving people had changed their financial fortunes by joining with Brother Roberts in a Blessing Pact. That seemed reasonable enough; but, when I reached the last page,

I read the following less palatable piece, written by the evangelist himself:

'What is your need? Is it spiritual? Is it for finances? Is it for a loved one? Is it for your body? Is it for harmony in your home? Whatever it is, God knows all about it and He wants to meet it by His miracle power. I challenge you to enter into a Blessing Pact with God, for I believe it will change your life. It's so scriptural and practical. It's not magic; it's just God working miracles as we release our faith to Him.

'Fill in the attached Blessing Pact Enrollment Card and mail it to me. When I receive it, I will mail you your free copy of the "Miracle Catch" painting* and the Blessed Pact Covenant book. Each month I will write you a personal letter and share with you from God's Word how to trust God and how to apply the Blessing Pact Scriptures to your actual needs. We will be partners together in our Blessing Pact with the Lord.

'Don't wait. Send me your enrollment card and prayer requests today. (See reverse side.) I know something good is going to happen to you.'

Obediently I turned to the reverse side; and very soon I understood what it was all about. The enrolment card read: 'Dear Brother Roberts . . . I am putting God first in my life and in my giving and I want to enter into my Blessing Pact with God. Looking to God as the Source of my supply, "I'll do it and I expect a miracle", I believe my depth is $ . . . . per month for the next twelve months. Enclosed is $ . . . . my first offering for my NEW† Blessing Pact with God . . . My personal prayer requests are . . .'

My first, somewhat over-cynical reaction was one of surprise that a prayer cloth had not been tossed in with the 'Miracle Catch' picture, the copy of the Blessing Pact Covenant Book and the monthly personal letter. My second was one of slight dyspepsia. Laying aside *Daily Blessing*, I picked up the *Tulsa Daily World* to search for some journalistic solace, like Charlie Brown and Snoopy; but there was no escape. Staring at me from one of its pages was a picture of Oral Roberts over a story which revealed that he had been made a member of the board of the National Bank of Tulsa. For one member, it seemed, the pact had worked, though the news did not send me scampering back to fill up the enrolment form, to take up the challenge.

On the contrary, I was feeling distinctly cool about the organization

---

* It shows the disciples hauling in nets bulging with fish.

† I wonder what happened to the old ones. Did they go stale, like photographic film?

at that moment of time. One lesson I had learned from my pilgrimage, however, was that I must beware of hasty judgements. I decided therefore that the sooner I saw the Rev. Dr Oral Roberts the better; and so, as the next day was Sunday, I made my way to his university where he was to preach at the morning service.

The campus, I found, was even more overwhelming than that of Ambassador College. Ultra-modern buildings rose on every side of me, world-of-tomorrow style, if I may borrow a phrase from the Rev. Herbert Armstrong. There was a low, gently sloping dome, like a huge, plump mushroom. There were tall superstructures with honeycomb contours. There were delicate, elegant pillars, supporting what seemed like acres of roof; and in the middle of it all was a colossal, star-shaped, sugar-plum-fairy edifice, covered in golden mirrors. Only later, when I was given a glossy information pack, did I learn that it was 'the spiritual heart of the university', a prayer tower from which a team of professional counsellors bombarded heaven, as they answered prayer requests right around the clock.

My target for the morning, however, was the service. Averting my eyes from the wonders around me, I was directed to what looked like a beautiful, medium-sized theatre, complete with a fine stage and six microphones. Beige curtains shielded the windows. A beige carpet covered the floor. The backcloth to the stage was pale blue. Here, I decided, was plush-lined, dress-circle religion and my decision was by way of a compliment rather than of criticism. The congregation was mixed—black worshippers and white worshippers, rich ones and poor ones, fur coats and skimpy, off-the-peg coats, a decent cross-section and a credit to the preacher.

An associate evangelist opened the service. Moving to the centre microphone, he said: 'We pray for every longing heart.' Then he recited the Lord's prayer with a clarity and intensity that is rare in more orthodox churches. When he had finished and we had settled back in our seats, he said: 'Would you greet the singers . . . the World Action Television singers?'

They stood behind him, scrupulously groomed, the boys in blue shirts, blue blazers and light grey ties, the girls in blue dresses with long chiffon sleeves. The congregation gave them a round of applause—the first I had ever heard in church—and they reciprocated with a hymn which they sang beautifully. When they had finished, the first speaker returned to the microphone and I learned that I had arrived for the last service of a four-day seminar, attended by Oral Roberts devotees from all over the country. For a while he spoke with quiet enthusiasm about their hours of work; but, when he reached the first major topic of the morning, the collection, his fervour increased.

'This is an exciting time,' he told us. 'You have heard over the past few days about planting a seed. This is the time when faith plants a seed, reaches out until the moment comes when a miracle happens.'

The seed, I gathered, was money; and, lest anyone should misunderstand, he offered us a jingle: 'They thought the man who gave had gone mad because the more he gave the more he had.' Returning to prose, he went on: 'This is World Action on the home front in the Tulsa area. You are going to be giving to buy Bibles for people in prisons or to help someone go to our Golden Age home. You will be giving to fill the gasoline tanks of the young who go to the Indians in the Tulsa area. Whether you have anything or not to give, just give your heart . . . but give more than you think you can and God will give to you. In the name of Jesus Christ this will be an offering of love, straight from the heart, a moment of meeting Christ and touching the source. Hear us now, as we give in the name of Jesus . . . amen.'

His delivery was beautiful and deserved the round of soft applause which greeted it. Then the collection was taken by students; and, when that essential piece of ceremonial was over, a tall young man with sideburns, wearing a handsome brown suit, stepped forward. With all the easy grace of a professional compère announcing the main act, he said: 'I would like to introduce a man I saw on television this morning . . . our speaker today . . . my father . . . *Oral Roberts!*'

Father stepped forward, a tall, well-built man putting on a little weight, perhaps, but looking much younger than his fifty-one years. He, too, wore side-burns and an even more exotic suit in midnight blue, relieved by a light grey tie. I sat up straight, ready to hear the man whom *Life* magazine had called the loudest and flashiest revivalist since Billy Graham and who was reported to have said of his own preaching: 'I become anointed with God's word and the spirit of the Lord builds up in me like a coiled spring. By the time I'm ready to go, my mind is razor-sharp. I know exactly what I'm going to say and I'm feeling like a lion.'

Half an hour later, however, I was sitting back, feeling slightly cheated. I had heard a folksy sermon, delivered with occasional hesitation and pitted with homely phrases, tract-like in their triteness—

'Don't live on the little end of Christianity. Live on the big end—the hem of plenty'; 'Don't get morbid about the Cross'; 'God is a good God, who loves me when I'm good and still loves me when I'm bad.' Where, I wondered, was the coiled spring, to say nothing of the lion? Where was the noise that *Life* had promised me and where was the flash? Had the switch from the Pentecostal Holiness Church to the Methodists put out the fire, or was my mind jaded by hearing too many sermons in the line of duty?

Whatever the reason for my lack of reaction, I must report in fairness to Dr Roberts that some were moved, for when he and an associate evangelist, called Brother Bob, exchanged communion on the stage, the silence was broken by a few emotional sobs.

The healing ceremony which followed was more impressive, for it seemed to make many people happy and give relief that was at least temporary to two of them. It was conducted with reasonable dignity and obvious sincerity, though some more traditional clerics might have disapproved of the rather theatrical air which was, perhaps, inevitable.

Here Dr Roberts was again the central figure, though this time he had a large supporting cast. His students lined up, face to face, their hands joined, forming a long, human tunnel. Those wishing to have healing hands laid on them passed through it and came out the other end, their faces glowing, a few with happy tears streaming down their cheeks. One old man hobbled away, shouting: 'Jesus did something for me! Here comes Jesus's offering! Thank you, Jesus!'

I asked him what Jesus had done for him. He said: 'I walked on crutches to this seminar. Now I can walk without them.'

A plump little woman, smiling ecstatically, sat surrounded by an excited throng. I joined them and I heard her say: 'I had a spinal truss for seven or eight years. The surgeon said he couldn't operate. I had this constant pain all the time and I prayed for years and years. Then yesterday it came over me all at once. Something told me I must go to Oral Roberts. I came here and it happened today, just like that. I don't feel any pain at all . . . no pain, no pain. I'd take off the truss, but my hose would fall down.'

Cynics may say, of course, that here were classic cases of hysteria, of people who would slump back into sickness once they were beyond the emotion of the service. What matter? They were experiencing a little relief at least and had a chance of more than that. As I listened to them, anyway, the scales in my mind, which had been tilted so heavily by blessing pacts, began to even up in favour of Oral Roberts.

The more I studied him, however, the more those scales see-sawed, for here is a character of many shades. There is Oral Roberts, the humanitarian, with a deep concern for people—the Indians, for instance, who have had and are having such a rough time in what was once their own country. There was Oral Roberts, the businessman, dealing with very large sums of money, though never failing to speak of it in spiritual tones. There was Oral Roberts who saw the hand of God in what seemed to me to be straightforward and highly efficient fund-raising ventures. He seemed to see himself as a man festooned with miracles, a success in a highly competitive field, despite a humble beginning.

The son of a poor Oklahoma farmer-turned-preacher, he contracted tuberculosis when he was sixteen. His parents prayed for him and one day his brother drove him to a revival meeting in Ada, Oklahoma. As he lay on a mattress in the back of the car, he heard God say: 'Son, I'm going to heal you and you are going to take My healing power to your generation.' Writing about that incident, he reveals no surprise, merely commenting: 'God not only healed me in that meeting, but gave me direction for my life.'

Anyway, he took the words to heart and became a preacher. Then, in 1947, by which time he was a pastor of a small church in the town of Enid and a married man, God spoke to him again and I must say that to me the manner in which He delivered His message seemed devious. Roberts, however, recorded the event, not flatly this time, but with high drama, or, perhaps, melodrama.

Describing how he was praying in his study, he wrote later, 'I poured out my soul, like water, before the Lord. Time merged with eternity. Slowly, almost imperceptibly, God began to take control of me. Suddenly I knew God was in the room with me. His hands were upon me and His power was coming into me. The old Oral Roberts began to fade as God took control. My struggling ceased. As I lay on the floor God spoke: "Get on your feet!"'

Here, I must comment, the Lord was more economical with His words than was His servant when he came to report them. From there on, however, the pattern of events became complex. When Roberts was on his feet, God said: 'Go get in your car.' When he was behind the wheel, he was told: 'Drive one block and turn right.' His curtain line to that scene—and it is a good one—was: 'When I reached the end of the block and started to turn right, God said: "From this hour you will heal the sick and cast out devils by My power." '

Let us pass lightly over the dangers of talking to a driver when he is turning a corner. What puzzles me is why God could not have delivered this comparatively simple, if important, message, when the preacher was in his study. What was so special about that spot on the right at the end of the block? Roberts gives no clue.

He obeyed the instructions, of course, though here he showed a prudence unusual in a young, idealistic evangelist. When he had hired a down-town auditorium for his first rally, he asked God for some material backing. He wanted, he said, an audience of a thousand; the power to heal so well that the congregation—'audience' is his word—would know that he had been called specially for this ministry; and, of course, the money to pay for the meeting.

All three requests were granted. He resigned from his church in Enid and moved with his wife, Evelyn, to Tulsa where, he said, he would begin a world-wide ministry. Though he knew few people there, his congregation grew quickly and within a year he was so successful that he decided he should buy a tent, rather than rely on invitations from different ministers. It would be, he said, a neutral place of worship for all denominations.

He raised the money for the tent by means which any energetic, enterprising minister—or businessman—would have adopted. Over the following few months, he asked one hundred people in each place he visited to give $10 towards the cost. With this backing, he went to a local bank, borrowed $9,000 and bought a tent that would hold ten thousand.

By that time, however, his mind seemed to have dug itself deep into the miracle mine. He maintains that here the amalgam of energetic fund-raising and a straightforward financial deal was further evidence that he was following God's plan.

Whether it was God or the bank directors who provided the money, however, he certainly moved fast from that moment. His congregations grew to nine thousand, which meant that he was playing to almost full tents; and by July 1948, he was in a position to make his ministry into a corporation, hire an advertising agency, buy radio time and blossom forth with rallies in other States.

He also was attracting the attention of influential people. At his rally in Miami, for instance, he met Lee Braxton, who had flown in for the meeting from his home town, where he was not only Mayor, but founder and President of its First National Bank. In addition he owned or held stock in several other businesses and corporations, a state of economic affairs so happy that he was just about to retire at the age of forty-four.

Having seen Oral Roberts in action, however, he decided that he still had work to do. He joined the Oral Roberts Evangelistic Association, Inc., bringing to it all his brilliant financial acumen. Roberts writes: 'Lee attended the Tampa, Jacksonville and Tallahassee crusades that immediately followed Miami. He then flew to Tulsa with me and helped us organize our office on a businesslike basis. He also approached me on a plan to increase the number of radio stations carrying our broadcasts to one hundred stations. This was a goal I had been praying and working toward. It seemed utterly impossible until this business-man came along and had the audacity to say it could be done.'

If God answered Roberts's prayers by sending him the shrewd and audacious Lee Braxton, He certainly showed keen financial judgement. That, however, will come as no surprise to the many evangelists I met, for most of them tell their followers with a monotonous persistence that He knows all about their money problems and can sort them out, if only they have enough faith to invest a little more than they can afford in His works.

Certainly Lee Braxton gave the organization a shot in its commercial arm. Soon after he joined, Roberts was working to extend the seating accommodation in his tent, which meant purchasing two more trailer trucks, 1,500 more folding chairs, a larger portable platform and a new lighting system. He does not record that he got all those extra trappings, but that, I think, can be taken for granted. Soon he became one of the first evangelists to use the medium of the infant television for his mes-sage, an enterprise which even in those days could not be launched with peanuts. Roberts, however, was able to pay sixteen stations to screen his programme and of the results he wrote: 'The response was immedi-ate. Overnight our volume of mail soared. This confirmed our con-viction that we were heading in the right direction.'

That last thought is a matter of opinion. His television programmes gave birth to the Blessing Pact which certainly was ingenious but not—in my view—particularly tasteful. Roberts thought of the idea when he was pondering how he could raise $42,000 so that he could have his crusades filmed for television. Of that time he wrote: 'The programs being filmed in a studio had no live crusade audience to "pull" the message out of me. I felt the people were not getting the real power and impact of the deliverance ministry.'

In fact I had gained a distinct impression that he believed God was pulling the message out of him; but perhaps He was just pushing it in, filling the coffee pot and letting others pour. One way or another, he needed $42,000 and he got it.

Of those hard times he wrote: 'I called a special afternoon service and shared this plan with my partners. I told them the Lord had given me a plan to enter into a partnership with each person who would help me to carry on our ministry. This partnership would be called a Blessing Pact. I pointed out examples of this in the Bible. The widow of Zarapath entered into a blessing pact with the prophet Elijah, when she grasped the principle of partnership with God—that it was based upon faith and miracles. She had to do something first, even though it was just a little. Then God performed a miracle for her in return and supplied her needs in abundance . . .

'Then I dropped a bombshell into their thinking. I said: "If I can trust God for the $42,000 to film the crusade, can you trust him for $100? I am asking four hundred and twenty people in this audience to make this pledge and, in turn, let me, as an instrument of God, enter into a Blessing Pact with you for one year" . . . I promised if at the end of the year God had not blessed them, I would return their money.'

He reported that there was an audible gasp in the audience, which frankly does not surprise me. Nevertheless, four hundred and twenty people of faith stepped forward; and after that it was camera, lights, action.

The audible gasp was heard in the middle fifties. The Blessing Pact, as I have said, is with us still and in *Abundant Life*, the Association's magazine, I found the usual plethora of financial miracles that were said to have flowed from it. They included a particularly appropriate one from a Newfoundland fisherman, who had been having poor hauls. So bad was business, in fact, that they had only two dollars left by the time they had sent off their first Blessing Pact offering. A few days later he was hauling up 'net-breaking, boat-sinking loads'.

Since those early days, of course, the Pact has expanded to embrace more than financial rewards. According to Roberts it can bring not only money, but love. This he revealed, when he published his answer to a woman who had written to him: 'I have prayed for at least twenty years for a Christian husband . . . Every time I read the promises of God I want to vomit because God has not kept His word to me . . . Why does God care so much about my soul and say so little about my happiness on this earth? I used to have glowing faith . . . I trusted God and He let me down . . . I don't even like God any more.'

Oral Roberts did not waver when faced with this fighting letter. Gently he wrote that she must trust in God and expect a miracle. Elaborating, he went on: 'Jesus said we ought to tithe, but He gave a higher law than tithing. The tithe is ten per cent of what we have already earned—a thanksgiving back to God. *Your Blessing Pact giving is a higher law of faith.* You give BEFORE you have received, you give as seed money for God to multiply back to you, you give as seed faith for God to increase back to you.

'In the future, each time you give, give expecting God to multiply it back IN THE FORM OF YOUR NEED—A HUSBAND! Sounds fantastic? Crazy? Well, I'm seeing it work for others, why not for you?'

To me it does not sound at all crazy. I would imagine that the Rev. Dr Roberts received many sacks of seed faith for the Lord from other lonely, unmarried women after the publication of those two letters. Marriages, after all, should be made in heaven; and celestial matrimonial bureaux presumably have just as much right to charge for their services as have their terrestrial counterparts, though whether the quality of the husband increases with the quantity of seed faith I am in no position to say.

The Blessing Pact plan, at any rate, seems to have been one of his most successful enterprises. It was so successful, indeed, that after a while he came to the conclusion that his 'money-back-if-not-completely-satisfied' guarantee was superflous and he withdrew it.

Certainly in the fifties it enabled him to screen his healing services, though occasionally there were snags. 'Some of the most marvellous healings in this ministry have never been shown because a piece of TV equipment failed and the last minute or two of the healing was not captured on film. When this happened, I have actually broken down and wept.'*

Television, as he says himself, gave a front-row seat in the crusades to millions. God, however, had even bigger plans. In December 1953 He

* That, presumably, is the devil of show-biz!

told him: 'You are to win a million souls in the next thirty-six months.'

Even for Oral Roberts that was massive block-booking. He wrote of it: 'I staggered and reeled under this command . . . Never before had anyone been asked to win a million souls in thirty-six short months. How could I do it?'

Do it, of course, he did—and in twenty-nine and a half months, which must have meant revving the conversion plant to unprecedented speeds. Then, before he had time to relax and congratulate himself, God raised the ante again. In seemingly casual tones, He said to Roberts: 'Son, if you will seek My pleasure, My joy and My faith, I will give you ten million souls in ten years.'

This time he reeled not, neither did he stagger. Instead he called his team together in prayer, presumably to seek guidance about how this enormous order could be filled. He got it, too, though I gained an impression that God spoke a little testily on that occasion.

'Oral Roberts,' He is quoted as saying, 'you're trying to be an American preacher. You think that no one can be saved in large numbers except the American people. My Son died for all.'

Verily, for Oral Roberts—who perhaps had accepted a little too readily careless talk about God's Own Country—this was a Great Revelation and there was more to come. Relaxing his tone somewhat, God gave him a Master Plan, what the evangelist called later 'our Seven World Outreaches'. They were the crusades, the overseas ministry, radio and television, the printing of Hebrew Bibles, work among North American Indians, the Abundant Life Prayer Group and his massive publishing enterprise. From that moment, all swung into high-powered action and Roberts was able to report: 'Our Second Million Souls Crusade began in January 1956 and was completed in fourteen and a half months. In March 1957, the Third Crusade was launched and twelve months later another million souls won to Christ was announced by our Auditing Department. When we announced in 1958 our desire to win the Fourth Million Souls to Jesus Christ in twelve months, we faced a tremendous challenge. But, to God be the glory, the task was not beyond the reach of faith.'

It was, however, tough sledding. Bearing in mind God's rather irascible words about the dangers of isolationism, he took his crusades out into the world, to France, Holland, Wales, Israel, South Africa, Australia, New Zealand and Formosa. He visited Poland and even the U.S.S.R., about which he wrote: 'Russian people are taught there is no

God; but I found those who still believe! I am expecting a great
revival to break out in that country.'

In Israel he was photographed sitting in the boat of some Galilean
fishermen, giving them 'personally autographed copies of the Hebrew
Bible', a picture which I felt drew a rather presumptuous parallel. In
Australia he was heckled and hissed. Crowds tried to overturn his car;
one of the tent ropes was cut; one of his trucks was set on fire; and,
when a newspaper carried a headline reading 'Fire Set At Oral Roberts's
Tent . . . To-night It Is Going To Be Burned Down', the crusade was
closed. Roberts wrote the inevitable epitaph: 'Well-known Communist
agitators were recognized, moving about, stirring up the mob.'

No serious damage was done to the tempered steel of his mission,
however, and Roberts moved smoothly into the Sixties, only to have
God cast another glove before him. He told him he must build a university and, to make the glove even heavier, He added: 'You are to
build the school out of the same ingredient I used when I made the
earth—nothing.'

Thinking, perhaps, how lucky the Israelites were, for they were asked
merely to make bricks without straw, Roberts set to work. His new
activity, however, was not greeted with wild enthusiasm by his associates, who felt that he was moving too fast, that evangelism and a university could not be combined. They faced him at a very extraordinary
meeting about which he wrote: 'It dawned upon me that I needed to do
some real communicating.'

There was, however, no better man for the job. He reports the success of his efforts in the following touching words: 'When I had
finished I was on my feet. I was churning inside and my spirit was
reaching out to these beloved men. Manford let out a gurgling sound
and burst into tears. Lee Braxton sat with tears streaming down his
cheeks. Bob DeWeese was broken up. R. O. Corvin was both smiling
and crying. I don't know how it happened, but in moments twelve
men were on their feet and we were embracing each other and praising
God.'

I think I know how it happened. Oral Roberts is one of the greatest
tear-jerkers since the day Al Jolson teamed up with 'Sonny Boy'. There
is no string that he will not pluck in the emotional harp, even if it
involves the private life of himself, his wife and his family. In the centre
spread of his autobiography, for instance, under the heading 'Evelyn's
Keepsakes', he prints personal letters which he wrote to them from

various parts of the world. They are sprinkled liberally with extravagant endearments, which I found embarrassing reading, but I have no
doubt that many of his devoted followers saw them as hall-marks of a
humble, loving, family man. Only once does the humility wear a little
thin and that occurs in a letter he wrote from Israel to the entire family.
It ends: 'I'll be home, Lord willing, by Dec. 15 or 16 . . . Should I be
called away, I'll meet you at my permanent address: Palace of the King,
New Jerusalem, Heaven . . . All my love . . . Your husband, father and
friend.' I gathered from these famous last words that he believed his
celestial seat to be reserved already, but perhaps I am doing him an
injustice. Where does faith end and proud self-confidence begin?

The quality of his publicity, of course, is a matter of taste. Its quantity
is a matter of remarkable fact. His television programme is seen now in
over 160 cities in the United States and Canada, much of it at expensive
prime viewing time. Over 25,000,000 booklets and pamphlets are distributed every year in 115 languages. The sheer poundage of all those
words and pictures could scarcely fail to work wonders and the university alone is a monument to their international value. I presume that
Dr Roberts started with nothing, in accordance with the Lord's
instructions, but obviously very soon he acquired something, for seldom can a seat of learning have sprouted so fast. Construction began in
1963. Two years later seven splendid buildings were completed, one of
them a remarkable hexagonal affair that encloses four and a half acres
on six floors, two of them underground. In May 1968, the first class
graduated; and by the time building has been completed, it will have
cost $21,500,000. Even now, when thirty per cent of the building
remains to be done, it can take 1,400 students, 1,200 of them residents,
though these figures have not yet been reached. Like Ambassador
College, it is equipped with ultra-modern teaching equipment—audio-
video apparatus on which students can dial lectures, experiments, plays,
films, language exercises and self-studies and receive them in colour; a
language laboratory where they can tape their own voices as they
speak; and a television studio, where several sections of a class may view
live telecasts and communicate directly by telephone from the classroom with a professor in the studio. Languages taught, incidentally,
include Russian, presumably in preparation for the great revival that
Dr Roberts has forecast will break out in the U.S.S.R.

Tulsa, naturally enough, is proud of this academic achievement by its
adopted son and the university staff recognize this pride. Conducted

tours are organized regularly, beginning with a brief colour film of college activities, shown in the private college cinema. It opens with solemn music and a pink glow. A commentator, stirring and inspiring, reels off the facts and figures of remarkable achievement . . . 'A recreation hall that holds 2,500 . . . a junior Olympic swimming pool . . . fine arts centre . . . closed circuit television . . . twin high-rise buildings for men and women residents . . . Station KROU, covering a four-state area with educational, classical, semi-classical and religious programmes . . . sports and the latest news . . . a university that has a spirit symbolic of the twentieth century . . . academic discipline with active Christianity . . . twelve students per faculty member.' Later I was to learn that its curriculum offers Bachelor of Arts degrees in thirteen majors, Bachelor of Science degrees in four areas, and a Bachelor of Music degree. There are pre-professional studies in dentistry, engineering, medicine, nursing and veterinary science.

It is an impressive record that has been recognized by the State of Oklahoma, which has given the university a full four-year accreditation; and I was delighted to learn that here was an academy that is completely integrated. The President of the students' body is Bob Goodwin, a young Tulsa Negro, which shows that Roberts was not merely murmuring platitudes when he told his television audience: 'God is colour-blind.' That comment brought two hundred letters from racists, but he refuses to compromise on this subject. For many years he has held integrated church services.

He is, in fact, a bewildering man, held captive to some extent, perhaps, by his own extravagant publicity. To find out more about him, I went to his Director of Public Relations, Gerald W. Pope. Pausing only to wonder whether or not the Association thought his name appropriate, I asked him about the healing services and whether there was any follow-up, when people claimed to have been cured.

'We have not much on our records about following up cases,' he told me, 'though it has been done with selected individuals, people who have been reported on from time to time. In a recent *Abundant Life* there was a story of a young lady who was healed away back when he first started with pictures of her then and pictures of her today.'

He gave me the story to read. It told how Ailene Green, a thirteen-year-old with a leg in irons after polio, had attended a crusade in Muskogee, Oklahoma. She went to Roberts and a few minutes later the irons were off and she was running down the aisle. Now married and mother of a little boy, she confirmed what happened in another section of the magazine. All that was lacking was medical evidence, but it was an important gap in this otherwise dramatic case history.

We turned to a more controversial aspect of the healing ministry. 'Is it true,' I asked, 'that he asks people seeking a cure to touch the television or radio set when a service is being transmitted? Does he get them to hold their children up to the screen?'

'Yes,' he said. 'When people lay their hands on the set, or get their children to touch it, there is a point of contact which produces in the individual a culmination of faith. At that one point in time the faith they cannot express will be released. The point of contact for people can be different things—voice contact, eye contact. His particular thing is a physical one—the laying on of hands; but that doesn't mean that it has to be physical. He stressed, of course, that healing can take time. When you are dealing with the physical, cures are not always instantaneous.

'Another point—for many years people have associated President Roberts with a ministry of healing that is purely physical. The concept is broader than that. Now that we are big on television with a different kind of programme, people are understanding a broader kind of healing—the healing of one's emotions and one's intellect and one's financial situation. It can also be healing in a social sense—changing the attitude of a racist student, for example. Think of the word "disease"—"dis-ease"; a person not right with himself.'

'But surely,' I said, 'this narrower concept of healing, which you mentioned, springs from your own publicity.'

'That's right,' he said, a reply which encouraged me to change the subject, to move into more pleasant waters. I asked him about the World Action programme, which seemed to be admirable.

'It is the real reason for the university being here,' he said. 'It is a programme that actively involves the students in the lives of people on a local, national and international scale. In the summer of 1968 two groups went overseas. One—the university choir—toured fourteen countries, including Estonia and Israel. They lived with the people wherever they sang.

'The second group went to Africa, where they participated in the crusade with the President.* Four graduates stayed and spent one year in Africa, each working in a different area in Kenya in village churches

* Dr Roberts is, naturally, President of the Oral Roberts University.

and schools. The summer before that they went to Brazil and to Indonesia; and in the autumn they went to Chile.

'At home—here in Tulsa, for instance—they get involved, too. They take part in an unemployment programme, which is sponsored by the Government and administered by a non-profit organization, which in this case is the university. We set up an office on the north side of town, the Negro section. Students do counselling work among hard-core unemployed and get local businessmen to participate. There is a training centre and the students are available at all times, seeing that the men get up in the morning and out to work and so on.

'Other students are involved in other ways. A large group is ready to go into retirement homes. More will go into schools for the mentally handicapped or retarded.'

This concern for the old, incidentally, is reflected in another Oral Roberts enterprise. He has built what he calls a Christian Retirement Centre beside the university. It has garden-cottage-type accommodation, a large apartment building with a dining room and a fifty-bed health centre, it is designed for those over sixty-two years of age. Roberts has announced. 'My own mother will be the very first resident ... She will sell her home and with the proceeds from the sale and her income, be able to secure life care.'

All those projects, of course, are admirable, provided, in the case of the Christian Retirement Centre, that there are beds for old people with small incomes and without much to sell. Certainly what I had heard had helped tilt those scales, but there still were a few question marks hanging heavily in my mind. I would have liked very much to have unloaded them before Dr Roberts himself, but this proved impossible, for he is a busy man and my stay in Tulsa was necessarily brief. Instead I talked to S. Lee Braxton, the bank president who had joined the organization when it was still an infant and who today is Chairman of the Board of Regents of Oral Roberts University, a job which he doubles with that of Radio and Television Director of the Evangelistic Association. Though now sixty-five years of age, he still pilots his own plane and offers splendid proof that evangelism is good for the body as as well as the soul.

First we discussed a problem that must face every evangelist in the Oral Roberts bracket, though not all of them recognize it. I asked Lee Braxton: 'Isn't there a danger that those who answer his call are declaring for Dr Roberts and not for Christ?'

'We are aware of that,' he said. 'We have started de-emphasizing him as a man. We even changed the name of the magazine from *Oral Roberts* to *Abundant Life*.'

'How about the Oral Roberts University?'

With a smile, he said: 'There was a strong sentiment that it should have a Biblical name, but the Board of Regents thought that the name of Oral Roberts would be a drawing power. The Board of Directors of the National Bank of Tulsa thought the same way. Remember we have 660 employees and 900 students. They bring in the money. They're a big economic factor and anything which introduces a payroll to this city is of interest to the bank.'

I paused for a moment, wondering why it was that the conversation so often slid off the subject when I was talking to evangelists. How had we leapt from the personality cult to the vested interests of the National Bank of Tulsa? There seemed to be no ready answer to that problem and so I bulldozed on. 'In Dr Roberts's book, *My Twenty Years of a Miracle Ministry*,' I said, 'there are ninety-eight pages. On those pages there are fifty-four pictures of the author. That does not suggest to me any particular humility.'

Looking at me with a new and amiable interest, he said: 'You counted them?'

'Yes,' I said. 'I have studied also a great deal of your literature. Whether he likes it or not, stories of Oral Roberts and pictures of Oral Roberts generally are central themes.'

'We have learned,' he said, 'and we have grown. We are going to up-date those books. In some of the books, for instance, physical healing is stressed out of proportion. Certainly it may be a physical thing, but it may be non-physical, too. Most people read into it what they want to read, but we are really talking about the totality of man, not just his money, but himself, his smile, his kindness.'

It had happened again. The conversation, like a toy train, had switched suddenly from one track to another, from Roberts, the man, to the blanket subject of healing. This time I decided to let it flow and said: 'There have been newspaper and magazine reports about a lady who thought that Dr Roberts had cured her diabetes, threw away her insulin tablets and died. Would you care to comment on that?'

'Everyone is going to die,' he said with a sad smile, 'but I don't think that story is true. The lady came against our wishes and against the wishes of her doctor. She, herself, elected to say that she had been cured.

Dr Roberts always recommends that people go back to their doctors, for all we do is pray for them.'

'I am interested in your blessing pact,' I said. 'Why did Dr Roberts withdraw his guarantee to send the money back if the donor was not satisfied?'

For a moment he toyed with a pencil. Then, tilting his head to one side, he said quickly: 'I presume you are familiar with the Holy Scriptures.'

'No,' I said, 'I am not very familiar with the Holy Scriptures.'

There was a longer pause before he said: 'Well, in the beginning people didn't know about the pact. When it proved itself, he was able to withdraw the guarantee. Some people wrote and said: "We want our money back." We returned it at once and some sent it back again with a note, saying: "We were just trying you out."'

It was, I felt, my turn to change the subject. I said: 'God told Oral Roberts that he was to win 10,000,000 souls in ten years. Has he done so?'

'Our records show that we have done it.'

'What precisely do you mean, when you talk of winning souls?'

'These are people who have made a decision through our efforts, people who are converted and join a church. Their lives are changed and they become Christians.'

My mind began wrestling with thoughts of filing cabinets filled with 10,000,000 cases of conversion, but it was an unequal contest. I asked Lee Braxton: 'How do you build these records?'

'We get reports and testimonials,' he told me. 'I have my own aeroplane and I travel a good deal. I get personal testimonies; and this year we got one million letters.'

Getting down to a subject that is never very far from a jet-set evangelist's mind, I asked: 'What is your annual budget?'

'About the same as Billy Graham's,' he replied. 'About $15,000,000 a year.'

'You publish no accounts?'

'Our accounts are available to any sincere inquirer. If there are groups which say that we are making millions, Dr Roberts will bring them down here and open his books to them.'

'How is Dr Roberts remunerated?'

'For many years he lived on what was called love offerings—contributions. Some people thought he was making millions. So, to avoid criticism, he petitioned the Board of Trustees to put him on a salary. At present he is not personally wealthy. The royalties from his books and his personal wealth he has given to the university. He owns no real estate, has no personal wealth now, though he is furnished with a car and a house, like any other minister. Personally I don't know that I agree with him, going on a salary, but, as I say, he wanted to get away from criticism.'

'What is his salary?'

'The last amount I heard was $18,000 a year. He takes no salary as President of the University.'

Most senior American executives would feel ill at the thought of being paid $18,000 a year, about £7,500; and it would not please many British bosses, either, for that matter. I felt no twinge of pity for Oral Roberts, however, for he had his perks. Bank directors and evangelists-in-orbit are seldom short of a crust.

The whole question of finance, of course, had been treated with a coyness and a vagueness to which I had become accustomed in my dealings with successful men of the cloth. Lee Braxton, it is true, had been frank enough about the switch from love offerings; yet his account of the event did not quite fit with the more soulful explanation offered by Roberts himself. According to him, Dr R. O. Corvin, one of his associates, asked him whether he was making the change because of criticism or because he felt he was being 'moved from within'.

'I said that I was taking this step as one of faith and through it to demonstrate to myself and to the world that my financial income did not in any way determine the course of my personal ministry,' he replied. 'I had vowed never to touch the gold or the glory. It is a good feeling to know the vow has been scrupulously kept. I wanted to leave a testimony that what I had done in the ministry was not due to either a small or a large income. I did it because I loved God and people.'

Had I been Dr Corvin, I would have repeated the question: 'Are you making this change because of criticism or because you feel you are being moved from within?' Having read Roberts's little sermon on self, I still am not sure of the answer.

Whatever his reasons for altering his financial pattern, he lives quietly enough, though comfortably. Because of his Pentecostal background, he is not wild about the theatre or dances, the use of cosmetics or alcohol. His favourite reading is said to be Western stories; and he has a 240-acre ranch—Robin Hood farm, south of Tulsa—where he raises

Aberdeen Angus cattle. He is a keen golfer, a member of the rather posh Southern Hills County Club, and enjoys riding whenever he has the time for it. Politically he is reported to be a Democrat; but so is Billy Graham, now so close to President Nixon.

In Tulsa I found that he was popular, though inevitably any local public figure of his calibre is bound to attract some criticism, even if it is muted. I met Tulsans, for instance, who felt hurt because he had not held a crusade in his adopted town for a long time and seemed in no hurry to do so. 'Maybe he has grown too big for us,' one said. 'He's a big shot now, of course, a director of the bank.' There was a feeling, too, that this coiled spring, this lion, this man who had been called 'the loudest and flashiest revivalist since Billy Graham' was ready to settle for plump respectability far from the sawdust trail to the altar. There would be no more crusades, I was told, no more histrionics in canvas cathedrals, no more frenetic shouts to save a mother's son from hell. From now on, the more cynical said, he would be a pillar of the church, a pillar of academy, a pillar of the upper-crust community, wrapped in the prim stability of the Methodist Church, divorced from the more colourful, more excitable, less socially acceptable Pentecostals into which he was born.

I raised these questions with Lee Braxton. Was he neglecting Tulsa, so far as crusades were concerned? Not at all, he said. The Association treated Tulsa like any other city.

Was he abandoning crusades altogether, anxious to immerse himself in the life of the university? This time the reply was long and more bewildering, but it left me with the impression that rumour was right for a change.

'We've held a number of one-day meetings,' said Lee Braxton. 'But a full crusade? We haven't a tent any longer. The only reason we had a tent was that there were no auditoriums big enough to hold the crowd. Since then there have been a wave of auditoriums and we have the facilities.'

'With these facilities, do you plan any full crusades?' I asked, feeling as if someone had just cut my guy ropes.

'We don't plan any just yet,' he told me. 'We've been giving attention to the university. We've had our graduating recently; and his radio and television programmes take up a good part of his time. We are devoting more time to seminars, where we invite people from all over the world. They come for four days as our guests, five or six hundred at a time. The day of the mass meeting, the rally, the crusade has been replaced by the printed word and television—especially television. This country has gone wild on it.'

'Why,' I asked, 'did he turn Methodist?'

'He felt that it would open a door to 11,000,000 people,' he said. 'It has proved to be one of the best moves he has ever made ... though not financially, of course. The President of Liberia is a Methodist. His son came over here and invited Dr Roberts to visit his country. That shows how the door has been opened to him.'

'Does it mean a change of heart?'

'One of the questions they asked when he went to be ordained was: "Why do you want to become a Methodist?" He told them: "I don't want to be a Methodist minister. I want to be what I am, what God has made me." Then they asked him why he wanted to affiliate with the Methodists and he replied that it opened a door to 11,000,000 souls. He repeated: "If you take me, I come as I am." They said: "That is how we want you."

'I was opposed to it because I didn't understand all the things about it. I told him: "If you do that, you are going to have a lot of repercussions from some of your people." But I wouldn't have him change back for anything in the world.'

'Were there repercussions?'

'The Pentecostals unfortunately were upset. I am a Pentecostal. I won't change. A lot of times they are small and uneducated and lacking in knowledge or vision. They stay small.'

I still did not know, of course, whether he had had a change of heart, though later I picked up a few clues which indicated that there was a lot of the Pentecostal in him yet. He was quoted as saying, for instance: 'I still speak in tongues daily.' By that he meant that he found himself using a strange language that generally neither he nor anyone else could understand, a sign to Pentecostals that a person is filled with the Holy Spirit. In an earlier interview, his wife—who says that she, too, is granted this facility regularly—elaborated further. She told a *Tulsa Daily World* writer: 'Because of his busy schedule he frequently prays very earnestly while he is shaving. It always amuses me when I pass by his bathroom and hear him bathed in the Holy Spirit and speaking in tongues.'

Time magazine quoted him as saying that his switch to the Methodists was 'the will of God', which was clear enough. It blurred the picture, however, by adding that he denied that he had abandoned any of his old beliefs. Bewildered, I read that piece again and I wondered whether there were times when Oral Roberts bewildered himself. Certainly, when I left Tulsa, those scales on which I had tried to weigh his ministry were still behaving like a see-saw.

There was so much to tilt them in his favour—his forthright stand on the question of race; his university and the manner in which he involved his students in the lives of so many people, giving them a grass-roots education; his old folks' home; his work for the unemployed and underprivileged in Tulsa and for the neglected Indians in the area.

Sitting on the other dish of the scales, however, were the eulogies about him that pour from his printing presses, obviously with his approval; his readiness to hail as a miracle any achievement brought about by the efficiency of his sleek organization; and, heaviest of all so far as I am concerned, his blessing pact.

That blessing pact weighs heavily in my mind, but I have decided that there is one sure way of finding out whether it is heavier than the more pleasant facets of his character and that is to apply a simple test which will give a mathematical answer. All I would have to do is to sign that pact with Oral Roberts, evangelist, and then ask Oral Roberts, bank director, for a material loan in anticipation of spiritual dividends.

4: HELL-FIRE ON THE RIGHT

ONCE upon a time there was a man called Joseph McCarthy, who became a United States Senator and expounded a theory that it was better to be dead than red. What his views on that score are now I do not know, for he slid quietly and scarcely mourned from this life in 1957 and has yet to produce any personal, post-mortem evidence in support of his drastic philosophy.

Nevertheless it is interesting to note that sufficient right-wing extremists remain in the United States to support a few unofficial chaplains; and high in this exclusive hierarchy are the Rev. Dr Billy James Hargis of Tulsa, Oklahoma, and the Rev. Dr Carl McIntire of Collingswood, New Jersey. Their temperaments differ widely, but their views match neatly. Both are fundamentalists, who interpret the Bible literally and can prise from its pages texts to meet any eventuality from nuclear war to a shortage of funds. Both thunder out sermons calculated to leave their congregations soggy with fear. Both must have cricks in their backs from looking under beds for Marxist plots, though they seem so shattered by what they see above-bed that I wonder why they bother.

Of the two I found Billy James Hargis the less unlovable, for his sheer aggression teeters constantly on the slippery brim of slapstick. Here I felt, as I watched him, was a dinosaur pup or cub or whatever, lashing its tail dangerously, but at the same time hilarious in its wild, brash abandon.

A well-upholstered man of forty-five, he was born in Texarana, a Texas town that used to boast of having the blackest earth and the whitest people. His parents did not smoke, drink or play cards; but they read the Bible a good deal and it was no surprise when Billy was ordained at the age of eighteen after just over a year at Ozark Bible College in Bentonville, Arkansas.

His early years as a pastor were quiet enough, apart from the time when he tried to convert the whole town of Ozark overnight. From the pulpit he accused the local school principal of having an affair with one of his teachers and for good measure castigated the church elders for going to the cinema. For that piece of evangelistic zeal he was fired.

He soon got another job, however, and he might be in a cosy pastoral seat still, had he not cottoned on suddenly to the alarming fact that Communists from both inside and outside America were about to take over the whole joint. Until then he had been preaching peace and world government; but he abandoned that line in order to save his nation from a fate worse than death. In 1948 he founded Christian Crusade, an organization which, he announced, would stand for God and Country and would oppose aggressively any person or organization whose actions or words endorsed or aided the philosophies of Leftists, Socialists or Communists. Senator Joseph McCarthy spoke at its first conference and its platforms since then have known the weight of Governor George Wallace and Robert Welch, President of the John Birch Society.

Despite this support from the Knights of the Right, however, Hargis's balloon did not lift properly off the ground—and I mean that literally—until 1953, when the International Council of Churches came up with a theatrical thought. It decided to float Bible texts and tracts into the Warsaw Pact countries with the aid of helium-filled balloons; but before I become immersed in that dramatic slice of history I feel bound to explain a situation calculated to bewilder.

The main communion of churches in America is the National Council of Churches, which is composed of thirty-three major Protestant and Orthodox denominations with a combined membership of 35,000,000. In 1941 Carl McIntire formed the American Council of Churches, which listed only fifteen Protestant denominations with a total membership of 1,500,000. Many members of the public, unaware of this churchyard jousting, confused the two bodies, particularly when McIntire popped up with his posse whenever the rival and original body came to town for a meeting.

A little later National Councils of Churches from many countries met in Amsterdam to join together in a World Council of Churches. Simultaneously McIntire arrived in this fine old Dutch city and formed the International Council of Christian Churches, which carried slightly less weight abroad among churchmen than his American Council bore at home. The lay public, of course, were even more confused by that time.

It was McIntire's International Council of Christian Churches—no connection with the much larger firm next door—that came up with the idea of airborne salvation; and it was Billy James Hargis of Christian Crusade who was the commander in the field. From Germany, with the aid of a following wind and a prayer, he launched his Bible-bearing balloons, a feat which earned him not only the rash of publicity he needed, but an Honorary Doctorate of Divinity from the Defender Seminary in Puerto Rico.

In 1960 he got yet another publicity hoist from a most unexpected source—an Air Force training manual for reserve non-commissioned officers. In the lesson on security education and discipline—which advised servicemen, incidentally, to cultivate the habit of saying 'I don't know'—was a warning against Communists in clerical collars. It went on to allege that the National Council of Churches— the major body that has nothing to do with McIntire, if I may be forgiven the boring, but necessary repetition—had been infiltrated by Communists and that thirty of the ninety-five Council members responsible for the Revised Standard Version of the Bible had been affiliated with pro-Communist fronts, projects and publications. To the huge delight of Billy James, two of his pamphlets were quoted in support of these odd charges— 'Apostate Clergymen Battle for God-Hating Communist China' and 'The National Council of Churches Indicts Itself on Fifty Counts of Treason to God and Country'.

The National Council of Churches, of course, protested at once and the manual was withdrawn with a fulsome apology from Thomas S. Gates, who was Secretary of Defense at the time; but Billy kept marching on, scattering the same charges like snuff at a wake until there must have been few Americans who had not heard of his Christian Crusade.

Despite these boosts, he still remained in a relatively minor league financially. When I visited his Tulsa headquarters, I found that it was modest compared with those of Oral Roberts and Herbert Armstrong. Modesty, however, is easy in the shadow of those flamboyant giants; and Billy's set-up was cosy enough, embracing, as it did, a modern church building, a publishing house, a film library, facilities for taping broadcasts, a chapel for the staff and further conveniences, including a Meditation Garden in which I found the motto, carved in stone: 'America is God's greatest country under the living Son'. Outside the church was a less heart-warming sign, which read: 'Beware Guard Dog'; but, as I had come to attend the service, I felt safe.

Before taking my seat, however, I had a brief and not very encouraging meeting with the Rev. Dr Hargis, who appeared dressed casually in a T-shirt and jeans. When he heard of my mission, he said: 'There have been twenty-eight books about me and all but one of them were critical. I presume what you're going to write will be critical of me too and critical of the Conservative cause.'

That, I explained, would depend largely on what he had to say to me, to which he replied: 'I'm very busy. I leave for Europe next

Sunday. After that I go round the world—to Teheran, to Bangkok.'
Decently enough, however, he agreed to see me before he saw the rest
of the world; and with that I joined the congregation, about a hundred
people, sitting on yellow metal seats in a circular church. The American
flag was predictably prominent, flanking the platform which held
yellow armchairs, facing out on to a vase of gladioli. Then the lights
dimmed; curtains at the back of the stage slid back silently to reveal a
large picture of Christ picking up the Cross; and a robust baritone sang
'God Is Real'. He was followed by a small boy wearing a blue waist-
coat with brass buttons. When he was lifted on to the chair, he sang 'A
Thanksgiving Prayer', the first two lines of which were: 'Thank You,
God, for father and mother... Teach... us... to love... one and other.'
Billy James, dressed in a smart suit now, smiled approvingly, though
events proved later that love was scarcely his central theme that night.

A prayer followed: 'Let us pray for the boys in Vietnam . . . Assist
them until they are granted an honorable victory against Godless,
atheistic, anti-Christ Communism . . . Forgive those young people who
would pull down our Government over this weekend and may their
eyes be opened to the Godless, despotic, tyrannical, dictatorial leaders
of Communism.'*

The adjectives, smooth with age and usage, slipped out like sheep
through a gate; but they were no more than spiritual aperitifs for the
Rev. Dr Billy James Hargis, who began with the message that tapes of
his sermon would be available for five dollars, about £2. Then, pausing
briefly to announce that the next congress would be held in Rhodesia
and would be addressed by Prime Minister Ian Douglas Smith, he
launched into a tirade of sombre prophecy and revelation that took us
round the sin bins of the world.

We started on the home front: 'The year 1970 could be the beginning
of the end for the United States and her free-world allies . . . I spent five
hours with Governor Wallace in Montgomery and we talked of everything except his Presidential Prospects . . . but I'm more worried about
Nixon than I am about the next election . . . Perhaps there won't be free
elections, if the anarchistic elements have their way.'

Here was scary stuff for his audience, provided, of course, that they
did not recall the words he wrote in his newsletter some time earlier:
'It is "do or die" in 1964. If we don't break this liberal yoke in '64, forget

* A reference to the March Against Death in Washington. The Government
survived this dangerous outbreak of peace fever.

about freedom and liberty. It will become but a memory in the hearts of an enslaved people.'

For Billy, the end of his world is always nigh, or so it seemed that night. 'The President of the United States is the only one to stop this drift,' he said. 'I would like to see a Statesman President, rather than a politician, a Winston Spencer Churchill of the United States, who doesn't give a hang about political expediency, but is concerned only with a Christian culture and the American dream . . . I hope we can push Richard Nixon into the role of Statesman.'

From America, placed in jeopardy by the dangerous liberalism of the pinko President, he switched to Britain in general and to me in particular. 'We have a British reporter here tonight,' he said. 'He may be seeing me at my worst; but I don't think we should give one dollar in foreign aid to any country which will not stand with us in the fight, any country that trades with North Vietnam—and that goes for Britain.'

There was a burst of applause. Heads twisted to examine me, symbol as I was of British ingratitude and perfidy. I smiled at the frowning faces, but got no response, as Billy James, arms held high, shouted: 'I don't see why we should prop up the Socialist Government of Harold Wilson.'

That won more applause, louder this time. Catching the mood, he went on: 'The British think the Chinese will respect the ninety-nine year lease they have on Hong Kong . . . They say it is a market place for Red Chinese merchandise; but that doesn't matter now because Nixon has lifted the economic embargo on Red China. Has he lifted the embargo on Ian Duncan Smith? He has not and Rhodesia is a Christian country. Ian Duncan Smith has made a greater contribution towards solving racial problems than any other country in Africa.'

That gem shone particularly brightly over his congregation; but Billy James still had a whole jewellery shop behind him. He spoke, for instance of 'that High Rasputin of Peace at Any Price Ralph Abernathy and his pro-red agitators'. He lashed out at 'nit-witted, traitorous liberals who will sell out for prestige or money'. He prayed for the moon-shot 'because the Communists could make great political hay, if anything happens to that machine'. He did not mention what would happen to the astronauts inside it.

Suddenly he cantered off in a new direction, zooming from space to sex. 'Take the sex revolution,' he said. 'I got concerned with it many years ago. The Communists will use sex as a weapon to demoralize the youth of America—sex both normal and abnormal!'

He paused, as well he might after that bombshell. Then, holding up a picture from *Look* magazine, showing a youth with his arm over a girl's naked breasts, he yelled: 'Another Beatnik! *Look* says that puritan America has gone for ever. I'll give my life to defend puritan America. Before Marxist-Leninist ideology comes sexual involvement. Why is there all this preoccupation with sex for children of seven years of age? It's a Satan-inspired revolution and Communism is a facet of Satan.'

His brow gleamed with sweat. More softly he said: 'How can these kids, all mixed up with sexual intercourse, homosexuality and lesbianism, ever be satisfied with Christ within the Church?'

It was a good question and everyone seemed to think it was a good curtain line. The organ sighed and the congregation rose to sing the final hymn. When they were half-way through the first verse, however, Billy shushed them and burst back into battle.

'There is sex identification in the name of art and folk music, performed by amoral, dope-taking artists,' he thundered. 'After all this sex I heard two of my little girls singing the theme song of that filthy show, *Hair*, a pornographic play on Broadway. Almost every movie is a homosexual film.'

The hymn, which had died in a hundred throats, revved up again. When it ended I left, watched cautiously by the worshippers, who seemed to be listening for the patter of cloven hooves, made in Britain by Harold Wilson's Socialist slaves.

That night, armed with a heap of Billy James literature, I learned a little more about him. There was a booklet called *Billy James Hargis Tells It Like This*, which set out the causes which he supported, rather than those which he opposed; and I had to admit that his sermon had left me rather ignorant about that aspect of his thinking. He spelled out his views in capitals and I learned first that Christian Crusade was for Jesus Christ, the Bible and Bible morality, news which did not surprise me greatly. Other headings, however, were less straightforward and less spiritual. I read: 'We are for dying on our feet, if need be, instead of dying on our knees'; 'We are for J. Edgar Hoover . . . He has the the right enemies . . . the Communists, the liberals, the far left, the amoralists'; 'We are for soap and water, haircuts and dresses'; and 'We are for the more affluent taking the leadership in solving America's race problem.' He revealed also that he was 'for the attitude, "I'd rather be dead than red"'; but that I had gathered already.

Having been told it like that, I turned to his biography, *Crusading Preacher From the West.* The cover showed Billy, holding an amiable white horse by the reins and gazing into the middle distance from beneath the rim of a stetson hat. Inside were pictures of him with President Syngman Rhee of South Korea and with Generalissimo and Madam Chiang Kai-shek.

From a variety of pamphlets I learned that his message was carried fairly widely on commercial radio and that he had a weekly newspaper, together with a monthly magazine. The magazine's Editor was the Rev. Gerald S. Pope, father of Oral Roberts's Director of Public Relations; and a further link between these two evangelists who had adopted Tulsa but were so different was L. E. White, known to his friends as Pete. Years earlier he had helped to publicize Oral Roberts; now, it seemed, he was doing a somewhat similar job for Hargis.

Financial support, I gathered, came from a variety of sources—his appeals on the air and in his literature; sale of his books and pamphlets; and holiday tours which he organizes for his supporters to the Orient, the Holy Land, Rhodesia, the Greek Islands, Italy, Germany and—for the really ambitious—right round the world. Those holiday tours were attractive and certainly showed initiative, a quality Billy James does not lack when it comes to fund-raising. On one occasion, for instance, his wife took over this chore and wrote to Crusade members: 'Recently, because of illness, I have not been able to visit the office as often as I would like, but I know the work is in great financial need right now. I can sincerely say that Billy's every thought is on Christian Crusade. He is always thinking what else can be done to get the message out, at the same time working day and night to provide the "ways and means".

'Won't each of you help to relieve some of this pressure by your contributions . . . He will be tired but a wonderful response from you, his friends, could lift a great burden from him. I pray the Lord will use me through this letter to help Christian Crusade, for I want so much to do my part during these critical days . . .

'P.S. The Office informs me that Billy has written a brand new booklet, called "American Socialism—Moving America Downhill!" His staff tells me this is the best thing he ever wrote, exposing all American "Liberals". Also, if you would like one, I would like to send a snapshot of Billy and the children.'

Buoyed up by this message, I went to meet Billy James the following morning. Before the appointment, however, I was taken on a tour of the premises by a courteous and kindly member of the staff. He showed me the massive organ I had heard the previous night, explaining apologetically: 'It's really a theatre organ, but we accepted it as it was donated to us.' Then I was shown the Edgar Scheubert Auditorium, where a blackboard bore the strange legend 'God Bless Spiro Agnew, Incorporated'; the library with its five thousand bound books; the shipping department, which sends out nearly a million pamphlets, booklets and magazines each month; and finally the museum, which held the pulpit from which Billy James preached his first sermon and a Toledo blade, given by General Franco to General Charles A. Willoughby, one of the Crusade's most staunch supporters. All in all, the tour got my adrenalin into a suitable condition for my meeting with the Father of Christian Crusade, who was relaxing in his office, his mood more genial than it had been the previous evening.

I asked him how many members he had and he replied readily: 'Well over a quarter of a million now, but that doesn't really mean anything. Think of it as 250,000 families with an average of four members each. I'm not in it for members, however. All I want is enough money to accomplish my mission in life.'

'Do you get enough money?'

'We took in about $1,500,000 last year,' he told me, 'but we're running into a hole this year. We've had some financial troubles. In the early fifties, you see, I had the field to myself. I was the first preacher in America to fight Communism in the name of religion. There was no Carl McIntire, no John Birch Society, though I don't think you could call the John Birch people a religious organization. Then all of a sudden I was faced with fierce competition from a dozen other organizations who were pulling my support. I don't mind, of course. My soul, I've no priority on Christian anti-Communism.

'I prayed about it, of course. I said: "Am I going to be twisted off a dying movement or exercise the faith I preach?" With no money I hired an architect and he made plans for this development here. The people supported me. This building cost a million dollars and the furnishings another quarter of a million. The building and property across the street is ours, too, and that cost a further quarter of a million.

'Now I'm going to open a college—we're calling it American College—to train Christian young people for leadership in our nation so that they can bring our country back to the Bible. We've had two big contributions for that already and we're launching a nation-wide campaign to underwrite it. It will mean finding another million and a half, but it will be worth it. Our school will emphasize Christian conservative training. Christians should get involved in saving the country.'

By that stage in my journey I had ceased to be surprised by the sound of evangelists talking blandly in millions. I had lost, too, any shyness about asking them how much they took out of the collection box for themselves, for I had found that they were not an over-sensitive breed. So I said to Billy James: 'Your own salary has been reported to be $12,000 a year. Is that true?'

Frowning slightly, he said: 'It's more than that, though I'm limited in what I take from Christian Crusade. I get an expense allowance that covers my travel, my meal bills, my hotel bills, two suits a year and my expenses on the road. I'm allowed a car with the gasoline paid and a house to live in.'

He pondered this list for a moment. Then wistfully he said: 'The house we live in belongs to the Crusade. It cost only $40,000 and in the United States that's a shack. The average home in Tulsa costs $70,000. My wife's tired of living in someone else's house. We'd like to have a home of our own. We really would, you know, somewhere we could change the colour of the walls, if we felt like it.

'We have our farm, of course—160 acres with twenty cows and one young bull. That cost $40,000 and I had to cash everything I had to make a down payment. Just now I couldn't write a personal cheque for a thousand dollars, if my life depended on it.'

'All the same,' I said, not exactly overcome by the pathos of the speech, 'you get free holidays from your conducted tours.'

'They're Christian Crusade tours,' he said. 'They're a major source of income for the organization. I'm taking 108 people out on Sunday night to the Holy Land and Greece. I'll be speaking every day as well as planning the menus and looking after the luggage.'

There he had a point. I thought of him, sitting on top of a heap of Tulsan luggage in Jerusalem, trying to write a suitable sermon with one hand and an edible menu with the other. Moved by the sad picture, I tried to cheer him up by introducing a subject I thought he would enjoy. I said: 'I gathered from your sermon last night that you don't think much of the British Labour Government.'

'You're right,' he replied. 'I think Harold Wilson has robbed the people of their destiny with his Socialist experiments. They've bankrupted the country. I don't like anything about the Socialist Government of Great Britain. Even the morals of the nation have declined since they took over at the end of the war.'

Gently I reminded him that there had been not only Labour, but Conservative Governments since 1945 and that the moral standards had not switch-backed noticeably with each change of the electorate's mind. His face bright with surprise, he said: 'That's right, of course. That Christine Keeler affair was under the Conservatives,* wasn't it?'

I nodded. Billy James smiled his acknowledgement; but the mistake did nothing to divert him from his purpose. Squaring his shoulders, he said: 'Man, I'm sure I'd die of blood pressure, if I lived in Britain!'

Lest even the thought of that amoral, leftist island might cause his heart to thump, I decided to settle for some small conversational change. I said to him: 'In some of your publications you have attacked the "Laugh-In" television show. Why?'

'Because,' he said firmly, 'they are a radical departure from home entertainment and Bible morality.'

'You have written that you stand for soap and water, haircuts and dresses. What do you mean by that?'

'Beards and long hair today represent another radical departure,' he replied. 'Even dress has become revolutionary.'

'But Christ had a beard and long hair.'

'It's important to me,' he said, 'that Christian young men maintain proper dress standards. Those who wear long hair and beards are aping Fidel Castro and Che Guevara.'

'I see,' I said, 'that you have had the Rev. Dr Ian Paisley speaking in your church. He is a man who holds fairly bilious views about Roman Catholics. Do you agree with him on that point?'

'Bob Jones from Bob Jones University in South Carolina brought him here,' said Billy. 'That guy Paisley, is a fantastic preacher, the most powerful preacher I've ever heard; but I don't want you to get the idea that I'm anti-Catholic. I get about twenty per cent of my support from Roman Catholics. As a matter of fact I asked Paisley to keep off the Catholic theme. "Just preach," I told him. "Just preach."'

Any man who can steer the Rev. Ian R. K. Paisley off his anti-Catholic theme must be powerfully persuasive. By accomplishing that

* Since then the Conservatives have ousted Harold Wilson's Socialists. I hope the news has reached Billy in Tulsa.

unique feat, he revealed a shrewdness that is not evident immediately
when he talks. His sermons and his replies to my questions might give
the impression that he is naïve, a small-town boy, trying to cash in on a
dying issue. Yet he cannot be dismissed too lightly, even though some of
his statements are so outrageous that they become hilarious. He realizes,
I think, that his anti-Communist act is not the five-star attraction that
once it was. So now he is adding to the script, introducing sex, which
is a much more permanent element than any political ideology. He
denounces the permissive society, sex education in the schools, student demonstrators and pop groups like the Beatles and the Rolling
Stones, though he still insists, for the sake of right-wing old-timers, that
all those diabolical manifestations are part of a monstrous Marxist plot.
He knows his followers, indeed, for the middle-class conservatives
that they are and he knows what they want to hear about beards and
Bolshevists and beats. So long as he continues to let them hear it he will
survive in comfort.

He is not, however, in the same intellectual bracket as the Rev. Dr
Carl McIntire, though they cling together in their fundamentalism,
their anti-Communist campaigns and their dislike of both the National
Council of Churches and the World Council of Churches. Where Billy
James will go out of his way to make friends and influence people who
may support his cause, however, McIntire has a superb knack of losing
friends and making enemies. Yet in spite of this foible, he is probably
more affluent than Hargis. Though he insists that those who are not one
hundred per cent for him are one hundred per cent against him, he
survives.

His headquarters are in the quiet, middle-class town of Collingswood, New Jersey, a spot where there is no business, except church
business, on Sundays; no liquor stores, no copies of *Playboy,*
True Romance or *Teen Confessions* on the news stands. There he has his
$600,000 church with a loyal congregation of 1,600, a broadcasting
studio which sends tapes to stations all over the United States and
Canada, a Bible school, a publishing plant, a bookshop to sell its wares
and the old Admiral Hotel, which was built in 1907 at a cost of
$1,500,000 and which he advertises as 'a year-round Christian and patri-
otic conference centre with 333 bedrooms, American plan, dedicated to
the glory of God'. His sermons are folksy, his writings less so, as the
following quotations from his book, *Author of Liberty,* show: 'We are
about to surrender liberty when we fuss over relatively small things,

such as benefits and security'; 'Imagine our founding fathers coming to this barren land with the purpose of setting up a government that would guarantee full employment to all people'; 'There is a limit to which Christians should help others because too much help encourages irresponsibility'; and—predictably—'Progressive and liberal are Satan's pet words.' Like Billy James, he knows his audience.

Today he is a prominent and wealthy citizen of Collingswood. The road to this affluence and influence, however, was rough, mainly because the Rev. Carl is so efficient with his verbal pick-axe and so sure that he is a little bit more equal than others. Born in Ypsilanti, Michigan, in 1906, he graduated from Park College, Parkville, Missouri and from there went to Princeton Theological Seminary, where he came under the influence of Professor J. Gresham Machen, a strict fundamentalist. When Machen broke with the seminary and formed a school of his own —the Westminster Theological Seminary in Philadelphia—McIntire followed him. In 1931 he graduated from this solid scriptural base, was ordained a Presbyterian minister and married his Southern-born sweetheart, who had the rather unfundamental name of Fairy. Three years later, when he was only twenty-three, he became Pastor of the Presbyterian Church in Collingswood and he has lived in the town ever since.

That post was a fine opportunity for a vigorous young preacher; but soon there was strife. Machen broke from the Presbyterian Board of Missions and set up his own Independent Board. McIntire sent his congregation's contributions to this new body. The Presbytery of New Jersey filed charges against them both for ecclesiastic disobedience and they were found guilty. Since then McIntire has been described frequently as 'an unfrocked minister', a description he dislikes because, he says, it is inclined to imply that he ran away with another minister's wife.

Despite the verdict, he continued to preach in the Collingswood Church. A new pastor was appointed, but the congregation, loyal to the Rev. Carl, would not let him in. Finally McIntire moved—to a huge tent just opposite the church. Most of the congregation followed him; and eight weeks later a new frame church, seating 1,500, had replaced the tent. A $250,000 Sunday school was built in 1948 and the present $600,000 church in 1960. Even in those early days he never thought of himself as a rebel, but as a pillar of the true Presbyterian Church. All the others were out of step; and soon he was unhappy about the way his old friend, Machen, was marching. He felt that the professor was not sufficiently strict—some of his followers smoked!—and they parted.

He owes his survival, perhaps, not only to his own shrewdness and tenacity, but to his supreme confidence in himself. When the National Council of Churches announced after the Air Force manual incident that they represented thirty-three major Protestant and Orthodox denominations with a combined memberhip of 35,000,000, while McIntire's American Council listed only fifteen denominations with a total membership of 1,500,000, he seemed to take it in his stride. As a gifted propagandist, he probably was well aware that few people read corrections or denials in newspapers and even fewer remember them. He continued to blast the National and World Councils through his two rival organizations; and even when he fell out with his associates in his own movements, he appeared undismayed.

Today he is head of the Bible Presbyterian Church, the Twentieth Century Reformation Centre, the Beacon Press and his bookshop, to all of which he devotes remarkable energy. He arrives at his broadcasting studio at six o'clock every morning to record his Twentieth Century Reformation Hour programme and, when that task is finished, he goes home to breakfast with Fairy, leaving the chores to his staff of eighty-five workers. They make copies from the tape and send them out to the commercial stations. Some of the station executives are worried about slander, because Carl McIntire is not given very frequently to soft words and has many targets. Glenn D. Everett, Washington Correspondent for a number of religious periodicals and an expert on religious broadcasting, wrote in *Concern* magazine:

This writer recently noted that, in the course of a single program, Dr McIntire denounced specifically by name no less than nineteen outstanding protestant leaders, starting out with Dr Arthur Michael Ramsey, the Archbishop of Canterbury, and continuing down the line through Presbyterian Dr Eugene Carson Blake and Episcopal Bishop James A. Pike—favorite daily targets—including Methodist, Baptist, Lutheran and Disciples of Christ leaders, sparing none a swipe of his tar brush.

His repeated thesis, according to Everett, is that the leaders of all major Protestant denominations, because of subversive teachings absorbed during seminary education, are engaged in a clandestine conspiracy to turn America towards Communism and atheism. It is no wonder that the studio executives feel unhappy, but most of them have found that Carl McIntire is a difficult man to shift, particularly when any move to do so can be translated so readily into an attempt to stifle free speech.

His nation-wide broadcasts, however, have created less concern than his international outpourings over a privately-owned station in Red Lion, Pennsylvania. It is powerful enough to cover the world and McIntire's broadcasts have caused considerable embarrassment to American diplomatic missions overseas and to the United States Information Service. While most Americans know that preachers buy time on the air, broadcasting in many other countries is controlled by the government. Listeners in these faraway places could interpret the words of the Rev. Carl McIntire as official policy. As he is inclined to suggest fairly firmly and frequently that both Church and State are about to be toppled by subversive elements, those words are not likely to encourage confidence overseas in the United States of America.

McIntire, however, seems unconcerned with such minor quibbles; indeed, if stories about his financial resources are true, he has every reason to be thoroughly satisfied with his work and himself. The *New York Post Daily Magazine* quoted him five years ago as saying: 'Our budget is easily a million dollars a year, but we have no fat cats. Our money comes in from the faithful and in small bills, but it keeps coming, it keeps coming.'

Robert T. Coote, Assistant Editor of *Eternity* magazine, wrote in its issue of May 1969 that his income from his radio stations alone was $3,000,000 a year and that his New Jersey complex was valued at $3,000,000. He continued: 'His 1968 Christmas drive for world relief brought in over $500,000 . . . To accomplish this, while running up a history-making list of disillusioned former supporters and rival institutions, is remarkable indeed.'

Certainly those he attacks cover a wide field. Apart from the National Council of Churches and the World Council of Churches—routine targets now—he has taken swipes over the past few years at such diverse bodies as the United Nations (a tool of Communism) and the Y.M.C.A. (for sponsoring teenage dances). Yet despite his uncanny ability to quarrel with those who do not stick firmly to his excessively narrow path, he still has friends who are widely known, though not always widely loved. He supports Barry Goldwater, despite the fact that the ebullient Senator said 'damn', while addressing the New Hampshire Primary in the last Presidential election, a slip which caused a right old tizzy among some of the lady members on McIntire's staff.

Like Billy James Hargis, he has shared platforms with prominent members of the John Birch Society and, when the Air Force manual affair was bubbling, the National Council of Churches issued a statement which read: 'Associated with McIntire at various times have been promoters of discord and hate such as William Denton, the Northern and Southern Knights of the Ku Klux Klan, Gerald L. K. Smith, Gerald Winrod, Edgar Bundy, Merwin K. Hart, Billy James Hargis.'

There is one man, of course, with whom he is extremely friendly and that is Dr Bob Jones, Jr., President of the Bob Jones University in Greenville, South Carolina, described in its literature as 'The world's most unusual university'. All fundamentalists love Dr Bob, for his academy is a cradle for their cause, sending thousands of faithful, dedicated workers from the campus into the mission fields at home and abroad. On his radio station he carries sermons by Billy James Hargis daily, by Carl McIntire from Monday to Saturday, and by Ian Paisley on Sunday. Both Hargis and Paisley have Honorary Doctorates from his university and that in itself was enough to send me to Greenville, South Carolina, to find out just how unusual it was. Briefly the answer is: very. I shall elaborate in the next chapter.

5: BIBLE-BELTERS

THE fact that Hargis, McIntire and Paisley—now there's a trinity for you!—all had close links with Dr Bob Jones, Jnr., was not the only carrot which lured me to his university outside Greenville, South Carolina, in the foothills of the Great Smokies and the Blue Ridge mountains. Earlier I had read the obituary notices—particularly that in the *New York Times*—of his father, the founder, and they alone contained enough fascinating information to make my journey not only necessary, but vitally so. Admittedly most fundamentalists and conservatives regard the *New York Times* as a pinko scandal sheet, but I had taken always a more kindly view, sloppy liberal that I am.

Dr Bob Jones, Snr., had died on 16 January 1968 at the age of eighty-five and, according to the obituary, had managed somehow to live a life that was both full and narrow. Right from his earliest days he had been drawn towards the Church and at the age of nine he was practising his preaching over the backs of a mule team, as he guided the plough on his father's farm in Dale County, Alabama. By the time he was thirteen, he had held his first revival meeting and he was licensed to preach by the Methodist Church two years later. Soon he was drawing crowds of 10,000, a phenomenal performance in those days of meagre transport and only slender lines of communication.

In September 1927 he founded his own school near Lynn Haven on the borders of Alabama and Florida because he was 'tired of leading boys and girls to Jesus Christ and then seeing them attend institutions which shake their faith'. His school, he said, would combat 'the atheistic drift in education' and 'dispel the old idea that, if you have old time religion, you must have a greasy nose, dirty finger-nails and baggy pants and that you mustn't shine your shoes'. To achieve his object, he drew up rules which were controversial even then and have become increasingly so ever since.

No black students were admitted because Dr Jones believed that separation of the races was ordained by the Bible. Drinking and smoking were forbidden. Mixed groups were limited as much as possible. If girls and boys had to be together, they were to keep their bodies at least six inches apart. Hollywood films were banned, as were cards, dancing and jazz. Students were required to report violation of these rules by others or face dismissal for being disloyal. Even today there probably are more ways of getting expelled from Bob Jones University than there are on any other campus. On the fly-leaf of the current

university bulletin, indeed, under the heading 'Important', are the
following solemn words:

> It is understood that attendance at Bob Jones University is a privilege and not
> a right, which privilege may be forefeited by any student who does not conform
> to the standards and regulations of the institution, and that the University may
> request the withdrawal of any student at any time, who, in the opinion of the
> University, does not fit into the spirit of the institution, regardless of whether
> or not he conforms to the specific rules and regulations of the University.

Here obviously was a man of single purpose and deeply entrenched
views, a combination which some people felt—and still feel—added up
to bigotry. The accuracy of their addition was reinforced when he
plunged into politics during the 1928 Presidential election and came out
with some speeches that make modern electioneering tactics seem pale
flowers indeed. His chief target was Governor Al Smith, the Democratic candidate, who not only had committed the unforgivable sin of
being born a Catholic, but had remained in that pernicious condition
long after he had reached the age of reason.

'Catholics,' Jones roared in one speech, 'believe that children of non-
Catholic parents are illegitimate . . . I'd rather see a nigger in the White
House than Mr Smith.' Then, scraping the bucket for even stronger
poison, he went on: 'I'd rather see a saloon on every corner than a
Catholic in the White House.'

Whether he hated drink more than he hated black skin I do not know
and happily his views on drunken non-white, non-Anglo-Saxon, non-
Protestants have not been published. At this point it is sufficient to say
that Al Smith lost; and Bob Jones, having played his spectacular, if not
very edifying, part in the democratic process, went back to the cloister
of his academy, which was beginning to stagger under the onslaught of
the depression. It survived, however, moved to larger premises at
Cleveland in 1933 and fourteen years later transferred to Greenville.
Today, according to the *New York Times*, it has over 3,800 students and
every year sends an army of missionaries, ministers and educators into
the wicked world to do battle with the liberalism, alcoholism, evolu-
tionary teaching and political decay that they believe infest American
life.

Intrigued by this fascinating slab of information and anxious to check
it with the university authorities, I wrote to Dr Bob Jones, Jnr., asking
whether he would grant me an interview. A week later I arrived in

Greenville, telephoned the university and was told by Robert Harrison, the Director of Public Relations: 'Dr Jones will not be interviewed by any member of the liberal press.'

'I'm not writing for the press,' I told him. 'I'm writing a book.'

'It's the same thing.'

'May I interview Dr Bob Jones III?' I asked. 'He's Vice-President. Surely he could help me.'

'No.'

'May I interview any member of the faculty?'

'No.'

'May I interview you?'

'No.'

I began to feel unwanted. He agreed to show me over the university, however, and a little later that day I was walking with him through grounds and buildings that were more solid, more dignified, even more expensive than the flashier establishments of Oral Roberts in Tulsa and Herbert Armstrong in Pasadena. As we passed by trim students— models of orthodoxy—and cars with stickers reading 'God Loves You', he told me: 'We built the new campus here in 1947 and since then we've expanded, nearly doubled, in fact. We kept the same architect so that the new buildings would blend with the old.'

He was right. Here was more than a university. Here was a small town, comfortably planned, beautifully executed, complete with all the urban trimmings—a radio station, a theatre of professional standard, a fine art gallery, an extensive library, a sports stadium, swimming pool and gymnasium, a laundry and shops where the residents could buy just about everything with the possible exception of clothes and the positive exception of alcohol and tobacco.

The efficiency of the place was staggering, as I found when we entered the dining hall, which seemed to cover acres. I said to Robert Harrison, who, I learned later, had been made an Honorary Colonel of the Alabama Militia by former Governor George C. Wallace: 'You could play football here.'

'You could,' he said calmly. 'It's the length of a football field, but not quite as wide. We can serve 10,000 meals a day here and for our Thanksgiving dinner we have over two and a half tons of turkey. It seats 3,500 and is one of the largest dining halls in the United States.'

Everything I saw, indeed, was the biggest or the finest and I must say that Harrison's gentle pride was justified. In the university theatre, which seats 3,000 and has its own Green Room, he told me: 'We have two major theatrical productions a year. Dr Jones, who is one of the leading Shakespearean actors and authorities in the country, often takes part in them. So does his son, Bob Jones III, who is quite an actor, too. We have one of the largest non-commercial operatic and Shakespearean wardrobes in the country and a collection of jewellery and armour that stretches over the ages. The stage revolves and there are lifts which can raise sections of it twelve feet high and lower them twelve feet down. I think that you could say that there is no college campus with a theatre like ours.'

I thought that I could and told him that I would. At that moment, however, his mind had been whipped momentarily away from me by the sight of a student with a beard. Urgently he explained: 'He has grown that for a film. We don't allow beards here. Not even the staff can wear them. Those with beards for the film wear badges to explain why they are not clean-shaven.'

As it happened, I had not noticed the beard, but obviously he did not want me to run away with the idea that here was a hot-bed of hippies. To sponge any vestige of such ugly thought from my mind, he went on quickly: 'We call our motion picture unit Unusual Films. We're known, you see, as the world's most unusual university. They've just released *Gateway to a Miracle*, a promotional film about the college with a script written by Dr Bob Jones III. They've filmed *Macbeth*, too, with Dr Bob Jones, Jnr., in the lead. Films by the unit have won a number of national and international awards.'

That is a feature of this remarkable establishment. Many people may not agree with its rules or its teachings; but few would deny that whatever they do, they do well. Their radio station—call sign WMUU for the World's Most Unusual University—may carry sermons which stick in the theological gullet of more liberal clerics, but it carries also fine musical programmes to a wide area. Harrison, mine of statistics that he was, told me: 'We have a 100,000-watt FM stereo station and a 5,000-watt AM station. We cover up to about 100 miles on the FM and we have two more stations in Atlanta. They are commercial stations, but we refuse all alcohol and tobacco advertisements; and there are no commercials at all on Sundays. The four stations combined can be heard in an area that holds 3,000,000 people and give students majoring in radio and television valuable practical experience.'

Like the theatre, the art gallery is far more than a cultural arm of the university. It is the pride of South Carolina, thirty rooms with over three hundred pictures, all of them with religious themes and some of them donated by well-wishers. In the few minutes I was there, I saw work by Van Dyck, Rubens and Rembrandt; and these were just part of a collection that is worth several million dollars.

Yet, despite all these impressive features, it is impossible to tour the Bob Jones University without stumbling from time to time over reminders that here there are facets which, to put it mildly, would not be found in more liberal establishments. In the Freedom Shrine—an odd name, I thought on a campus so claustrobic with rigid rules—I saw a book with the aggressive title *The History of Romish Treason and Usurpation*. Near by was a Public Service Award for Leadership and Patriotic Courage in the Cause of Freedom and Dedication, presented to Dr Jones, Snr., by the Texas Detective Bureau. Farther on was a gift from the Rev. Ian R. K. Paisley—sermon notes of a long-dead fundamentalist preacher. To me these exhibits symbolized the unyielding attitude of the place; and the severity of them was emphasized rather than softened by the presence of intimate family souvenirs which should have breathed some humanity into the air. I saw newspaper cuttings reporting the founder's early revival meetings, the hymn book and razor which his father carried throughout the civil war, and sermon notes of Billy Sunday, base-ball player-turned-evangelist, daddy of all hell-fire revivalists and a close friend of the Jones family. Softly my guide said: 'Dr Jones was very sentimental. Billy Sunday spoke at the school, you know, and we've named one of the four dormitories for women students after him. The auditorium is named after his song leader, Homer Rodheaver.'

As I brooded on the sentimentality of racists—'Massa's In De Cold, Cold Ground'—he whisked me to the library, which contains not only a highly valuable collection of rare and historic volumes, but ten volumes on the history of the Roman Catholic Church and the lives of its Popes. There was plenty of contemporary material, too, of course, including newspapers and magazines. I asked Robert Harrison whether they took the liberal press and he said with a sigh: 'Anything at all today is liberal.' As if saddened by the thought, he moved on to a large, pleasant, comfortable room and said: 'This is our social parlour. Students can bring their dates here.' I thought of the rule that insisted on six inches of space between the sexes and wondered what would happen if they were caught taking them anywhere else.

Out we went then into the open air, of which there is plenty on this 180-acre campus. We walked past lush lawns, past fountains that seemed so much more discreet than those at Ambassador College, past rose gardens and lawns that looked as if they had been brushed and combed and trimmed—just like the students, indeed. Then suddenly, amid this peaceful orthodoxy, I came across a symbol of un-American activity: a soccer pitch.

'You play soccer here?' I said. 'No American football?'

'Football with all its equipment is too expensive because we don't play other colleges,' he said. 'We believe only in intra-mural games. We're known as a Christian school, after all, and we don't want students coming here just because we're a good football school. People know Notre Dame, for instance, as a football college.'

He paused. I waited. Then, to his credit, he came out with what I gathered was a more potent reason for this isolationist policy. He said: 'We have certain standards here. There is no smoking. If other teams visited us, it might be difficult. After some football games, of course, it goes far beyond smoking. There is . . . drinking.'

I must record that Robert Harrison helped me to the best of his ability, confined as he was by the instructions which his President had given him about interviews. From him I learned that they had more students from the Northern States than they had from the South; that their day-to-day teaching operations were financed by students' fees; and that they taught evolution as a theory, but not as a fact, preferring to stick to the Biblical version. In the restricted circumstances of our meeting, however, it was inevitable that I should leave the campus with many gaps in my knowledge about its activities.

These, however, were filled from a variety of sources, which helped me to clothe the rather spare image I had of Dr Bob Jones, Jnr. I learned, for instance, that he was an author and a poet, as well as an administrator, teacher and preacher. I had heard of his acting ability, but I did not know that in his earlier days he had resisted the lure of offers from Broadway and Hollywood. He may have been matinée idol material, but I doubt if he would have had the temperament for the wicked world of show business. On one national television network, he said: 'Any degenerate should welcome the "new morality". It gives him a licence to cheat, kill, rape, practise sedition and at the same time it gives him a quasi-respectable cloak of pseudo-intellectualism to hide behind while doing these things.' Apart altogether from the fact that he holds those strong views, it is unlikely that he would have been able to take part in that well-known old Hollywood party game of musical marriages. Obviously a staunch believer in long engagements, he courted his future wife for eleven years before they married. They are, I can report happily, if unnecessarily, still together.

Other snippets of information I gathered told me that the theatrical wardrobe is valued at $300,000 dollars; that the university war memorial chapel contains paintings which George III commissioned for Windsor Castle and which Bob Jones, Jnr., bought at Sotheby's; that the film unit is so good that it is invited to do outside contract work and that it accepts these invitations, provided the subject is right; that Bob Jones students may learn to fly, if they wish; and that in a survey by *McCall's* Magazine, BJU was voted America's Most Square University, though it could make only third place in the contest for the title of 'Most Conservative University', being pipped by Brigham Young University, the Mormon academy in Salt Lake City; and West Point Military Academy. When news of these accolades was announced to the assembled students, they received it with thunderous applause.

I was given an insight, too, into the lives the students lead. Their movements are controlled by a bell which rings forty-three times every day, getting them up, calling them to classes and meals and sending them to bed. Laughingly, they have given the bell the name 'Sing-Sing'. At weekends, hundreds of them visit towns and cities to preach in jails, at street corners, youth rallies, rescue missions or Sunday schools. In Greenville itself, they hand out gospel tracts outside stores and theatres, according to the *Greenville News*, which adds somewhat cryptically: 'One of the first of dozens of recurring rumors was that each Bob Jones student was expected to talk to at least three persons a day about "being saved".' There are few students from Greenville, most of them coming from outside South Carolina altogether.

It is difficult, of course, for a university with rules like ingrowing toe-nails to avoid clashes with the broader concepts held by government educational authorities; and in this sphere the BJU has had its problems. The last major bust-up came in 1966, when the U.S. Office of Education ruled that, because of its policy of segregation, the university had not complied with the Civil Rights Act of 1964. It cut off the supply of Federal money that was available for student loans and demanded that the $700,000 supplied for this purpose between 1959 and 1965 be returned. The university replied that the money was loaned for periods of ten years under the term of the original agreement, that it had been approved before the Civil Rights Act, and that the Government could not demand repayment in a shorter period. I regret that I cannot record the final verdict, but I think it is safe to assume that the battle was and maybe still is vigorous.

There have been internal problems, too. In 1953, indeed, there was the nearest approach to a campus revolt that BJU had ever seen; and it came, not so much from the students, but from members of the Faculty who wanted more academic freedom. The Jones family, however, knew how to deal with mutineers. Theodore C. Mercer, registrar and assistant to the President, was fired after thirteen years with the institution. In protest, two deans of the college, eight faculty members and the President of the student body left, but with that the civil war ended. The empty faculty seats were filled quickly; and the number of students increased.

Despite the rigid rules and the loss of Federal loans, indeed, the Bob Jones University continues to grow more rapidly than most other academies. Neither fratricidal strife, nor the clipping of financial wings, it seems, can harm it. Its fees are lower than the national average; yet the cost of operating this highly sophisticated learning machine must be enormous, as, indeed, is the capital investment. They have just completed a $400,000 hospital and a $1,000,000 apartment building for faculty and staff members in addition to a $4,000,000 expansion programme that was completed a few years ago. Today, according to Dr R. K. ('Lefty') Johnson, business manager of BJU since 1935, the campus plant is worth $30,000,000 and is completely free from debt.

How has it been done? 'Lefty' Johnson's answer to that question was the same as those offered to me by a dozen or more run-of-the-mill evangelists. When I had inquired how they had been able to build their little empires, they had pointed solemnly towards heaven and they had said, as 'Lefty' says: 'God has led us . . . He has performed miracles to enable us to reach this point.'

Others, hedging their heavenly bets, give a degree of credit to Mammon, too. One commentator wrote: 'By the very virtue of his position in control of BJU's purse strings, Dr Johnson has been in more intimate contact with Greenville's business men than any of the other BJU people. And they, almost without exception, like him and admire his keen business abilities. But they know, too, that he can be a rod of iron when it seems necessary.'

How could they help liking and admiring him? The building programme at BJU was worth millions to Greenville. On one job alone,
when men had to work round the clock to get a building completed
before the term began, he admitted that it probably cost the university
$150,000 in overtime. I wonder what the basic was.

Apart from construction work, there are nearly four thousand students spending their money in the town. They and faculty members
own a thousand cars between them and many of them were bought in
Greenville. Even imported machines are welcome, however, bringing
happy smiles to the faces of those who own service stations and garages.

This BJU manpower keeps local barbers happy, too. It has been
estimated that the male population on the campus gets at least 25,000
haircuts a year. At the rate of $1.75 a haircut, about $38,750 is spent by
students on these trimmings every year. Luckily for the local barbers,
the fundamentalist teaching staff does not seek to impose the Biblical
story of Samson on its students, perhaps because there are not many
Delilahs on the campus. Certainly they have friends in the town;
when they were planning their $400,000 hospital, for instance, they
announced: 'It is possible to honor the memory of a loved one or friend
through a contribution to the hospital fund. A gift of $100,000 will
build one floor; $10,000 will build one room; and $2,500 will furnish
one room. A lovely plaque bearing the donor's name will be affixed in
each room or hall in memory of the one he is honoring. Names of those
making $500 donations will be inscribed on a plaque in the lobby. Those
wishing to contribute any amount may send their gift to the Hospital
Fund in care of Bob Jones University.' I saw the hospital. It is a beautiful
building.

I must not be too harsh, however, on present-day BJU administrators
who claim miracles with such facility. They are merely following the
example of their founder.

Even when the university first opened its doors, it was not lacking in
support from the top brass. It was born, not in Greenville, but in
Florida; and among guests at the inaugural banquet were the Governor
of Alabama, Bibbs Graves, and former Congressman William D.
Upshaw.

That was in 1927. Two years later, when the school nearly sank in the
depression, Bob Jones, Snr., paid off the floating debts by cashing in his
life insurance; but he looked elsewhere for running expenses, barnstorming the country to raise funds.

A few years later Dr Jones and various members of his board of trustees began discussing a move to a more centralized location. On a trip to Cleveland, Tennessee, his son noticed a Holston Methodist Conference school that had been closed for seven years. It was dilapidated, but that was no problem. Dr Jones, Snr., simply contacted the local Chamber of Commerce, whose members promptly agreed to spend $10,000 in remodelling the property; and more aid came from individuals throughout the nation.

That was in 1933. Later, when the trustees were considering yet another move, God, presumably taking time off from moving mountains, worked overtime, nudging the plump elbows of chambers of commerce, City Fathers and wealthy businessmen. At any rate, there was an almost indecent scramble among various American cities to get his custom. Boston offered the school 1,200 acres of land, if they would move there. Kansas City proposed a city park for a campus. Friends in Orlando, Florida, offered a million dollars to be given over a period of time, if the school would consider returning to Florida. Both Asheville and Hendersonville, North Carolina, sent delegations to make bids and further carrots were hoisted in Atlanta. One man offered the school a donation of $100,000, if it would stay in the State.

Greenville won through sheer persistence. The Chamber of Commerce telephoned constantly, urging the Bob Jones board to do nothing until they had discussed the matter with them. Finally they flew a special delegation of their Chamber of Commerce to Cleveland to clinch the deal. The Chamber offered to buy all the land bordering the roads, approximately 170 acres, which would cost them $170,000; and so the University found a new home, selling its old one for $4,200,000 to the Church of God.

For those who wish to start a liberal arts college, the moral of the story is clear: approach half a dozen chambers of commerce through God or *vice versa*. Then stand back and pick the best miracle available.

Whether God or Mammon deserves the credit, the Bob Jones University today seems virtually impregnable. It can afford to blackball even Billy Graham, who studied there in the early forties and later was awarded an Honorary Doctorate of the Humanities. Because he holds crusades that are even partly under the auspices of the National Council of Churches, Bob Jones students have been forbidden to attend his meetings. The penalty for disobedience is dismissal.

The old reliables, of course, remain unshaken in their faith. Former

Governor George Wallace of Alabama has an honorary degree from the BJU. The well-known gospel song-and-dance act of Hargis and McIntire are devoted subjects still. So is the Rev. Dr Ian Robert Kyle Paisley—perhaps more devoted than all the rest, in fact, for not only does he broadcast regularly on WMUU and hold an honorary degree from the university, but he is on its Co-operating Board, a distinction shared by only four other Europeans and not achieved as yet by either Hargis or McIntire.

What has Paisley got that so many home-grown fundamentalists lack? A clue, I think, may be found in the university itself, where plaques hang, inscribed with some of the founder's folksy sayings. One of them reads: 'A man who has no enemies is no good. You cannot move without producing friction.'

The Rev. Ian moves fast and in recent years has produced more friction than most clerics. Indeed, he has won international notice through his firebrand activities in Northern Ireland, where he champions the true-blue Protestant cause and finds time to mourn the loss of an Empire which most Britons were glad to see handed back to the original owners. His actions have been criticized widely by many eminent people, including Dr Ramsey, the Archbishop of Canterbury, who told David Frost on his television programme: 'I wouldn't call Ian Paisley a man of God. He's a religious and political partisan. He doesn't help us believe in God, exactly.'

Asked by Frost whether Paisley helped at all, the Archbishop replied: 'He doesn't help me at all. Not a scrap!'

His comments, I thought, were reasonably mild. Paisley, after all, had called him 'a Romaniser, an idolator and a blasphemer'.

His rumbustious gallivanting on a relatively local front is but one reason why I mention him here. His international links—particularly in America—are wide; and in the autumn of 1968 he announced that he was going to broadcast daily on the powerful station used by Carl McIntire at Red Lion, Pennsylvania. His words, said the announcement, would be heard around the world—in Europe, the South Pacific, the Far East, Central America and the Caribbean area, Africa, the Near East, South America, Canada and the U.S.A.

For those who have not heard him speak, that piece of news may not sound very disturbing. I, however, have heard him and I found the sound unpleasant. The occasion was a rally which he addressed at the foot of the beautiful Mountains of Mourne in Co. Down, Northern

Ireland, and the following excerpt from the shorthand notes I made at the time gives some idea of the style of oratory which he can adopt when he feels like it:

Churchmen are going to see old 'Red Socks'. They're saying to him: 'Hello, Pope. How's Mrs Pope and all the little Popes?' They're slobbering over his slippers. The Archbishop of Canterbury goes a bit higher. He kisses him, that man of sin in the Church, that man of perdition! That is what they call the Pope in the Westminster Confession of Faith, the basis of Presbyterianism. That is what our forefathers said and where we stand today.

There was a good deal more in similar vein—sombre meanderings about the Whore of Babylon and so on. The words were so grotesque, indeed, that they would have been comic, had their effect not been so saddening. He was speaking at a time when four Catholics had been murdered simply because they were Catholics. The emotions he aroused could have turned to violence easily, as the authorities knew well, for they had posted strong forces of police in all the laneways surrounding the field where the meeting was held. The sight of them may have been a restraining influence; nevertheless, it was unpleasant to hear middle-aged men and women shout emotional hallelujahs to his sermon of vinegar, while young girls chanted 'To hell with the Pope'.

It may be argued, of course, that this all happened quite a while ago—in the autumn of 1966. Since then, however, Paisley's influence has grown to such an extent that, when he opposed the Prime Minister at a recent general election, he came within inches of defeating him; and time has not mellowed his tongue. Recently a writer from *Nusight* magazine in Dublin attended one of his meetings in the Ulster Hall, Belfast, and provided readers with the following even more unappetizing quotations: 'The Protestant people of Ulster are seeing the wonderful works of God in this very hour . . . Jesus stands among us . . . He has risen us up to fight the forces of Romanism and all its allies.' 'Our cause is righteous and is washed in the Blood of the Lamb.' 'We are here to defend the Gospel, not to preach it . . . We will defend it with our blood like the martyrs of old who would not bow to the forces of Popery and the scarlet whore drunk on the blood of the churches.'

Again there were the hallelujahs, the shouts of 'Glory', the low murmurs of 'Praise the Lord'. Again the temperature rose among an audience that was well dappled with middle-aged, middle-class people. The words worked; and if he were to use similar words in broadcasts to small, ill-educated African communities, they could work even more powerfully and much more dangerously, particularly if there were a Catholic mission school near by.

It is because of his international ramifications, as I said, that I believe his background is worth reviewing here, for some facets of it may come as a surprise even to the Jones family in Greenville. He was born in Armagh, North Ireland, in 1927, the son of a Baptist preacher who subsequently formed a breakaway Tabernacle. For a while he worked as an assistant in a bakery shop, but in 1943 he enrolled at the Theological College of the Reformed Presbyterian Church in Belfast, where he passed his examinations with credit after a three-year course. In 1946 he was ordained by his father, began his pastoral works in Belfast's dockland and found time to study at the Barrie School of Evangelism in South Wales.

Over the next few years he popped into the news from time to time, generally because of his vigorous protests about liberal Protestants who in his eyes were selling out to Rome. After a disturbance at Ballymena, where the Rev. Lord Soper, a Methodist peer, was pelted with a Bible and rosary beads, he was charged in court and fined $12. His first big international incident, however, came in 1962, when he went to Rome for the opening of the Vatican Council. His mission, he said, was to protest against Protestant ministers 'selling out to Popery on the Reformation', but he extended his own mandate a little by sending a telegram to the Pope, informing him that his claims and doctrines were contrary to the word of God. When he returned to Belfast, he was escorted to a police station for questioning. Soon afterwards he organized a protest march to the Italian Consulate and stuck posters on the B.B.C. building, accusing that staid organization of being 'the Voice of Popery'. In those days he was quite a clown and nobody took him seriously.

By 1966, however, he was funny no longer except for those with a rather sick sense of humour. His flamboyant speeches caught the mood of extremist Protestants, of which Northern Ireland had more than its fair share. There was violence resulting in death; and the authorities began to take a serious view of him. When he made yet another trip to Rome to protest against the visit of the Archbishop of Canterbury to Pope Paul, he was not allowed to enter the city and was sent back to London Airport, where he was kept in custody for twenty-four hours.

A few months later he led a march in Belfast on the General Assembly of the Presbyterian Church to protest against its 'Romeward trend'. It degenerated into a severe riot after which Paisley was charged with unlawful assembly and sent to jail for three months. Over two thousand of his followers gathered outside Crumlin Road Prison and the police who tried to shift them were pelted with petrol bombs. Armoured cars which were called out were set on fire.

During the battles of 1968, 1969 and 1970 in Northern Ireland—serious riots in which a number of people, most of them Catholics, died and which went on, despite the fact that British troops were sent over to restore order—he played an active political part, rallying the forces of extreme Protestantism, presenting himself as the valiant defender of their faith. Again he was sentenced to three months in jail for unlawful assembly, but was soon released under a general amnesty.

Throughout all these upheavals, of course, he maintained constantly that he was a man of peace, defending his embattled co-religionists from the bloodthirsty hordes of Rome.

Inevitably, however, his presence on the scene and his colourful oratory attracted many British journalists to Northern Ireland; and, coming from a country where religious controversy seldom causes heavy breathing, let alone bloodshed, they were bewildered by what they saw and heard.

Some decided that they would like to know a little more about the background of Dr Paisley—where, for instance, he had obtained his doctorate. They were told that he held degrees from two evangelical colleges in the USA, the Pioneer Theological Seminary, Rockford, Illinois, and Burton College and Seminary, Manitou Springs, Colorado. The Pioneer Theological Seminary, which had granted him his Bachelor of Divinity Degree, subsequently gave him an Honorary Doctorate in Divinity in recognition of the fact that he was First Moderator of the Free Presbyterian Church in Ulster. In March 1958, he had obtained his Master of Arts degree by thesis from Burton College.

When a couple of journalists investigated further, however, they learned that both these centres of learning had been condemned by the American authorities as 'bogus degree mills' where degrees could be bought.

When I was in the United States, I took an even closer look at these establishments and their pupils.

I learned, for instance, that another well-known theologian, Billy

James Hargis, was a graduate of Burton College in Manitou Springs. His biography describes how he searched for a college through which he could get a degree by means of a correspondence course. Various schools turned him down, but finally he struck academic oil. Later he wrote: 'I discovered the Burton College in Manitou Springs, Colorado, Dr Fred Stemme, President. At this time, Burton College had not been attacked as a "degree mill" by a liberal administration, as was later done . . .

'I wrote to Dr Stemme and he said that Burton College would grant me a degree if I would write a thesis and if the thesis were acceptable to the school. Also I was required to spend one summer at the school for resident work.'

Billy James wrote his thesis. So that he could spend his summer in residence, he organized a series of crusades in the Manitou Springs area, which must have cut into his studies somewhat. Nevertheless, after one thesis and one summer in residence, he was awarded a Bachelor of Arts degree and a Bachelor of Theology degree.

Just for the record, I contacted the Division of Higher Education of the U.S. Department of Health, Education and Welfare in Washington and asked them to confirm that Burton College and the Pioneer Seminary had earned their disapproval. They not only did so, but let me have an official list, headed 'Degree Mills' to prove it. Both were named in it; and with the list was a statement which began: 'In the United States no reputable institution of higher education confers degrees solely on the basis of correspondence study.' It went on:

The lax chartering laws in some States permit the existence of correspondence schools whose practices amount virtually to the sale of degrees. Such organizations are commonly referred to as degree mills, a degree mill being defined as an organization that awards degrees without requiring its students to meet educational standards for such degrees established and traditionally followed by reputable educational institutions. Most of these degree mills operate solely by mail. In many cases staffs and plants do not even exist.

Degree mills are a serious threat to American educational standards in several ways. They damage, by misunderstanding in the public mind, legitimate and reputable correspondence schools. They defraud those who honestly believe they have received recognition from a legitimate institution of higher education. They lower American prestige abroad by deceiving foreign students.

I decided that in the line of duty I should visit one of them. I chose the Pioneer Theological Seminary in Rockford, a town, I discovered on my arrival, spread thinly on the ground, but over a wide area. The college could scarcely be described as conveniently situated, indeed, for it was out in the sticks six miles away. When, not without some difficulty, I finally unearthed the Rev. Dr Ian Robert Kyle Paisley's Alma Mater, I found that it was not quite up to the standards of other theological colleges I had visited. There was no fountain, no film unit, no complicated computer system, no theatre, no radio station, no faculty, no students—not even a prayer tower. It was just one building, No. 122 Concord Avenue, a comfortably battered, green-washed house, overgrown with creepers and facing on to a dishevelled garden that held five garbage cans.

I knocked and a large genial coloured man opened the door. A mass of cheerful children peered round his legs, smiling at me. When I asked for the Rev. Robert Hansen, who, I had learned, had been listed as the President of the College, he beamed and said: 'The Reverend? Why, he died some years back.'

I asked whether his church was still operating. He shook his head and said: 'It's been pulled down.'

'Is his wife still alive?'

'Which wife?' he asked, his grin broadening. 'He was divorced by one and then he married her sister. His first wife lives in a caravan not too far from here.'

I thanked him and went away to contemplate a situation that seemed to grow more confusing every minute. Over a cup of coffee in a snack bar near by, I asked again about the Rev. Robert Hansen. The lady behind the counter had never heard of him. A customer two stools away was more helpful. Scratching his memory, he said: 'I recall the guy. He had a church that isn't there any more. There was something about him and his correspondence course in the newspapers. Apparently, if you were in a bit of a hurry and paid your money, you got yourself a degree good and fast.'

He paused and gazed heavenwards. Then he said: 'He had a bad heart and he just died one day. I hope he had the dollars for the entrance fee when he got up there.'

It was, I felt, time for me to pay a call on the Reverend's ex-wife, or perhaps I should say first widow. I returned to the ex-academy to find that the new owner was just about to drive into Rockford. Without any hesitation he offered to drop me off at her caravan, even though it took him on quite a detour.

The caravan was set back from the road in Carbaugh Avenue, off Auburn Street. The door was opened by a grey-haired lady in a flowered frock. Her voice was tired, her manner gentle and she invited me in rather hesitantly, for obviously she was a little unsure of strangers. Very soon, however, she was talking readily about her ex-husband and I learned that she had been widowed twice. After her divorce from the Reverend, she had married a Mr Nance, who had died since.

'He built that church himself,' she told me, 'the one that's been pulled down. Before that he was minister in another church—Lincoln Park Church of Christ. That was in the thirties and he had his correspondence college there, too. He never had pupils on the premises, of course. It was a good business, that correspondence course, but things went wrong. He thought he was doing the right thing, but he wasn't. I don't know why. They closed it, anyway, some time before he died.

'I'd divorced him before that. We both married again. He had two children by his second wife, but none by me. He was only fifty-two when he died.'

She mused a while over happier days before saying: 'He was a good speaker. One of the best speakers I ever heard. Boy, oh boy, could he preach! But he was mentally deranged in some way. It was too bad, too bad.'

'Did you ever hear of a man called Ian Paisley?' I asked. 'I've heard that he got a degree from the college.'

'I never met him,' she said. 'He never visited and I never heard my husband talking about him; but I saw a write-up in the paper about him. I've got it somewhere here.'

She produced a box full of souvenirs . . . family snapshots, hymns and poems she had written as a girl. At last she surfaced with a cutting from the *Rockford Morning Star* and handed it to me.

It was reported that the Rev. Ian Paisley had claimed as an alma mater the Pioneer Theological Seminary and went on to give some fascinating details about both the college and its founder.

On 5 September 1960, it stated, the Seminary had been charged by the Federal Trade Commission with misrepresenting Bible theology and philosophy home study courses. These charges included a claim that the college gave diplomas to anyone willing and able to pay for them.

But the F.T.C. charges came after the death of the seminary president, the Rev. Robert Hansen, who died on 28 July 1960. Two others were named on the complaint, Hansen's widow, Verna L., and his brother, the Rev. Carl C. Hansen. Both agreed to a consent order from the F.T.C., but the three firms had not been active after Hansen's death.

Prior to his death, Hansen had pleaded innocent to a federal indictment, charging that he sent obscene literature and photographs through the mail.

I handed her back the cutting, but she waved it away. 'Keep it,' she said. 'I don't want it.'

Late news flash: as this book was going to press, the Rev. Dr Ian Robert Kyle Paisley was elected a Member of Parliament of both the Northern Ireland Parliament at Stormont and of the Mother of Parliaments at Westminster. What a pity his old Professor at the Pioneer Theological College, Rockford, Illinois, is not alive, for he would have been proud, indeed, of his pupil, who showed such early promise.

6: 'CHURCHES IS PEOPLE'

SHOULD the Rev. Ian Paisley, D.D. and bar, wish to collect a few more spiritually academic (or *vice versa*) distinctions to add lustre to himself and his church, he will not have to overstrain his active mind. This field is lush in America because not only the Federal Government, but most State legislatures develop nervous twitches at the slightest suggestion that they are interfering with the religious freedom of the citizenry. As a result, the laws throughout the land are lenient to the point of licence. Churches sprout and flourish in wild, gorgeous profusion, their branches heavy with ordination certificates, doctorates and exotic spiritual titles.

For twenty dollars, for instance, about £8, he could get a Doctorate of Divinity from the Very Rev. Dr Kirby J. Hensley, a fifty-eight-year-old illiterate preacher, real estate owner and ex-carpenter, who founded the Universal Life Church in Modesto, California, in 1962. Since then he has ordained 250,000 ministers—men, women, children, dogs, a cat called Frankie Utt from California and, at approximately 2.30 in the afternoon of Tuesday, 11 November 1969, myself. In two years' time he prophesies that he will have a million ministers throughout the world and shortly after that he plans to become President of the United States, a post for which he has sought election twice already.

The first reports I received about his activities were a little garbled and subsequently turned out to be laced fairly generously with the truth. I was told, for instance, that thousands were becoming ministers to evade military service and/or tax; that others were getting half fare on airlines on production of their ministerial credentials; that these credentials could be used also for getting prices cut in a variety of stores; and that the Very Reverend Kirby J. Hensley, known locally as the Modesto Messiah, was serving a sentence of one year in jail for selling Doctorates of Divinity for twenty dollars.

Only that last dispatch proved utterly untrue. I was in Los Angeles when I made my first contact on the telephone with the Universal Life Church in Modesto and the High Priest himself answered the call. He cackled with delight at the very idea that any authority would be sharp enough to find reason to incarcerate him and even on the phone I could sense that here was one of the most irreverent Reverends in a large nation that has a fair glut of them. Accordingly, three days later I was on my way to Modesto to spend what turned out to be the most hilarious day in a tour of research four months and 15,000 miles long.

His church, I found, was not particularly imposing. It was, in fact, a rather ramshackle affair in a comfortable sort of way. The offices behind it were not very splendiferous, either. I found one vast room, filled with utilitarian tables, desks and chairs; a smaller outer office, where his wife Lida, his secretary and his daughter were working at the not inconsiderable task of packaging the five hundred ordination certificates which are sent out daily. Finally I entered the tiny episcopal sanctum, where sat the Bishop, a gnome-like figure with a stewed-prune face and his feet on a desk of magnificent clutter.

With a grin that sliced diagonally across his face and in a voice straight from the Beverly Hill-Billies, he told me immediately and succinctly his philosophy. 'The sooner we get rid of the big churches, the better,' he said. 'I don't believe in preachers, sittin' thar, earnin' soft livin's, talkin' about what happened two thousand years ago. They don't know from nothin' what's happenin' in the world today, what's happenin' to people.

'So I'm goin' t'make everyone a minister—men, women, children, cats, dogs, monkeys. I'm goin' t'cut the ass out of this whole preacher business.'

There are moments in a writer's life when he realizes that he must get a stranglehold on an interview before the words overwhelm him, like a stampeding herd of cattle, leaving him broken, bleeding and bewildered. Here was such a moment; so I said as firmly as possible: 'Reverend . . . let's start at the beginning. How did you get your calling?'

He told me that it was a long story and I did not doubt him. Lazily, but fluently, he went on: 'I was born the seventh child of a seventh child in a two-roomed log cabin in the foothills of the Blue Ridge Mountains, near Burnville, North Carolina. Near where Billy Graham lives now, matter o' fact, but he's a bit richer than what we were. We were poor enough, but I don't remember it botherin' me much.

'I went to this one-room school, but not very often. I never learned to read or write because mostly—when I was there, that is—I jest stood at that blackboard with my nose in the circle. When I was fourteen I gev it up and decided to see what was on the other side of them hills. I went to New York. Then I spent a few years ridin' the rails, working here and there. Then back to Low Gap—that was what they called the place we lived—but somehow it wasn't the same; but I joined the local Baptist Church and that was where I found my first interest in religion.'

The local Baptists, however, did not satisfy him, a point which I accepted readily. He tried other churches—the Pentecostals, for instance, but had no better luck with them. So he thought it might be a good idea if he became a preacher himself.

'Trouble was, o' course,' he said with his water-melon grin, 'that I couldn't read or write; and to be a preacher I'd have to learn me the Bible. So I reckoned I'd get some feller to read it for me because I've a good membry and could store it all up there in my head.

'Next thing I bought me this Bible, but I'd travelled 1,500 miles before I met someone who was ready to read it to me; and he says: 'That ain't no Bible. That's a Webster's dictionary.'

That little misunderstanding was soon cleared up, however. He got himself a real Bible. Now he claims—and I was not going to contradict him—that he knows the entire New Testament by heart and the Old Testament in story form.

By that time he had acquired a trade as a carpenter. He joined the Church of God and told me that he had built eight churches for them, though whether he meant spiritually or materially I was not quite sure. It is unimportant, anyway, because this liaison lasted no longer than his partnership with the Baptists and the Pentecostals.

He married, had two children, but in 1948 was divorced by his wife. Alone, he moved to California, where he met his present wife, Lida. In the meantime, he had begun building houses, selling them and buying himself some real estate.

It sounds simple, when said quickly; but it was not so easy for Kirby J. Hensley. He told me: 'When I first started out to build, I could only read the inch on the rule. I didn't know from nothin' about half an inch or three-quarters of an inch or three-eighths of an inch. Then I broke my back twice. Fell off a house. So I gev up carpentry and buildin'.

'Then Lida and me, we moved to Modesto. We'd two boys and a girl by that time. I bought me this bit of property and I converted the garage and put up a notice beside it, saying: "Church". When people asked what kinda church, I'd ask them their religion. If they said they was Baptists, it was a Baptist Church. If they said they was Pentecostals, it was Pentecostal; and so on. Then in 1962 I got this idea of a universal church—the Universal Life Church.'

'And what, Reverend,' I asked, 'is your doctrine?'

'Easy,' he said, chuckling hugely. 'You jest have to believe in what is right. We hold that heaven is here and now. When you have what you want, that's heaven. When you haven't, it's hell! You can forgit the rest.

We're the only church that offers folk somethin' before they die, not after. 'I've jest got written out five commandments which explain it all. The first is: Thou shalt not interfere with thy neighbour's way of doing his religious thing. The second is: Thou shalt not aspire to be holier than other holy men simply because you look pretty holy to yourself. The third is: Neither shall you harass the little man and let the big operator go hog-wild. The fourth is: Render unto Caesar what is his and then let him stay the heck out of the church business. The fifth is: Thou shalt not covet thy neighbour's free-will offerings, for he, too, is worthy of his hire.'

He paused to ordain me, a simple, moving ceremony, which entailed for the Bishop the task of finding a blank ordination form. He signed it slowly and laboriously in the spidery, unformed hand of a child and then he slung it cheerfully across the desk to me with an identification card to show that I was a minister and a fact sheet with which to confront anyone who might have the temerity to question the fact.

It summarized the doctrine, which did not take up too much space, and went on to state that the church would ordain anyone without question of their faith for life for a free-will offering to help defray the cost of handling and mailing. The licence and ordination papers, it insisted, were legal and recognized by all States in America and by many foreign countries. Universal Life Ministers could perform the same services that any minister of any church could perform—wedding ceremonies, funerals and even ordinations. Here, however, was a warning that in California ministers had to be twenty-one years of age before they could perform marriages and a suggestion that new Reverends might check their own State laws concerning that point.

Then came ground rules for establishing a church under the ULC charter. They read:

The ULC will provide anyone with a charter, if he or she wishes to open a church. The Headquarters of Universal Life Church will keep records of your church and file with the Federal Government and furnish you a tax exempt status and all you do is to report your activities to Headquarters four times a year. We will keep these records for you for $1 per month. When a church is established, they decide upon the types of meetings that they wish to have. We have no control over the church. We recognize everyone's beliefs. One needs only a Pastor, a Secretary and a Treasurer to have a legal church.

It ends with a further mild mention about free-will offerings and suggests that anyone who wants to become a minister should write to the Universal Life Church at 601 Third Street, Modesto, California, 95351.

In fact Bishop Hensley is not too fussy about free-will offerings for ordination. In addition to ordaining me free, he gave me a couple of signed certificates for friends in California. Press cuttings about him— and he claims to be getting more publicity than anyone in America, except President Nixon—show that more often than not he ordains for nothing. Recently, indeed, he has held a number of ordain-ins at Californian colleges, creating with a wave of his hand 2,000 ministers among the students at Sonoma University; 3,000 at Stanford; and 5,000 at S.F.S.

With the legal situation concerning the establishment of churches like tangled wool, why was he having trouble with the authorities? Why the stories about him going to jail? When I asked him, the grin grew impossibly wide and he said: 'That wasn't about the ordinations. That was about me makin' people Doctors of Divinity for a free-will offerin' of $20. That includes a ten-lesson correspondence course, though it's not very long. The first lesson is important, though. It quotes Article One of the Amendments to the Constitution. Here . . read it yourself.'

He thrust the course across the desk to me, a couple of sheets of closely-printed paper. I read Article One, which stated: 'Congress shall make no law respecting an establishment of religion or prohibiting the free exercise thereof, or abridging the freedom of speech or of the Press; or the right of the people peaceably to assemble and to petition the Government for a redress of grievances.'

I read, also, a few of the other lessons, which told the Modesto Messiah's students how to establish a church, and how to keep within the law, and gave them a brief outline of a short wedding ceremony that might come in handy. In keeping with the liberal traditions of ULC, the lesson stresses: 'You do not necessarily have to use this ceremony, but it is very popular.'

Hauling the slippery conversation back to real business, I said: 'But how did you tangle with the law?'

'The law?' he said. 'I was forgittin'. One day this police sergeant from San Jose—I think he was one o' my ministers—swore this charge against me for issuing degrees. I fought it and I beat it. Then thirty days later they re-opened the case and the judge, he found me guilty and gave me a 500-dollar fine and a year in jail. I appealed and it's coming up on Thursday. What'll happen I don't know, but we'll take this to the Supreme Court, if necessary.'*

I asked him whether he was worried about the case. He stamped his feet with laughter. 'Worried?' he said. 'It don't bother me a bit. There ain't nothin' you can't do, if you've the Lord and a good lawyer on your side. Looky here . . . the Government would like to see me dead. The big churches, they'd like to see me dead. They all hate my guts . . but the man in the street, he likes me.

'Why, I've had 'em coming at me from all sides. The State authorities, they're after me. So is the F.B.I. So is the Secret Service. So is the Internal Revenue. Anyways, they can't git at me no more about the Doctor of Divinity thing in California. I've opened an office in Phoenix, Arizona and I'm issuing them from there. Anyone who wants one jest has to write to ULC, Box 3528, Phoenix and enclose that little old free-will offering of $20.'

'Why are the F.B.I. after you?'

'Because of the draft,' he chuckled. 'Ministers of Religion, they don't have to do military service, if they don't feel like it. There's quite a few of my ministers who don't feel like it one bit. That's their business, o' course. I don't go out and bat for them; but because of this the F.B.I. fellers call round here pretty regular. Some are nice enough. Some have even become ministers. Same with the Secret Service.'

'And the Internal Revenue people?' I asked. 'Why are they breathing down your neck?'

'We-ell!' he said, singing two or three syllables into the word, 'they kinda reckon that I should be payin' taxes. I keep tellin' them that I'm a non-profit makin' religious organization. So far they ain't bin able to prove me wrong.'

I decided to see whether I could do any better, which showed, I suppose that I was ideal raw material for martyrdom. I should have known it was going to be like shooting the wings of mosquitoes in flight.

'Looky here . . . I mean look here, Reverend, how can you justify issuing Doctorates of Divinity when you can't even read or write?'

His eyes pranced with delight. 'What's a Doctor of Divinity?' he said. 'He's a feller who's supposed to know about God. Now all those professors in all those big colleges, they just think they know about God.

* Sight nor sound I have not had of my Bishop since; but I'll bet my surplice to a pint of bat's blood that he is not a compulsory penitentiary chaplain.

They can't prove nothing, I've studied the Bible and I've bin around and I've got my own ideas about Him. I reckon I'm entitled to my own opinion and I told the court that, too.'

I tried another ploy. I said: 'It has been reported that you are making between $5,000,000 and $7,000,000 dollars out of the Universal Life Church.'

He waved an expansive arm and said: 'Jest you look around. This ain't no palace. I ain't no millionaire, but I ain't broke, neither. I take no salary out of the Church, though I could if I felt like it; but people seem to forgit that it costs me $100 a day jest gittin' those certificates out. Matter of fact the Church has bin in the red for a while, but this year I'd say we're in the black.'

Certainly his offices were a slum compared with those of many other ministers I had met in my travels. I sought, however, a further chink in his armour. I said: 'How many Doctors of Divinity have you . . . created?' It was not, perhaps, the best verb, but I was flagging.

'I reckon 'bout 5,000, give a few, take a few.'

'That means 5,000 free-will offerings of $20,' I said. 'That makes a total of $100,000 or about £40,000 in my money.'

I could see that he was forcing back the laughter. I knew that he had heard all these questions before. With a beautifully wicked grin, he said: 'But not all of 'em paid.'

'Reverend,' I said, 'how many church charters have you issued?'

'Reckon about 5,000, give a few, take a few; but we don't set much store on buildins. Churches ain't buildins. Churches is people.'

How right he was! Nevertheless I had a job to do. I said: 'You offer to keep their records for them for one dollar a month. That makes $60,000 a year, about £25,000 in my money.'

'But not all of 'em accept the offer; and not all of 'em pay.'

I know when I am beaten. I flung the financial towel into the ring and got back to more colourful subjects. 'Reverend,' I asked, 'how do your ministers dress?'

'Anyways they like,' he told me. 'I told you we ain't got rules for them. Some wear cowled cassocks. Some wear robes of Eastern religions. Some make up their own; but usually a minister wearin' a dog collar can git a bit further than if he's wearing jeans.'

The Bishop himself dressed casually and comfortably, when we met. On occasions, however, he can put on quite a show. At one meeting, for instance, he flowered forth in a luminous neon-green suit with a fluorescent orange tie. When he ordained the multitudes at Sonoma University, he wore a lounge suit and flowers in his hair, a sight so inspiring that one young girl student rushed the platform and kissed him on the back of the neck.

Who joins ULC? The Bishop told me: 'All sorts. We've got a lotta doctors and lawyers and the like—you know, liberal folk. The Beatles, they're members. And the Rollin' Stones. And Jack Benny. And quite a few fellers who are just out the pen . . . the penitentiary, that is . . . are ministers. And preachers are leavin' their organizations and comin' to me. Matter o' fact we were goin' to offer Bishop Pike the Vice-Presidency, if he hadn't gone and died.

'We have our own flag, too. Jest two stripes of gold and white. The white's for peace and the gold's for prosperity, the golden age that we're tryin' to bring around. We hope to get people to fly it and have a positive way of thinkin'. It's goin' to unify everyone and that's what everyone on earth is dreamin' of. This flag is just one step towards heaven here and now.'

Never had I heard so many logical illogicalities, magnificent sweeps of hickory rhetoric. I said to him: 'You say you have your own ideas about God. What are they?'

I stood back from what I felt was bound to be an avalanche; but Dr Hensley was quite restrained. He said: 'I don't believe in any feller with a long, white beard somewhere off in the blue. I believe God is a substance . . . something you use, not something that uses you. God is everything. I believe in reincarnation, too. In past lives I was a lawyer and a comedian.'

I saw no reason to argue about that last life. Instead I said: 'Tell me about your Presidential plans.'

'I ran first in 1964,' he said, 'I got my name on the ballots of sixteen States and a quarter of a million people voted for me. In 1968 I was on a few more ballot papers and I got me 4,500,000 votes. Nixon, he won't make it no more. Teddy Kennedy's the next one; and after that it's me and my Universal Party. The Republicans and Democrats will be all washed up by then.'

'What,' I asked, 'were the main planks in your platform?'

'There were quite a few,' he said, 'but the Press seemed to seize on two of them in particular. One was that I was goin' to abolish income tax.'

'And the other?'

The grin was almost wolfish. He said: 'I was calling for civil treatment and protection for people from other worlds visiting our planet in their machines without interrogation, leading to immediate commitment in our jails.'

On that note, the interview ended. I reeled away happily and only when the wild aura of my Bishop had faded a little did I start checking up on some of the stories surrounding him.

Do his ministers manage to evade the draft? There is one report which the authorities are trying to trace that one of them was actually sent home from Vietnam when he produced his ULC credentials. Some undoubtedly got away with it in early days, but Top Brass is well aware now of the Modesto Messiah. Col. Paul Feeney, deputy director of the Massachusetts Selective Service System, stated not so long ago: 'Several Massachusetts men have tried to get classified 4D ministers of religion on the basis of their ULC ministry. Such exemptions are only given to people who devote their full time to religious duties. Mere ordination or title is not enough.'

Can his ministers marry, bury and ordain people? Mary A. R. Hines, commissions clerk in the Massachusetts Secretary of State's office, said: 'We've had a lot of queries. The answer in each case is: "No!"'

In Vermont, however, a probate judge can give the minister of an out-of-State church permission to perform a wedding; and, according to Bill Davis of the *Boston Globe*—or I should say the Rev. William Davis, for he, too, is one of my brother ministers—some ULC clerics have performed marriage services.

A number of airlines in the past have given half-fare rates to the Modesto Messiah's missionaries, but the market is hardening as news of his unorthodoxy spreads.

Is there nothing to stop him ordaining youngsters of tender years? I think I should ask Pat Smiley of the Clarke Press, Portland, Oregon, to answer that one, because his seven-year-old son, Tige, is a ULC Reverend; and, what is more, he registered his credentials at the local courthouse. When Pat asked Roger Thommsen, Washington County director of registrations, whether there was any reason why they should not be registered, he was told: 'There is no law to stop it.'

What about the local authorities in Modesto itself? Naturally enough they have had quite a few queries about the Very Rev. Kirby J. Hensley, D.D. Each time they have answered with a sigh: 'His church is as legal as mother's milk.'

Bill Davis, the Beatles, the Rolling Stones, Jack Benny, numerous lawyers, doctors and ex-prisoners, Frankie Utt, the Californian cat, and I will be glad to hear that. So will Tom 'Inky' Stokes, a black male kitten, of whose ordination I have just learned, as I write.

I would not advise anyone to try berating the Bishop for extending the Cloth to our four-legged friends. He has his answer ready. He says: 'The Bible's full of animals. You ain't going to keep 'em out of heaven, are you?'

Was he joking when he said that? Was he joking throughout this and all the other interviews he has given? Is the whole idea of the Universal Life Church a magnificent, star-spangled send-up of pompous prelates throughout the United States, throughout the world? On the other hand, could he be serious?

I neither know nor care. For me he was an oasis of humour and broad humanity in a long series of interviews that too often were memorable only for their lack of laughter and their narrow intolerance. I only wish that a number of the clerics I met would take note of two remarks by the Very Reverend Kirby J. Hensley.

The first was: 'I don't believe in preachers, sittin' thar, earnin' soft livins, talkin' about what happened two thousand years ago. They don't know from nothin' what's happenin' in the world today, what's happenin' to people.'

The other was: 'Churches ain't buildins. Churches is people.'

I saw so many buildins in those four months and 15,000 miles.

7: GOD'S TEETH!

FOR me it was an unusual situation, if I may be permitted a chronic understatement. There I sat in a large, blacked-out bus, driving through the Arizona desert from Miracle Valley towards the Mexican border, while my fellow-travellers drowned the noise of the engine with a frenzy of hymn singing, militant, passionate, every word tingling with rabid sincerity.

Already—and we were just starting out—the fervour of it all seemed sufficient to give the bus angelic wings, to send it soaring over the giant cacti that made the countryside look like a background to a Western set in Tombstone City, which, as a matter of fact, was quite near by. The hymn, however, was only a preliminary, a resounding overture to an even greater religious ecstasy. When it ended, the voices took up a new theme, personal, intimate pledges of utter devotion: 'Sweet Jesus, I love you', 'Lord, I adore you', 'Dear God, come to me and fill me with your Spirit'.

To me, detached, isolated, not only by the darkness, but by the mood, it seemed that the atmosphere was tinged with something very near to hysteria, a comment, incidentally, which implies neither criticism nor mockery; and then, just as I felt this spiritual passion had reached its peak, the paeans of praise were swelled by strange, garbled voices uttering weird, unintelligible words that resembled no language I had ever heard. The passengers, pure Pentecostals every one of them, were speaking with tongues, a sure sign, according to their faith, that the Holy Spirit was truly within them. Only myself and, I am happy to say, the driver were silent, for had he caught the fervour, we could have flown most unangelically off the road and buried the bus in the bowels of a giant cactus.

It was, of course, no ordinary bus, but the property of the Miracle Valley Bible College, an adjunct of an evangelistic organization run by the Rev. A. A. Allen, a quaint and paradoxical man, who somehow has managed to superimpose brash modern business methods on the old-fashioned revivalist formula of another era. The passengers were students from the college on their way to the border town of Douglas, where they would practise what they were learning to preach. The hymns and all that followed were reinforcing them for the moment when they would walk the streets, stopping total strangers and asking them: 'Are you a Christian? Do you know the Lord? Are you saved?'

I had travelled to meet them after I had read a magazine article which said of the evangelist: 'Today—particularly now that Oral Roberts has

dropped out and turned Methodist and Billy Graham has become Richard Nixon's guru-in-waiting—A. A. Allen, 58, is the nation's topmost, tent-toting, old-fashioned evangelical roarer.'

It went on to describe the healings and the wild heights of enthusiasm that enlivened his rallies, which certainly seemed rip-roaring affairs; yet there was nothing in the least frenetic about his headquarters at Miracle Valley, some miles from the small Arizona town of Sierra Vista.

Miracle Valley, of course, is not the original name of the spot, but merely one bestowed on it by the Rev. Allen for the very good reason that he claims to have acquired the land by a miracle. It is really the San Pedro Valley, three miles from the Mexican border in the shadow of Mule Mountain, so called, it is said, because in earlier times Indians sporadically attacked Federal soldiers, whose mules escaped to the hills, roamed, bred and became wild.*

To get there I had to take two buses—one from Tucson to Sierra Vista and another on to the centre. I arrived in the early afternoon; and, as I stood with my bags on the empty road, I saw a large sign announcing 'A. A. Allen Revivals, Inc.'; a cluster of scattered buildings; and, dominating all, a church with an orange, green and blue dome, plump and garish like a huge beach ball that had been sliced neatly in half. Trees and tropical oleanders mellowed the slight air of desolation and the Huachuca Mountains, Mule presumably among them, hovered, a hazy blue in the distance, symbolizing somehow a barrier that kept the rude world at bay. It was stark, compared with the proud extravaganzas I had seen at the shrines of the Doctors Roberts and Armstrong; but it was infinitely more restful, though the sight of two light aircraft in a nearby field struck an oddly material note.

Those who received me were restful, too; courteous people who obviously had an almost reverential devotion to the Rev. Allen. There was the Reverend Dr Roy M. Gray, Dean and Instructor since 1958 and once a co-worker with the incomparable Aimee Semple McPherson, an experience which could hardly fail to mould any personality. A sturdy, quietly spoken man with silver hair and a small moustache, he lectured me amiably and happily about Pentecostal principles for a while before I could lure the conversation round to the College.

'The Pentecostal movement,' he said, 'was a world-wide spiritual revival. Jesus told us in his parables that the history of the Church would be mottled, that new movements would arise from time to time.'

* I had always thought that mules could not breed. Another miracle?

'How long has the College been here, Doctor?' I asked. 'Have you been with it some time?'

'The feature of the Pentecostal Church on to which most people fasten,' he said, 'is speaking with tongues. That, however, is not the central feature of the movement, merely a manifestation of it. It is a great inward blessing. Your whole attitude has been taken over by God within.'

'I understand, Doctor. Now about the College . . .'

'I was nineteen and a Presbyterian, when I went to this prayer meeting in British Columbia. There I received the baptism of the Holy Spirit and suddenly I began speaking with tongues. My vocal apparatus was taken over completely. I spoke for perhaps an hour and a half, stopping only to say "Send for mother". And I wept because I felt myself to be preaching to heathen peoples . . .'

'But, Doctor . . .'

'It is an experience when God unites Himself with you without robbing you of your own personality. St Paul says that it edifies the person and the Church. Once I was speaking on a platform in a tent and had a tremendous blessing and began speaking with tongues. Mr Harris, an Indian gentleman, was present and he turned to his wife and said: "He's speaking Navajo!" Innocent little Indian children have been heard to speak in fluent English, though they know not a word of it; and sometimes you speak in languages nobody would know.'

'Doctor,' I said as firmly as I could with politeness, 'everything you say is absolutely fascinating; But I have come here to learn about the Miracle Bible College and the A. A. Allen Revival organization.'

He smiled a sincere apology, abandoned reluctantly his favourite subject which was, of course, his faith, and, as he talked of the academy of which he was Dean I soon realized that the lack of gloss and chromium in no way affected the efficiency of the school. I learned, for instance, that what I had taken at first to be a cluster of buildings was a fairly complex plan. There were, he told me, six substantial buildings, specially adapted to the climate and terrain of Southern Arizona. There was the administration centre which contained the offices of the dean and the school staff, the reception lobby, the registrar's office and the library. A main auditorium accommodated close to a hundred students and was fitted with audio-visual equipment. The senior classroom held fifty. There was a chapel to seat the whole school, a bookstore for all supplies and separate restrooms for men and women. All these buildings were heated automatically by gas and cooled by blower-type coolers, adapted to the desert. There were two dormitories with eighty rooms and eight apartments to house the students, the men's and women's superintendents and married couples. There was even a laundry, the overall plan making the college an island in the desert.

'Here we have a Pentecostal school, where we teach a Pentecostal gospel with Pentecostal power and results,' said the Dean. 'Over a two-year course we provide a good foundation in the inspired Bible, as written by God. We aim to shape the whole life of the student, not just his head.

'The day begins at 7.30 in the morning and we pray until 8.45. Then there are classes until 4.30. In the evening they are in their rooms from seven o'clock until ten to do their study and to pray. We believe a lot in prayer—good, old-fashioned, down-on-your-knees prayer.

'The college is co-educational and inter-racial. We never have more than ninety students because we haven't the facilities for more. There are more white than black, but it's very close to half and half; and we have only three main teachers.'

It all sounded economically austere; but then I remembered the two light aircraft and mentioned them to Dr Gray. As if planes in a seminary set in a desert were commonplace, he said: 'We have an airstrip here big enough to take the biggest planes. One of President Lyndon Johnson's planes landed here once. And people fly in to buy cattle.

'Those two planes you saw? They belong to two of our students. But most of the others have meagre financial resources and work in the college to pay for their tuition—on the farm, on the construction of new buildings or in the printing works, perhaps.'

Then, steering me gracefully and perhaps unwittingly from the subject of birdmen in this former Indian country, he went on: 'These youngsters have a practical training, too. They take their bus, you know, and go over to the military base at Fort Huachuca to hold meetings for the servicemen. They bring them back here to the church—it holds 2,000—and then we have some real gospel singing.'

'And the Rev. Allen?' I asked. 'Does he play a big part in the college?'

'He comes here twice a year,' said Dr Gray, 'for our camp meetings in February and August. People come from all over the country and we give them bed and board for three weeks.'

I was about to mention that it could be construed as a little strange that the Chairman of the College Board should be seen so seldom on the campus, but I refrained. After all, it was a good man who could delegate authority and somebody had to be out earning the money to keep the academic wheels turning smoothly and regularly.

Instead I asked: 'What happens to your students, when they graduate?'

'They become pastors to churches, missionaries in Africa and Canada and on Indian reservations,' he said, enthusiasm mounting in his voice. 'They make their own way—by faith. Sometimes one will go to a town and just start preaching and if people like what he has to say, they may form a corporation. Others just rent halls. Some travel round, preaching in other churches. One of our graduates is over in the Philippines, flying our helicopter into the jungle, taking the Gospel to the natives who have never had a chance to know it. The helicopter is the only plane we own.'

Again my mind, perhaps, unkindly, leaped back to lucre at the thought of this Pentecostal whirly-bird; but the mild Dr Gray spoke of it smoothly, proudly, as if it were merely a mechanical missionary, an aerodynamic agent of the Lord and not a highly costly piece of machinery. He had the knack or, perhaps, the grace, to imbue material matters with a spiritual aura; and this he managed even when talking of money itself—vast sums of it.

His voice was tender when he told me: 'The Corporation here gets two or three million dollars a year from free-will offerings. We are dependent entirely on people all over the United States, Canada and other countries. It comes mainly in small offerings—one dollar, two dollars—from people who see Brother Allen on television or on the radio.'

I turned the figures over in my head. In sterling they represented between £800,000 and £1,200,000. The Reverend Allen was not in the Armstrong/Roberts/Graham league, but neither was he preaching for nickels. Before I could pursue this sordid theme, however, Dr Gray was talking of the college again and I found myself studying the prospectus.

It was a fascinating document which made clear that austerity and purity were all part of the training. Under the heading 'Conduct', I read: 'Complete and wholehearted obedience to those in authority is absolutely indispensable . . . This obedience is not limited to the larger issues of daily life, but will be evidenced in all the minor and seemingly trivial matters . . . An accumulation of such seemingly unimportant disobediences may necessitate the student's withdrawal from school.

'Our calling demands a deep sense of the stern realities of life and eternity incompatible with "foolish talking" and "jesting", which are not convenient.'

Under 'Social Life' were further stern warnings: 'Experience has shown that, when friendship of the sexes is allowed to develop, interest in studies and prayer wanes . . . For this reason social contacts leading to such friendships are forbidden . . . Engagements or marriages are not to be entered during the school year. Infringements of this rule will result in immediate dismissal from school. Students engaged before entering school are subject to the same rules as other students. The superintendents will arrange for any necessary meetings together . . . dishonorable dismissal from the school is the penalty for any effort on the part of any student to make and develop a friendship, where one is of the opposite sex.'

In the unlikely event of any hippy of either sex seeking admission, the hurdles presented by the section on personal grooming are high. For men it says: 'Hair is to be kept cut and no extreme haircuts will be permitted. Students are to keep themselves clean shaven. All men students must wear dress suits or dress jackets and slacks and dress shirts and present a well-groomed appearance at all Sunday church services and Sunday meals. Western-type dress clothes are acceptable. Levis and blue jeans are not to be worn to church at any time.

'All men students must wear ties on Sundays, including street services. Short sleeved shirts must not be worn on the platform at any time. Clothing worn to classes may be of any type, so long as it is neat, clean and modest . . . Trousers and slacks must not be tight-fitting.'

The rules for girls are even more stringent: 'Hair should be worn in its natural colour, even if it has turned grey or white. There are still many who feel that short hair is a mark of an immodest and unspiritual woman. Hair which will not or has not had time to grow can be dressed in such a manner as to show a willingness to wear it long . . . Lipstick, rouge, eye make-up and colored fingernail polish are not to be used . . . Dresses and blouses must not have low-cut necklines front or back, nor be extremely form-fitting. Materials must not be sheer.

'Sleeves should be of such length as to be at least closer to the elbow than to the shoulder . . . Skirts must be long and full enough to cover the knees when standing or seated and not form-fitting nor clinging. Because of high winds at certain seasons of the year, skirts should not be too full . . . slacks, pedal pushers, toreador pants or shorts are not to be worn at any time.'

It was under the heading 'dormitory life', however, that I found the most remarkable rule. It read: 'Firearms are forbidden.' Don't, presumably, shoot the teacher; he is doing his best.

Apart from the gun-toting regulation, these rules would be enough to cause considerable turbulence in secular colleges on either side of the Atlantic, or, for that matter, in a few seminaries that I came across in my travels; but the students at the Miracle Valley Bible College, far from seeming truculent or rebellious, appeared quite happy in their ultra-cloistered environment. They were quietly spoken, friendly in a reserved fashion and obviously completely dedicated to their calling.

It was only when I met the Reverend Dale Moran, Dean of Men Students and Instructor in Evangelism, a slim young man with deep blue eyes, that I saw a more worldly side to this organization. I am not suggesting that he, personally, is worldly; on the contrary, he is so deeply dedicated to his mission that he accepted a lower salary to work at Miracle Valley than he had had in his previous job.

It was he, however, who showed me the powerhouse behind A. A. Allen Revivals, Inc. Proudly he told me: 'We have our own banking system here. And an IBM system for our mailing department. We have about 400,000 names on our mailing list, you see, and each month they receive our literature. On top of that, there are another 40,000 letters a month to handle. We have, of course, a typing pool.

'There is a contract post office here, too, handling the mail for the whole district. The Government pays part of the staff salaries and we pay part. We have our own trucks and our own construction crew to put up new buildings. We make our own concrete blocks. And there is an underground cellar for storing freshly picked fruit and vegetables until we can process them. We have four square miles here, you know, good cattle country, but we only raise about sixty-five head—just enough for our own needs. We raise about 6,000 chickens and have our own dairy, but we never sell any of our produce because we are an entirely religious organization. To sell would be secular business.'

For a moment I was not listening any more. Here was the first of a number of paradoxes I was to find in the A. A. Allen organization. Half an hour earlier Dr Gray had told me that people flew into the airstrip to buy cattle. Now I was being told that the Corporation spurned such commercial transactions. I let the point pass, however, for unworldly men are bound to get their lines of communications crossed occasionally.

The Rev. Dale Moran, anyway, was off on another tack. 'We have our own volunteer fire department,' he said. 'We are building a new fire truck instead of buying one. The Lord has blessed us in giving us all these different people with all these different skills. We have an engineering department, in fact, which can maintain and repair all our equipment.'

Trade unionists, of course, would call this use of cheap labour a curse, rather than a blessing; but before I had the chance to develop a debate on industrial relations, the Reverend Moran said in strange, non-sequiturial fashion: 'This valley, you know, has less atomic radiation fall-out than any other part of the United States, according to the National Geographic Magazine.'

I was tempted to suggest that it was a rather biased God which gave more protection to one part of the world than another, but resisted the urge. Now, anyway, we were in the radio and television department, from which the heart of the Reverend A. A. Allen throbs loudly to many millions. Maps on the wall plotted the radio and television stations which carry his message and, as I studied them, he explained: 'It's one of the best networks in the United States. It covers the country six days a week, except for half of Montana and parts of Idaho. We're on sixty-nine radio stations for fifteen minutes every day. Brother Allen sends us the master tape from wherever he is preaching and we make the programmes here for mailing to the radio stations. We do all our own TV films here, too. They are photographed during the rallies and edited here. After they've been used on TV we make them available to any church organization on a free-will offering basis. At the rallies we have three cameras, sometimes four, one a remote control job that can be operated from a distance of two hundred feet.

'And we have our own record processing department. It can produce a hundred records an hour with double staff working sixteen hours a day. Most of the recordings are made at the tent meetings, as Brother Allen preaches or the choir sings.'

Altogether it was a set-up which would have won the admiration of N.B.C. or B.B.C. technicians; and it was matched in technical excellence by the printing department, where my enthusiastic guide told me: 'Each of these printing machines cost between 50,000 and 60,000 dollars. We print 400,000 copies of our magazine every month and do most of the colour work ourselves. We would do it all, but we can't keep up with the work, though here again we have two eight-hour shifts working every day. So we send out about twenty per cent of our work.'

He gave me some samples of their recent work; and when I had time to study them I realized to the full that A. A. Allen Revivals, Inc., has a secular sophistication that certainly is not reflected in the puritanical prospectus it sends out to potential students at its Bible College. I was shown, for instance, a list under the scarcely humble heading 'Dynamic Books by A. A. Allen'. There were about forty-eight of them—twenty for a dollar, which is about eight shillings, two for seventy-five cents, twenty at fifty cents, five at twenty-five cents and one at ten cents.

Nor were the titles very demure, though I have no doubt that absolute purity reigned between the covers. Here are some examples: 'Demon of Lust', 'Demon Possession Today and How to Be Free', 'Except it Be for Fornication', 'Self-Invited Troubles', 'Flesh and the Devil', 'How to Renew Your Youth', 'My Besetting Sin', and 'Seven Women Shall Take Hold of One Man'.

As a tradesman in the world of words myself, I felt a sliver of admiration for the dynamic A. A. Allen's exquisite 'come-hither' technique with his titles. Who could resist picking up a book about seven women holding one man, even if some of the more sensitive customers did so a little shyly?

Another aspect of his monumental literary output, however, would not be inclined to win the admiration of the average book-seller. That Brother Allen's books are dynamic is a matter of opinion. That the three I own are very slender volumes indeed, far slimmer than any seventy-five cent paper-back, is a matter of fact; and they are selling at a dollar each. Nice work, I suppose, if you can get a dollar for it, but maybe I speak with my mind clouded by the sin of envy.

His autobiography *My Cross*—and here again the title does not exactly exude humility—is but ninety-five pages long. 'Bargain Counter Religion'—which contains, incidentally, some fairly abrasive phrases about other churches, scarcely an exhibition of Christian tolerance—is fifty-five pages long. 'Is It Religion or Racket—Faith or Fear?' which contains a few hefty side-swipes at his fellow-evangelists, has but thirty-three pages. These may be petty points, but it is as well for A. A. Allen Revivals, Inc., that books are not sold by weight.

Pamphlets pour off the presses in an even greater flood. Most of them are fairly ordinary modern evangelistic material—warnings that Communism is infiltrating the Churches, vague attacks on other Churches, including some Pentecostals—this in a nice, scary, red, black and white leaflet, called 'Satan Behind the Pulpit' with a picture of Lucifer reading the Lesson—and a piece about the witches who are working among us now. Brother Allen claims considerable success over witches and demons, indeed, and in another pamphlet states that among the messages he received personally from God was: 'Behold I give you power over all the power of the devil.' This is a direct quote because, he says, he wrote the words down as they were spoken to him.

I must say, however, that Brother Allen interprets this personal message fairly broadly. This is made clear in another pamphlet with the tantalizing title 'The Power to Get Wealth—How You Can Have It!' At first I thought it was no more than the old Rev. Ike technique which I described way back in Chapter One—give your money to God through me and soon you'll be swamped with the stuff. The evangelist from Miracle Valley, however, goes a little further. He says: 'God has anointed me to deliver His People from the demon powers of poverty.' He adds: 'The devil has many Christians backed into a corner, beat down by bills, debts and hopeless poverty. It is time to resist the devil; claim the promises of God and say: "Old devil, you have kept me poor and in debt long enough. God is going to destroy your power over my life, FOR IT IS GOD THAT GIVETH ME POWER TO GET WEALTH."'

Then at the end of the pamphlet come the punch-lines: 'In the Philadelphia tent meeting, God said to me: "I want you to line the people up across this tent and lay your hands on every one who pledges a hundred dollars for this Miracle Ministry! And those who pledge in faith, not just for money for themselves, but for the Glory of God and to preach the gospel . . . as you lay your hands upon them you will find that I have given you an anointing and the power to bestow upon them the power to get wealth'.

In other words, if the Miracle Mission gets rich, God gets rich. Everybody gets rich. Inevitably the pamphlet includes a ready-made letter to Brother Allen, the operative words of which are: 'I am enclosing $ . . .', 'I am pledging $ . . .' and 'I will send $ . . . each month on this pledge.' There is also a personal message from A. A. Allen, reading: 'The name of each person sending or pledging one hundred dollars will be placed in the special BOOK OF REMEMBRANCE in the Big Tent. Please enclose a small photo or snapshot of yourself, if you have one available.

I will lay my hands on your photo as I ask God to bless and prosper you.'

In the body of the copy there are even more encouraging words. They read: 'Just this afternoon a man who pledged a thousand dollars to God in the service last night, brought in his pledge this afternoon and he increased it to twelve hundred dollars!' Would I be wrong in assuming that God worked so fast, prospered him so quickly, that he was able to afford to give even more than he had promised? That old demon poverty must have got a right old shock, if that were the case.

This question of pledges, however, I raised with the Reverend Dale Moran. He told me: 'At our revival meetings, we have people who make a pledge to pay $100 or $10 dollars. We don't hold them to it. We just leave it to them and to the Lord, for this is a faith ministry. We keep a record and a file on each person, of course, and we send them a letter of reminder.'

I asked the Reverend Moran how many pledges were on the file and he told me: 'About 48,000. Some of them are for only $25, of course, but some may be for $500. A lot of times people set their own amount. They say: "Lord, I'm going to give your work so much money." Sometimes we set the pledge. We say: "We would like so many people to give $100 pledge." But they have the option of crossing it out.'

While I was considering this last magnanimous statement, another little paradox suddenly reared its niggly head. Earlier Dr Gray had told me that most people sent small offerings—one dollar, two dollars. Now the Reverend Moran was talking in terms of $25, $100, $500. Again the lines of communication seemed to be getting snarled, but what are a few hundred dollars between friends?

At that point I felt the conversation was becoming a little embarrassing and yet there was one aspect of it which I felt I could not leave. I said to the Reverend Moran: 'Why all this emphasis on personal wealth? Why this pamphlet, telling people how to get rich? Surely Christ and his disciples were poor and didn't kick up much of a fuss about it.'

'That pamphlet,' he said, 'is to prove to people that it is not God's will to let them live in poverty. It is Brother Allen's answer to the anti-poverty movement.'

What a man, this Brother Allen! He finds time to think of everybody and everything. That last thought, I feel sure, will gladden the hearts of the thousands of black children who are suffering from malnutrition in

Mississippi. Perhaps some day he will produce another pamphlet for them and call it: 'The Power to Get Food.'

The Reverend Moran's reply, at any rate, seemed to me a perfect curtain line to a conversation about a subject which obviously we viewed from somewhat different angles. Turning to livelier matters—anything, but anything for a change after what I had just heard—I picked up the witchcraft pamphlet and asked him whether they had been having much trouble from that source lately.

'We do a lot of preaching on this,' he said. 'We get a lot of correspondence from England about it. Many people are troubled by witchcraft.'

I gathered from him that there was a lot of it about. So wrap yourselves up well in Brother Allen's pamphlets. A couple of pledges will help to keep the broomsticks at bay, too.

I must admit, however, though it may sound foolhardy, that I carried no wooden stake with me on my way back to my motel that night. Witches, anyway, seldom wear tall hats these days—as Brother Allen points out in another pamphlet, they could look just like the girl next door—and I might have plunged the damn thing into the heart of a perfectly innocent woman taking her cat for a walk.

Instead I bore away *My Cross*, the autobiography of Brother Allen, for I wanted to learn as much as possible about this extraordinary man. The sub-title was intriguing: 'Personal Secrets and Hidden Truths, Never Before Published, Now Revealed.' The sub-sub-title read: 'The Book Thousands Have Waited For.'

If those thousands were expecting a good sob-story, they certainly got it. Brother Allen told of his struggle, his poverty, his faith and his courage, pressing hard on the emotional pedals until I expected to come across the line: '"God bless us, every one," said tiny Tim.' Personally I found it a rather embarrassing record, though there was one part which intrigued me: his description of his conversation with God.

He was pastor of a church in Colorado at the time and he decided that he must hear from heaven, that he must learn why his ministry had not been confirmed by signs and wonders. He felt that he could gain this knowledge by staying in a prayer closet and fasting.

This he tried several times, but always he was beaten by hunger. At last he asked his wife to lock him in the closet and not let him out until he had heard from God.

I admire his determination and, according to his autobiography, it brought results. He wrote: 'The glory of God began to fill the closet. I

thought for a moment that my wife had opened the door as the closet
began to grow light. But my wife had not opened the door of the
closet—JESUS HAD OPENED THE DOOR OF HEAVEN and the
closet was flooded with light, the light of the glory of God . . .

'Then, like a whirlwind, I heard His voice. It was God! He was
speaking to me! This was the glorious answer for which I had waited so
long!'

There were only two snags. In the first place, God was speaking very
quickly and of this Brother Allen wrote: 'My heart cried out: "Speak a
little more slowly. I want to remember it all!"'

Secondly, God had so much to say that the pastor was afraid he
would not be able to remember it all and he had omitted to take writing
material into the prayer closet. He faced up to this frustrating situation,
however, with ingenuity and fortitude.

'I began to feel in my pockets for a pencil,' he wrote. 'At last I located
a short one, but the lead was broken. Quickly I sharpened it with my
teeth. I searched for a piece of paper. I couldn't find any. Suddenly I
remembered the cardboard box filled with winter clothes which I was
using for an altar. I would write on the box.

'I asked the Lord to please start all over again at the beginning and let
me write the things down one at a time—to speak slowly enough so
that I could get it all on paper. Once more God started at the beginning
and spoke to me one after another the many things He had already
mentioned. As God spoke to me, I wrote them down.

'When the last requirement was written down on the list, God spoke
once again and said: "This is the answer. When you have placed on the
altar of consecration and obedience the last thing on your list, YE
SHALL NOT ONLY HEAL THE SICK, BUT IN MY NAME
SHALL YE CAST OUT DEVILS. YE SHALL SEE MIGHTY
MIRACLES AS IN MY NAME YE PREACH THE WORLD, FOR
BEHOLD I GIVE YOU POWER OVER ALL THE POWER OF
THE ENEMY."'

The next major miracle that I find Brother Allen recording is the
acquisition of the land at what he was to call Miracle Valley. Again God
spoke, not to him this time, but to a young rancher called Urbane
Leindecker.

One day in 1956, Urbane was attending a Rev. Allen tent rally in
Phoenix, Arizona. Suddenly God said to him: 'I want you to give this
ranch to Brother Allen for My glory.'

'This ranch' is now the headquarters of A. A. Allen Revivals, Inc.

From then on, according to the evangelist's magazine, miracle has piled upon miracle. Inevitably perhaps, in these circumstances, the name of the magazine is *Miracle* and interesting reading it makes. The first point that struck me about it, however, was not the enthralling material between its brightly coloured covers, but the remarkable resemblance between this official organ of Rev. Allen and the official organ of Rev. Ike. Testimonial followed testimonial. Appeal followed appeal. The major difference was that the claims of the evangelist from Miracle Valley, Arizona were even more exotic than those of the evangelist from Washington Heights, New York.

Rev. Ike, for instance, offers no Help Kit. Rev. Allen does—and for only four dollars, post paid. It is designed specially for those who wish to be delivered from tobacco, alcohol or narcotics and certainly seems to be a bumper package deal. It contains, for instance, an unbreakable 'Miracle Help' record which brings right into your own living room 'momentous on-the-scene deliverances and amazing testimonies'; three books (two priced at twenty-five cents and one at fifty), innumerable tracts and a copy of *Miracle* magazine. Each of these items, of course, can be bought separately and I must confess that I have not totted up the individual prices to see whether they add up to more or less than that of the do-it-yourself Help Kit.

Like Rev. Ike, Rev. Allen dispenses prayer cloths, one of which—again I quote the magazine—cured a homosexual drug addict of both his problems. Rev. Ike, however, does not offer to his readers Holy Bibles, imported from England for only ten dollars—£4—post paid; and in two major respects he lags away behind his Arizona brother.

In the first place he has not claimed yet, so far as I know, that his prayers will move God to fill teeth. Rev. Allen reports under a big red heading: 'God Is A Dentist! Miracle fillings in East St Louis.' There follow a couple of testimonies to back up this amazing piece of news.

Secondly, Rev. Ike has yet to intercede with God on behalf of those who wish to lose weight. Rev. Allen has a couple of testimonies on that score in his magazine, one under the breezy heading: 'She Used God's Reducing Plan!'

Naturally he wishes as many people as possible to benefit from these remarkable blessings. So in another section of the same magazine, he has a special message for them; it reads:

Special anointed cloths. Dental Needs—Reducing. In the East St. Louis Campaign Evangelist Allen felt inspired of God to have sponsoring ministers and those who had received fillings in their teeth to join him in prayer and in laying on of hands (1 Tim. 4: 14) to anoint miniature cloths especially for people who need a miracle for their teeth and for those who need to lose excessive weight. Do you need one of these specially anointed cloths?

If you have faith, write for one of these miniature handkerchiefs today. One could be the means of bringing God's blessing to you. Remember, there is no charge for these cloths. As Paul says in Acts xix; 11, 12, we also minister by means of anointed cloths to those who are not able to attend services. This is a faith work. The approximate cost to process and mail the cloths and instructions is one dollar. Fill out the blank below and, if you can, include an offering. It will help us continue this ministry.

The blank below has two little squares. Opposite one are the words 'For a miracle for my teeth'. Opposite the other, it says 'To lose excess weight'. All the faithful have to do is to put a tick in the square which interests them most. There is, of course, another square, but that has nothing to do with medical miracles. The words beside it are 'Offering enclosed $ . . .'

Rev. Ike has yet to offer recordings of prophetic music which will drive evil spirits from the minds and bodies of those who listen to them. Rev. Allen can let you have one for $2.95 (about 24s.), two for $5, or five for $10; and there is even an easy order coupon!

I would not like it to be thought, however, that Rev. Allen is away ahead on points over Rev. Ike. The score cards, indeed, are levelled up by one item which appears in both their magazines. It is that little piece in small print, and the *Miracle* Magazine version reads, amid a fairly long preamble:

Accounts of healing, deliverance and miracles, as printed in *Miracle* magazine are testimonies of those who report to have experienced the same. Detailed attention has been given in reporting and editing these testimonies to avoid distortion or exaggeration of the original personal or written declarations. Utmost care has been taken to assure the accuracy of all testimonies before publication and A. A. Allen Revivals, Ltd., and *Miracle* Magazine assume no legal responsibility for the veracity of any such report, nor do they accept responsibility as to the degree of permanency of reported healings, deliverances or miracles.

Admittedly it is difficult to give a written guarantee that miracles will be delivered by mail order, that wonders can be switched on like central heating. Nevertheless, I would have imagined that both Rev. Ike and Rev. Allen would have checked their facts before breaking into such exotic prose that seemed to offer so much hope for so many. It is reasonable, I think, to suggest that readers might be so dazzled by the vast headlines that the warning light might be overlooked. Certainly here was a point I thought well worth pursuing. It is the 'heads-I-win-tails-you-lose' gambit again. 'The management will not be responsible for any item of clothing lost or stolen in this restaurant . . .'

When I left Miracle Valley in that spiritually explosive bus, I had made up my mind that my life would be empty, indeed, were I not to have the unique experience of meeting Brother Allen. When I reached New York a couple of weeks later, he was in Chicago, holding three revival meetings daily; and, when I phoned the Coliseum Stadium, which was his base, the news certainly seemed encouraging. I spoke to the Reverend Don Stewart, one of his assistant ministers, and was told that I would be welcome any time I cared to call. He suggested that I should contact the Reverend Garry Beeney, Public Relations Director of A. A. Allen Revivals, Inc., and immediately I wrote to him, telling him that I would be in Chicago in a few days' time. I added that I understood just how busy they all were with three services a day, but that I would be grateful if he could arrange an interview for me with Brother Allen.

When I arrived at the Coliseum in Chicago on a bleak, bitter morning, the Reverend Beeney on his own was just concluding the morning session with a moving testimony about the rent they had to pay for the place and the high expense of holding rallies anywhere and everywhere. The congregation, understanding the situation, contributed suitably.

Immediately after the service, I introduced myself. He flung a brotherly, expansive arm around my shoulder and, as we walked from the vast stadium we chatted amiably about my visit to Miracle Valley. I asked him about the possibility of meeting Brother Allen and he told me that he would be present at the afternoon service to give out the pledge cards, though precisely what time he would arrive was difficult to say.

That afternoon I arrived in good time. The second service was just beginning, though the hall was far from full, understandably enough, as the star preacher was not speaking. I wandered around the back, where I found the vast, silver, trailer-cum-office which had carried him so many hundreds of thousands of miles around the country; but of Brother Allen himself there was no sign and nobody seemed to know for sure whether he was due to arrive at all. So I waited . . . and waited . . . and waited . . . and at last I was rewarded.

A short, stocky figure, wearing what looked to me like an astrakhan coat, swung into the bare, bleak area behind the stage. He walked with a slight roll, like a retired sailor or an old-time movie big-shot gangster. We shook hands briefly and, having told him who I was, I reminded him of my talk with the Rev. Stewart and my letter to the Rev. Beeney. His mouth remained taut. His face showed no flicker of welcome. His eyes scanned me with pugnacious suspicion, as if I might be a witch; and there was always the possibility, of course, with the unisex vogue so popular and his personal knowledge that witches no longer carry cards showing that they are fully paid-up members.

Briskly, he walked into his trailer and sat down at his desk in the cramped space. I followed, which was a little rude because I had not been invited. I watched him ruffle around among the scattered papers, find my letter and read it two or three times.

Then he said: 'Why can't you read my literature, my books? You'll find all you want there.'

'Rev. Allen,' I said, 'I have read your literature.'

'What have you read?'

'I've read your autobiography, for instance.'

'Who wrote it?'

I had to ponder that one very carefully. At last with some temerity I said: 'You did.'

He paused for a moment before saying: 'Yeah . . . of course . . . that's right.'

It was the first time that he had agreed with me and, I regret to say, the last, for after that the conversation became a little bit gritty, though I did all that I could to keep it velvet. Without looking up from the desk, he said: 'I'm a preacher. I'm not a businessman.'

A cynical demon tried to insinuate some doubt into my mind on that score, but I rejected him. I said: 'Reverend Allen, I am a writer and I would like to interview you, the preacher.'

He snapped on my words, like a trout after mayfly: 'I know writers. All writers are after the buck. All writers are infidels, though, mind you, I'm not saying you are. But they're all chasing the buck.'

Again that demon was at me. 'Go on,' it whispered. 'Tell him he's after the buck, too. Ask him about all those pledges. Ask him about the prayer cloths and the teeth-filling and all that heave-ho.'

'Get thee behind me, Satan,' I whispered. 'Don't be rude.' To Brother Allen I said: 'We try to make a living. I am writing about your organization and naturally I would like to interview you about it.'

'I'm giving no interviews,' he said. 'You'll have to talk to my business manager. I'll phone him and he'll fly in at a moment's notice. All the way from Dallas.'

He erupted from the desk and brushed past me out of the trailer. I followed. Suddenly he swung round, stared at me hard from under bushy eyebrows and said, George Raft fashion (or was it Bogart . . . or Cagney?): 'I'm not a fool.'

With utter sincerity I replied: 'That was the last thought I would have had about you, Reverend.'

He disappeared into a phone box and stayed there for about five minutes, occasionally flicking sharp glances in my direction. Though I was engaged in writing down quickly my first impressions of this man who had talked with God—I had writing material, but then it is my job—I smiled back at him each time. His face remained stern, totally unrelaxed and that saddened me. I was beginning to get the distinct impression that Brother Allen did not like me.

Then he bustled out of the box, jerked his head over his shoulder at the phone and said: 'My business manager is on the line. From Dallas. He's flying in to see you. Talk to him . . . to Mr Hoekstra.'

Off he swung to give out the pledge cards, for the service, which had been a loud but suitable background to our brisk, brief conversation, was ending. I picked up the phone and was greeted by a warm, friendly voice. Mr Hoekstra would be delighted to meet me. Was looking forward to it. Would arrive at O'Hare Airport, Chicago at 10.30 the following morning.

The contrast was confusing, but welcome. I arranged to meet him at the airport so that I could fly on to New York immediately after our talk. Chicago, lovable city though it is in many ways, suddenly had begun to pall upon me.

As I left the box, Brother Allen was striding past, pledge cards off his hands. As monosyllabic as ever, he said: 'You fixed up?'

'Yes, thank you,' I replied. 'Everything's fine.'

Down came the bushy eyebrows. Out thrust a finger, pointing at my heart. He looked rather like an angry Old Testament prophet in an astrakhan coat and I waited for him to tell me to prepare to meet my doom, for the end of the world was nigh. Instead he said: 'You'll meet a good businessman'; and he was gone.

The next time I saw him was that night at the service, where he was the star. The hall, which had been comparatively bare for the morning and afternoon services, was packed, alive with anticipation. On the stage were the preachers, a pianist, a drummer, an organist and a group which included a tall, handsome lady, magnificent in flaming orange. Already the organ was pounding out a beat, tantalizing the emotions, Brother Love fashion. I thought the devotions were about to begin, not realizing that there was an essential preliminary. A speaker—I think his name was Brother Bob—went to the microphone and said: 'Before we start, have a look at our bookstall. Just have a look at that gold and silver Bible. And our recordings. Slip up there right now because we've only a dozen of some of those records left. But don't leave your purse on your seat because there may be an old devil around. I've had people coming to me and crying that their purses have gone and I've told them "But I warned you!"'

In a few minutes the stall was surrounded. I picked up a copy of *Miracle* magazine and was charged twenty-five cents for it—about two shillings. The service did not begin until the last customer had cast a lingering look at the books and the pamphlets and the records and the gold and silver Bibles; and then we were off into the warm, heady world of supercharged revival, the group singing its spirituals with a resounding fervour, the organ shrilling its heart away, the audience expanding, melting into the mood with a speed that would have made Brother Love pale with envy. They sang. They danced. They waved their arms. Then the Reverend Don Stewart, the friendly one I had phoned from New York, was up there, reaping the harvest of the music, scything the air with arms and words, fertilizing the frenzy with a vigour that verged on violence.

'The cold, dead churches are dead today because they don't want God's blessing,' he shouted. 'That's why they're losing members. They don't want God's blessing . . . but WEEE want it . . . yeeaah!'

'Yeeaah!' they roared back. 'WEEE want it. Hallelujah! Thank you, Jesus!' Already he had them out of their seats, into the aisles. In front of the stage a dozen or more, men and women, black and white, old and young, are bouncing around in wild bunny-hops. They are not in the Coliseum now. They are not in Chicago. They are out of this world in their own, private, half-way house to heaven.

'God says: "I want you to choose life,"' says Brother Stewart. '*Choose life*! CHOOSE LIFE! But you can have the curse, if you want it. He raises the poor up from out of the dust and the beggar from out of the dung-hill. Did He say that?'

'Yeeaah!' they respond. 'Yeeaah, He sure said that! He said it!'

'Money?' bellows Brother Stewart, making it sound like a dirty word. 'Hold on to it and it makes you poor. Give it away to God and He makes you rich. Riches are an evil. God says when you keep it, it will hurt you, but when you give it away, it will bless you. It's not the the money that's a sin. It's only a sin when you don't give it away to God. There were men in the Bible who chose the curse instead of the blessing and went to hell!'

As he swirls out the words, they dance and jiggle and hop. One little old lady, all in white, a spangle in her hair, trots round the perimeter of the stadium, like a marathon runner training in an indoor stadium, an ecstatic smile on her tender face. Another, quite hysterical, jiggled up to the stage. Brother Allen rose, arms held high, and shouted: 'Just look at this little woman. She can't keep still. She's having a great blessing!'

'Jesus Christ chose poverty,' said Brother Stewart. 'He didn't have no place to lay his head. This is the day of prosperity. This is the day of riches . . . yeeaah!'

The last word was pure Satchmo, vibrant, sensual, almost wolfish. On and on he went on the evils of riches for about ten minutes—and then came the pay-off, the time to call for pledges. Brother Allen went down to give them out, while the organ throbbed and the drum beat and the tambourines jingled. The crowd moved forward and queued to take their pledge cards; and when they had settled back comfortably in their seats again, Brother Stewart, arms folded, said in a calm, quiet voice: 'Now everyone who took a pledge come forward here and we'll pray for you. Take a pencil from the usher and sign the pledge now. First thing to do is put your name and address on the pledge. You can pay your pledge right now or post it; but why not put it in the envelope right now?'

Obediently they went forward again. Brother Stewart had done well; and now that the business part of the evening was over, it was time for the sermon from Brother Allen.

He stood there, a small, sturdy figure in a gleaming yellow shirt. For a moment my mind went back to the Bible College prospectus with its strict rules about modest clothes, but soon I was gazing in wonder at this man, for he had changed not only his clothes, but his skin. The brusque, tough and not over-polite character that I had met a few hours earlier had disappeared; and in its place was a simple man, a humble man, a man who had suffered. A tear-jerker, like the man who had written the autobiography.

'One pair of shoes was all I had once a year, when I was a little boy . . . a big package from my dear old daddy and stockings for my four sisters and long underwear . . . In the spring we went barefoot to save our shoes . . . and my poor old mother, she couldn't go to the dime store and pay fifteen cents for half soles we were so poor . . . So she used to go to the city dump and find old shoes and repair them on an old last . . . My two sisters, my own two sisters were drop-outs at the sixth grade they were so poor and I quit at the eighth because I was ashamed of my clothes . . . Often I had to steal a nickel to buy the tablet to do my homework on.'

Hearts and flowers and sweet violins; and they loved it. They were still loving it, when ushers carried round pledge baskets and Brother Allen, his voice breaking with emotion, growing softer, softer, went on: 'Jesus, come among your children with your blessing of prosperity. You've been so good . . . so good . . . so good.'

He sat down. A singer called Eugene Martin, sang 'Walk Around Heaven All Day'. The pledge baskets filled. The hearts and flowers faded away and back we were to the old beat, the old frenzy, the old Hallelujah. The atmosphere, which had sunk to a whisper, was whipped to white-hot heat in a matter of minutes; and a new Allen appeared, a frenetic, joyous Allen, jumping up and down on the stage, shouting: 'Go on . . . go on . . . so good . . . so good . . . yeeaah, so good that if it was any better, we couldn't take any more . . . just like honey . . . honey!'

As I watched him, I realized that here was an artist. One minute he had them near to tears. The next he had them wild. A few minutes later he calmed them again, for the time for healing had come.

He went to five people in invalid chairs. 'Walk, for Jesus's sake,' he implored, his hands pressing on frail heads. 'Walk in the name of Jesus . . . Thank You, Jesus . . . He'll make you walk.'

Four stood and tottered a few paces. The fifth jerked and strove, but couldn't make it. Now others with other ailments were lining up. Brother Allen went to each of them, clamped his hands on their foreheads. A dozen of them collapsed in a faint or a trance, to be caught by the waiting ushers who were ready, for they had seen it all before; and while Allen exhorted the Lord to heal, three other worshippers, still gripped by what had gone before, lay writhing and jerking by the stage. Nobody paid any attention.

At last it was all over. Slowly the crowds filed out. Did he heal that night? I do not know. I can but refer you to the small print in his magazine. I can say that, when I went back into the hall, three of the invalid chairs were occupied again. Two were gone. Had they been wheeled away empty, while their one-time occupants walked? Again I do not know. I wonder does Brother Allen.

Next morning at the airport I met Mr Raymond G. Hoekstra, a big, breezy man, wearing a wide stetson hat. He told me that he was Brother Allen's adviser on fund raising and that he advised some other churches too. 'I run the Twentieth Century Advertising Agency,' he said, 'but I only take religious or patriotic accounts . . . accounts of the conservative type.'

We got right down to business. I said: 'Why this emphasis on making people wealthy? Was Jesus wealthy?'

'Jesus came that man should live more abundantly.'

'Didn't He mean that spiritually?'

'He meant it both ways.'

'What do you say about his claim that God will fill teeth and help people to slim?'

'It amazes me more than anything. I have heard many testimonies, which I have no reason to doubt. Slimming? I suppose it could happen in several ways. God is not all emotion and mystery. He is mind and intelligence as well. Prayer could cure obesity, if a person were cured of a physical imbalance; or if he were cured of emotional problems which could make him an obsessive eater, or it could be done by a miracle, for all things are possible with God.'

'Why does he think it necessary to have that piece in his magazine, absolving his organization from all legal responsibility in connection with the truth of the testimonies it prints?'

'It would be possible for an impostor to give a phoney testimony. If someone wanted to harm his work by injecting a fraud, it could be done in this way. The stories, of course, are checked by the magazine; but they receive so many hundreds of testimonies that it would take a large staff of investigators to check them all.'

'If the secular press cannot confirm a story, they leave it out.'

'In a magazine like this, you must depend on the witness's word.'

'What is Brother Allen's annual budget?'

'A minimum of 2,500,000 dollars a year. We normally think of it as a minimum of 50,000 dollars a week.'

'Does he take a salary?'

'No. He lives on love offerings and so do all members of the team.'

'One national magazine quotes him as saying that he believes people can be raised from the dead by prayer. Is that true?'

'I'm sure it is possible. There are well documented instances of it in South Korea and Indonesia in recent years.'

'Documented by whom?'

'Evangelical leaders connected with such people as Billy Graham and World Vision.'

'Where were they reported?'

'I've seen them in evangelical publications. I know that Brother Allen stresses that Jesus Christ healed the sick and raised the dead and commanded the disciples to do the same.'

'Did he command the disciples to raise the dead?'

'Yes . . . at least I think so.'

Here I ended the interview and caught the next flight back to New York. On the way I was thinking of the simple, shy students, who sang and spoke with tongues in the bus on the way to Douglas on the Mexican border. They were nice people.

As this book went to press I learned, from the *San Francisco Examiner*, of the death of the Rev. A. A. Allen in front of a television set in his fourth-floor suite in San Francisco. The Coroner, Dr Henry Turkel, said that he had died of 'acute alcoholism and fatty infiltration of the liver'.

A pathology and toxicology examination disclosed a blood alcohol content of ·36 per cent, enough, it was said, to produce deep coma. He was fifty-nine years of age but to me he looked much younger. The burial was at Miracle Valley.

8: DOOM, GLORY AND GRAHAM

I do not know who said that it was tough at the top, but Billy Graham, senior whiz-kid in the fiercely competitive world of jet-set evangelists, almost certainly would respond to that sad sentiment with a deeply sincere 'amen'. A routine response to the news that I was writing a book about the salvation business was: 'I suppose you'll have a go at the Graham circus.'

That, I soon learned, was a rather unfair comment, yet understandable. Having spent months whittling away at a yardstick—or consumer guide—to measure the weight and size and strength of those who strive for souls, I would say that his methods are a good deal more ethical than those of many others I met. Yet because he is so widely known internationally, because some of his critics have never heard any other chromium-plated revivalists, they dismiss him as a slick commercial, who uses every showman's trick to make friends and influence people for his financial benefit and his ego. The spectacular success of the man has backlashed.

Certainly he is a high-pressure salesman. He proved that early in life, when he was the best Fuller's Brush traveller in North Carolina; and today he insists that he is selling the greatest product on earth. It is true that the commission he draws from his work—it is a salary, in fact—keeps him comfortably; but that is fair because he puts everything he has got into it. I agree that he stirs emotions and appeals for funds frequently in highly professional fashion, that he sells books, record albums and song sheets. It is all comparatively straight-forward business, however, even down to a key ring containing scripture texts, complete with Billy Graham signature. The somewhat tasteless blurb reads: 'This handsome eighteen-karat gold key ring contains twenty memory verses. Durable and practical. Certainly a unique gift! Price: one dollar.'

To his credit, however, he has no truck with blessing pacts or prayer cloths. His magazine, *Decision*, which outstrips in circulation all its rivals, boasts of no miracles. He has never said: 'Come and join me and you will be cured of your physical and mental ills, freed from your creditors and loved by all.' I certainly am not enthralled by his pulpit tactics and am even less excited by his publicity methods; but I have chalked up some points in his favour which other evangelists lack and which, oddly enough, do not seem to be widely known.

He is not a bigot, for instance, and rejects any school which claims a monopoly on God, which is one reason why he stayed only briefly at the Bob Jones University. Of that early episode one of his biographers, Curtis Mitchell, writes in *The Making of a Crusader:*

Billy began to feel increasingly uncomfortable. On campus you were not permitted to speak to girls except during certain hours. You were not allowed to loiter. You could not leave the campus unless you signed a book. Upper classmen might have cars, but they could not drive them on Sunday. Violations were mysteriously reported and demerits awarded. If you got so many more, you were shipped home in disgrace . . .

Another trouble galled him. The Bible was used to settle every dispute. It was the ultimate authority. Billy.had always accepted the supremacy of the Bible and he had no wish to change now, but insistence on the precise meaning advanced by the school became a heavy cross. One day he violated a rule by crying: 'Don't we ever have the right to figure things out for ourselves?'

He left voluntarily, but he could not have been more than one jump ahead of the sheriff, Bob Jones, Snr., who told him angrily: 'If you're a misfit at Bob Jones College, you'll be a misfit wherever you go.'

When the inaccurate prophet of such gloom died thirty-two years later, Bob Jones, Jnr., sent a telegram to Graham, saying that neither he nor his personal representative would be welcome at the funeral.

Perhaps the most important point in Graham's favour, however, is publicized least. Though he is a Southerner, born in 1918 to parents who retained a deep suspicion of Yankees, he constantly has taken a brave stand against racial prejudice. He has denounced it publicly as 'a product of man's sinfulness' and refused to hold a crusade in South Africa because the authorities would not allow mixed congregations. Since 1950 he has been addressing—insisting upon, in fact—integrated rallies in the Southern States, which not only has cost him support among diehards, but has been positively dangerous. He spoke in Little Rock and New Orleans, when the atmosphere was particularly tense; in Clinton, Tennessee, after a racist's bomb had destroyed a school; and in Birmingham, Alabama, despite threatening letters and telephone calls.

It was in 1963, however, after murders in Selma and Montgomery, Alabama, that he took his most determined stand, though he was ill in hospital in Honolulu when he heard about them.

Dr Martin Luther King had organized a protest march to draw attention to the fact that Selma's black population had only one per cent of the vote, though they made up fifty per cent of the population. Major John McCloud of the State police ordered the protesters to return to their church. Instead they stood in silence. State troopers, Selma posse men and sheriff's deputies thrashed into them with clubs and mopped up with tear gas canisters.

Two nights later, the Rev. James Reeb and two other ministers were beaten in front of the Silver Moon Café. Reeb died. Graham, who had been following the sickening sequence from the radio by his hospital bed, telephoned his Atlanta headquarters and instructed two of his closest associates, the Rev. Dr Walter Herbert Smythe and Stanley Monneyham, to visit Selma and other Alabama cities to organize meetings. They reminded him that he had appointments in Europe. Graham said: 'They can be cancelled.'

Ten days after James Reeb died, Dr Martin Luther King led a civil rights march from Selma to Montgomery. Those who joined with him included a cripple, a blind man, a nun and many preachers. They reached Montgomery on 25 March and that night Mrs Viola Liuzzo, a civil rights worker, was murdered by Ku Klux Klan members. Immediately Graham announced that he was taking his crusade team into Alabama.

Normally his organization needs between eight and twenty months to organize a crusade. The Alabama campaign opened five weeks after Mrs Liuzzo's death. On Saturday, 1 May, he spoke in Dothan. The following Monday he preached at the University of Alabama where, some time earlier, Governor George Wallace had stood with his back to the door to prevent two black students from enrolling. On Tuesday morning he held his rally at Auburn University and that night he spoke at Tuskagee. Then he flew to Denmark, where he had an unbreakable commitment; but in June he was back again in Alabama, opening another tour in Montgomery, speaking for several days, often several times a day. At any one of those meetings he could have been murdered, for any Southerner who preaches integration is a quisling in the eyes of white supremists.

There at any rate was a splendid, blood-and-guts Graham. It is a pity that it takes violence to reveal this fine side to his character, to spur him into action against social injustice. His voice is powerful, though here I am not referring to its decibel content.

His preaching style, however, is worth examining, for it reveals how he has changed over the years. Like Oral Roberts, he has abandoned open exhaust evangelism in favour of a quieter line, a sincerity-with-dignity touch. No longer does he cut the air to ribbons with his **arms**

and fade out finally with a winsome: 'God bless you all . . . real good.'
No longer does he wear the garish ties that once were the banners of his
religious razzle-dazzle. Instead he prefers the sober suits of an elder
statesman; but then he has walked with Presidents—five of them.

Certainly his organization purrs along now with all the smug power
of a Rolls-Royce rather than the rasp of a sports car. In Minneapolis, the
financial headquarters of the Billy Graham Evangelistic Association, his
old friend and fellow-worker, George Wilson, presides over a multi-
million dollar complex with a devotion that is both spiritual and commercial in an atmosphere that is redolent of both worlds, as if the Chase
Manhattan Bank had opened a branch in St Patrick's Cathedral. This
illusion is heightened by the sight of a Bible on his large desk, side by
side with the *Wall Street Journal*.

Wilson, a short, plump, happy man in his middle fifties, is ideal for
the job and properly proud that he can keep both God and Caesar well
serviced. Smiling and relaxed, he told me: 'I started here with a staff of
one twenty-six years ago. Now we have more than 350, working three
shifts round the clock and I still find time to do a bit of lay preaching. I
suppose I could have gone into business, but what would I have made,
except money? I don't have a lot of that now, but there's nothing I need
that I haven't got. I've no ulcer department. I've never had an ache or
a pain in a quarter of a century . . . all that and the pleasure of seeing
people's lives change.'

He gets obvious pleasure, too, out of the powerhouse he has helped
to create in those buildings which look so modest from the street.
Simmering with energy, he whisked me round the printing and publishing departments, the filing and mailing sections, the spiritual counsellors' offices, the personnel department, the chapel, the cinema and all
the expensive toys that keep them moving so quietly, so quickly. There
were impassive computers that could—and did—tell their masters, for
instance, the day and date of Easter over several centuries in several
minutes or maybe it was seconds. There were magnetic tape machines
that could infile and outfile 2,500 names a minute instead of a thousand
a day. There were . . . but why go on? Just take it as read that George
Wilson has every dazzling electronic aid that he feels will pay for itself
in the long run, while spreading the gospel now.

As I trotted at his twinkling heels, he kept up a rapid-fire commentary: 'Our magazine, *Decision*, has a circulation of nearly four million . . .
two English editions, published in London and Australia . . . a Japanese

edition in Tokyo . . . baseball is very big there . . . a Spanish edition in Buenos Aires . . . a French edition in Paris . . . a German edition in Frankfurt . . . We publish two or three million copies of the radio sermon each year and give them away or sell them on a cost basis . . . and the Gospel of St John as follow-up material for people who make decisions at the crusades . . . We sell books and record albums, mostly to evangelists and make some money out of it, but it's just nominal . . We do all our own photographic work, colour as well as black and white.

'Then there's our radio ministry . . . started nineteen years ago . . . Now there's an "Hour of Decision" programme on 900 stations every Sunday . . . biggest radio network in the country . . . and we've forty-five stations in Australia . . . and fifty short wave stations in foreign countries . . . We own a station in Honolulu and another in the Black Mountains . . . no commercials . . . supported by listeners . . . and we've television, of course, on between 200 and 350 stations across America . . . prime viewing times, video tapes direct from the crusades . . . in Australia as well . . . first colour television they ever saw . . .

'Films, too . . . our unit's called World Wide pictures . . . based in Burbank, California . . . beautiful, downtown Burbank . . . One film, *The Restless Ones*, has been seen by nearly five million people . . . 360,602 people made decisions for Christ after seeing it . . . *For Pete's Sake* has been shown 643 times to a million and a half people and there were 67,373 decisions . . . Cliff Richard, the young British star, featured in *Two a Penny*, made last year . . . He gave his name and time for nothing . . . We've just finished another in Israel . . . distribute them ourselves from here . . . We may rent a theatre or a hall to show them . . . and we hire them out for five or ten dollars, maybe . . . the whole operation is subsidized, not commercial at all.'

We reached the chapel, a sanctuary for me, for I was flagging. George Wilson, still effervescing like a bottle of tonic water, touched a button that gently dimmed the lights and sent the curtains before me sliding back, slowly, silently. A picture of Christ picking up the cross filled the screen and, as an organ played, a voice, deep, comforting, commanding, told the story of the crucifixion. Then the lights began to glow again, symbolizing the resurrection, while the organ reached for a crescendo in 'The Battle Hymn of the Republic'.

'Will you accept Him or will you reject Him?' asked the voice sternly. 'This is life's great decision.'

Then out we went again to the workaday world and the commentary, lush with statistics: 'This is the mailing department . . . We handle 25,000 letters a week . . . and up to 100,000 a day when we're on television . . . Here's where the spiritual counsellors work . . . Sometimes people come in off the street . . . We get letters addressed to Billy Graham, c/o Archbishop of Canterbury . . . or c/o the White House . . . one was to Billy Graham, Many Apples . . . Now here's our filing department . . . We use magnetic tape that costs thirty dollars and carries 150,000 names . . . That's a bit cheaper than five filing cabinets at 300 dollars each . . . Here's the personnel department . . . applicants for jobs have aptitude tests here . . . On religious grounds? No . . . but they don't usually stay if they're not practising Christians.'

There was more, so much more, but I think I have made it clear that the Billy Graham Evangelistic Association wastes no time, no money, no opportunity to further its mission. All I wanted to know at the end of the tour was how this electronic empire was maintained, how it was possible for the Bible to marry the *Wall Street Journal*. I was not really surprised when George Wilson made it sound very simple.

'In 1967 we worked to an annual budget of $10,000,000,' he told me. 'Now it's over $15,000,000—about £6,250,000 in your money. Sure we're a business operation, but that's not our sole purpose. It takes money to do our kind of work and we make no apologies for it.'

'Where do you get your money?'

'From sales of our magazine and books and from offerings . . . mainly small offerings. A few people make fairly large contributions, but mostly they average about seven dollars each. We get their prayer support, too, of course, because a lot of people believe in the message Mr Graham is giving and the way he is giving it. We're in the jewellery line of Christian giving, however. If there's an economic squeeze, people quit buying jewellery, but still buy other goods. They carry on giving to their Church, but we feel the pinch. That's the way it should be—the Church first and us second, though it means we have to keep a close eye on our budget.

'Actual cash in hand? We normally run with about enough in the treasury to take care of the payroll for about two months. That's good business.* We have no bonds or stocks, no endowments. If people give them to us, bequeath them to us in their wills, perhaps, we sell them as

---

* Do not ask me why it is good business. To understand the *Wall Street Journal*, I would need not only an abacus, but a code book.

soon as possible. We feel there are other ways of retaining a balance without having funds in something that can rise and fall. We've got to be careful because we're merely trustees for these funds. We have an obligation to every donor.'

'How about property?' I asked. 'Do you invest in real estate?'

'We buy property only when we intend to use it, only if we absolutely need it. We never buy it as an investment.'

'How do you spend the $15,000,000 a year?'

'We buy television and radio time. We put out a good deal of publicity. We have wages to pay and we have a correspondence school which is a follow-up in Bible studies for those who make decisions for Christ. We don't bring a baby into the world and leave it on the doorstep. We try to nurture it, to feed it with the sincere milk of the word. There is no fee for this. If people want second, third, fourth or fifth lessons, they get them all free. That's good business, too, the Lord's business; and the Lord's business should be done efficiently. We've the greatest product in the world. Why shouldn't we present it in as fine a fashion as others present soap chips or cornflakes? We're dealing with human lives. Why shouldn't we try to make them better churchmen, give them something which will make them want to study and read the Bible?'

I had not contested the point, but obviously others had. When he felt that he had made it with sufficient strength, he went on: 'Then there's our school of Christian writing, an adjunct of *Decision* magazine. We've had several of them here and a couple abroad—in Melbourne and in London. It's an annual three-day thing to encourage writers in the religious field and we get right down to the nitty-gritty. We've experts to teach them how to get an article in the paper, how to write a story, what to do when they get a rejection slip. Out of 900 applications a year, we take about 250 and, though we charge a small five-dollar fee, it covers only part of the cost.'

'Do you make money out of your crusades and rallies?'

'When Mr Graham accepts an invitation to hold a crusade in a city,' he said firmly, 'he insists that those who invited him must set up a non-profit corporation to receive and dispense funds. When the crusade is over, they must publish their audited accounts. We're not even on the board. Some of our men may go in and help set up the budget, but we're not there to raise money. We're in the soul-saving business.'

That was an interesting, but not a complete answer, though I am not suggesting that George Wilson was short-changing me. From a formidable information pack which I was given later, I learned that Billy Graham personally receives no money from any crusade or rally. The statement went on, however: 'It is hoped that the budget will be met before the crusade concludes and that at least the final two offerings can be designated for the Billy Graham Association. Any surplus should be designated for the Billy Graham Evangelistic Association to assist in any number of their world-wide ministries.'

I had but one more question for George Wilson. 'Until 1950 Billy Graham accepted love offerings,' I said. 'Then he went on a salary. Could you tell me how much he earns?'

'Certainly,' he replied. 'He gets $24,500 a year—a little over £10,000 in English money. That's the highest salary in the entire organization, of course. If he were in business, he could make $100,000.'

That is true. According to John Pollock, an English biographer of Graham, he has turned down at least three film offers which could have made him rich. Apart from such obvious gold-mines, it is clear that his undoubted abilities, coupled with his fame, would make him a very useful addition to any board of directors. I think that it is fair to say, however, that he does not seek excessive wealth, merely the comfortable living which he earns by working extremely hard. One of his team put it reasonably enough when he said: 'Too much work done in the name of Christ is run-down, baggy-trousers stuff. Billy believes in going first class.'

He has some personal income from family property in Charlotte, North Carolina, where he was born, and from book royalties which are put into a special trust for his wife and family. He has no control over this trust and, so far as the Association is concerned, he refuses even to write a cheque for it. His home at Montreat in the foothills of the Blue Ridge Mountains on the borders of North and South Carolina was a gift from friends. It is no millionaire's mansion, but, according to most reports, it is more than cozy with a beautiful view and oceans of peace. On the lawn in the summer, where he practises his often erratic golf swing, are two rocking chairs, presents from Lyndon Johnson when he was President. When he reaches the metal gates at the bottom of the drive on his way home, he touches a button on the dashboard of his car and they swing open. Visitors are faced with two warning notices, one announcing that 'vicious' dogs are let loose at night, the other stating:

'Trespassers Will Be Eaten'. Generally they conclude that both the spelling and the messages are meant as a joke.

It is here, presumably, that he will retire. There seems little likelihood at this stage in his career that he will be forced to sell out and move to more modest premises when he is too old to preach and that, of course, is as it should be. Similarly, though George Wilson in Minneapolis may shake his head over rising costs and a tight budget, I cannot see the Billy Graham Evangelistic Association closing its doors for lack of funds. When the liner *Queen Elizabeth* was for sale in 1968, indeed, the Association toyed with the idea of buying it for use as a floating evangelical school. The price mentioned was $4,800,000 and George Wilson was quoted in *The Times* as saying: 'We would have to set up foundations in the States. We don't have that kind of money available.' He gave the impression, however, that he did not think it would be too difficult to raise it, that foundations could be set up. Both Graham personally and the organization generally have many influential and wealthy supporters; and even without them I imagine that millions of little people would chip in willingly, if they felt that there was any real danger of bankruptcy.

How has he achieved this position in the hearts of so many people, eminent and otherwise? It is not by charm alone. Governor John Connally, who was wounded in Dallas when President Kennedy was assassinated, has said: 'Billy Graham is more than a preacher, more than an evangelist, more than a Christian leader. In a greater sense, he has become our conscience.' That could be true in America; and even the British, a more inhibited people, were won over in their thousands by this man, despite an initial coolness. Personality and superbly professional production methods may have played their part, but so great was the response that there must have been something more.

In an attempt to find out what that something was, I watched a colour film made for television of a Graham crusade, shown for me by George Wilson in the cinema of the Minneapolis headquarters. As I sat back in a blue seat that tilted like a rocking chair, a splendid voice said softly, almost reverently: 'This is the crusade in Portland, Oregon . . . the beautiful City of the Roses . . . May we encourage you now to call a friend and invite him to watch? We hope that the programme tonight will be a very special blessing and will meet the needs of every single one of you . . . And here now is a new song which conveys in a very wonderful way the message which young people are singing today; "The Flag to Follow and the Song to Sing."'

The choir, white, white shirts for the boys, white, white blouses for the girls, sang it beautifully, though I could not imagine it becoming the anthem of the deeply involved young people I had met on my journey. It was followed by a blatant commercial: 'In this wonderful little book, you will find the living Psalms and Proverbs . . . para-phrased edition . . . 745 pages just full of the truth of God . . . yours for the asking, if you just take a few minutes tonight and write to Billy Graham, Minneapolis, Minnesota . . . and include your gift of confi-dence and trust. Thank you for caring and staying with us.'

Graham opened his sermon with a superlative, which was true to form, for he is a great man for oratorical extremes, seeing in life the greatest, the tallest, the finest, the worst, the lowest, the wickedest. Firmly, but with the intimacy that is part of him, he said: 'This may be the most important hour you have ever spent . . .'

A little later he slipped in another commercial for the book, ending it with: 'We hope you will send some financial help to put on this telecast. If ever a series of telecasts was needed in America, it is now. We don't know how long we'll be able to do this . . . And now I would like you to turn to Mark's Gospel . . . "What shall it profit a man, if he gain the whole world and lose his own soul?"'

It was the moment of loud, intense truth. Leaning forward, blue eyes glinting, Graham said: 'It has been estimated that the real estate of the world is worth thirty-seven trillion dollars. Jesus said that your own soul, living inside your body, is worth more than that put together . . . Mao Tse Tung said: "It is not enough to have loyalty. We must possess the soul of the people . . ." Even our teenagers are asking about life and death and soul . . . about heaven and hell and the future . . . and the devil . . . Oh, yes, there is a devil . . . There was a play in England called *To Lucifer, a Son*. It was written with the theme that a personal devil does not exist, that no intellectual can accept him . . . but seventy-one per cent of the American people say they believe in the devil and so do I. . . .

'I know thousands of people who live below the poverty line in American, who are happy as they can be because they have Christ . . . We have a tremendous responsibility, of course, to those in trouble . . . People say: "You will have happiness, if you have a higher standard of living" . . . Tonight Satan is bidding for your soul . . . Some of you have sold your souls to the devil very cheaply . . . Why didn't you hold out for a higher price? People say to me: "Do you believe there is a hell, Billy?" I tell them: "Yes, because the Bible teaches it. Jesus says there is a hell and I believe Him . . . I'm going to heaven, just like you, not because I've preached to millions round the world, but because Christ died on the cross for us . . . the real poverty is a spiritual poverty . . . I've been in places where really genuine, terrible poverty exists and we should do something about it in this rich country of ours . . . but there is a worse poverty . . . a spiritual poverty. . . .

'I'm going to ask you to make this your "Now Time" and declare for Christ . . . This is your Rubicon . . . This is your Armageddon . . . You hang in the balance . . . Which way will you go? My friend, Jack Nicklaus* says: "Think positive after a bad shot" . . . I am going to ask you, in spite of your sins, to get up out of your seats and come forward and say: "I want to know my soul is saved . . . I want to know my soul is saved."'

The organ began to play very softly. The voice reached out, not so much to the crowd, but to every single individual in it, beseeching them, urging them, perhaps luring them: 'I'm going to ask you to come and stand here . . . I'm going to ask that nobody leaves, but that they just stand in prayer while you come.'

A girl moved forward, crying. Others followed, slowly at first and then in greater numbers. Graham said: 'Those of you watching on television can receive Christ in your hearts, receive Him just now and let Him into your life and let him forgive your sins. Write a letter to me and I'll send you some literature which I'll give to these people tonight . . . God help you to make your commitment tonight.'

The programme ended with another plug for the book. The lights went up and I was left with the impression that Billy Graham plays on the emotions of his audience and his viewers with all the skill, all the art of a great actor supported by a fine cast. The only difference is that he is playing himself, for this is his life. I have no reason to doubt his sincerity, but, as I left the cinema, I had a strong feeling that reason can dissolve in tears at these crusades. I decided, however, that I would postpone my decision on that point until I reached Atlanta, Georgia, where I hoped to meet the evangelist himself.

Accordingly I asked George Wilson whether he could arrange an

* Graham is a great name-dropper; but aren't we all?

interview and he promised that he would mention it to the Rev. Dr
Walter Herbert Smythe when he saw him in a few days' time. That
encouraged me, for Smythe was not only Crusade Manager—the man
who set up those explosive Alabama meetings, indeed—but a friend of
Graham's for nearly thirty years and his best man when he married Ruth
McCue Bell, a missionary's daughter, in 1943.

I left Minneapolis on 17 October. By 8 November I was in Del Mar,
California, having trundled my way there via Salt Lake City, San
Francisco and Los Angeles. I wrote to Dr Smythe, explaining my
mission and asking him whether he could arrange an interview with
Billy Graham, apologizing for the fact that I could give no specific date
for my arrival in Atlanta, as I had a good few whistle-stops to make on
the way. On 19 November I telephoned his office from Tulsa, Oklahoma, and was told by his secretary that Billy Graham was making no
appointments until after the New Year, by which time I would be on
the other side of the Atlantic. He was resting, she explained, after many
months of hectic work, which had included crusades in New York and
Los Angeles.

Naturally I was disappointed, but felt, nevertheless, that Dr Walter
Herbert Smythe would be a more than adequate substitute since he had
known him so long and was never very far from his elbow. On 24
November I arrived in Atlanta to find that Dr Smythe was out of town;
and at that point the situation began to come apart at the seams in a
fashion that bordered on the comic.

I was put through on the telephone to the Rev. Gil A. Stricklin,
Billy Graham's Press Officer and a man who had travelled hundreds of
thousands of miles with him. He was sorry, he said, but he did not know
when Dr Smythe would be back in Atlanta again. Would it be possible
for me to reach him by telephone? Unfortunately, no.

Sighing, but blaming nobody because I had been unable to give any
firm date for my arrival, I said: 'May I come and interview you?'

'I'm afraid not.'

'But you're the team's Press Officer.'

'I'm sorry, but I can't answer your questions.'

Now that rang a bell. For a moment I was back in Pasadena, California, listening to Dr Garner Ted Armstrong of Ambassador University, telling me that I would find the answers to all my questions in his
magazine, *The Plain Truth* at a time when he had no more than a bare
outline of my business. I said to Gil Stricklin: 'How do you know that

you can't answer my questions, when you don't know what I'm going to ask you?'

'It makes no difference,' he said. 'I can't answer them.'

I had expected and, indeed, had received no more than reluctant co-operation from a number of other evangelistic organizations on my tour; but I had not anticipated that Billy Graham's light would be thrust so firmly under a bushel. What was behind this modesty? I still do not know.

He agreed, however, to show me over the team headquarters and the following afternoon he was shaking my hand firmly and saying: 'I sure am glad to see you, sir.' We walked briskly round the offices, which were trim and unostentatious except for some rather large photographic colour portraits of the team. I saw Billy Graham's office, decently utilitarian with his name-plate—a rather unnecessary touch, perhaps—on the large, tidy desk. I saw what Stricklin told me was the chapel, though it looked to me more like a board room with a series of dark, wooden tables fitted together and surrounded by solid, black, leather chairs. The tour did not take long and soon I found myself back at the lift. My visit, it seemed, was over, for Gil Stricklin shook my hand again, smiled and said what a pleasure it had been.

He was way ahead of me. My poor mind was chewing still at the problem of the light and the bushel. In an effort to help it, I said: 'Am I right in thinking that nobody in this building can answer my questions?'

'Nobody but Dr Smythe.'

'And he's not here.'

'No.'

'You are the team's Press Officer. You send out information to newspapers and magazines all over the world and run one of the most efficient publicity outfits in the country.'

'That's right.'

'And you can't help me.'

'I passed you on to Dr Smythe.'

'But Dr Smythe isn't . . .' I stopped because we were back at the starting gates again, conversationally and now physically because the lift doors slid open behind me. Gil Stricklin was still smiling as I stepped into it, and so was I. I felt like a man who had gone into a bar and been told that they only had water.

All, however, was not lost. When I reached New York a few days later, there was a message waiting for me to ring Dr Smythe at the Billy Graham offices there. I did as I was bid and talked to Bill Brown, an Associate Crusade Director, whom I had met many weeks earlier and who had helped with me with amiable efficiency. Dr Smythe, he told me, was in town and would be glad to meet me.

I still do not know what had happened in the meantime. The good Dr Smythe, however, I found a genial and fluent talker, though obviously—and perhaps inevitably after all the years they had been together—he regarded Billy Graham as something a little more than man-sized.

'It has been suggested,' I said, 'that Billy Graham's crusades are top-heavy with emotion.'

'No more so than Anglican or Presbyterian services,' he replied, 'and I am a Presbyterian myself. The emotion comes from the crowds. You can't have thousands of people gathered together without it. Why is it, I wonder, that people are quite prepared to let themselves go at a football game, but clamp the lid on their feelings when they're dealing with spiritual matters?'

I suggested that it might be because the result of the football game was less important. To my surprise, he agreed with me. Then he went on to analyse the people who went forward at the crusades to make a decision for Christ.

'Our records show,' he said, 'that between fifty and sixty per cent come to make a first time commitment. The others come for a great variety of reasons—perhaps because they have not been faithful to vows they had made earlier, or because they're conscious of the sin in their lives, or because they've gotten away from God. Some come because they have problems at home, or personal problems and some because someone else comes forward. Others, perhaps, have been "prayed in".'

'How many remain within the Church afterwards?'

'As I travel throughout the world,' he told me, 'I meet people all the time who have remained faithful. When we went to Australia, for instance, in 1959, we visited every capital city and every country town and all the time we were meeting people who had come to us two years earlier and were still with the Church. A bishop in Sydney told me that out of forty clergymen in his diocese, fifteen were converts in the 1959 crusade. Dr Maurice Wood of Oak Hill Theological College in London says that ten per cent of his student body are people who were converted at Billy Graham crusades.'

'Is it not possible,' I asked, 'that some people come forward in the emotion of the moment? Up there on the platform is a handsome man, a fine orchestra. A magnificent choir sings. Could it not be dangerous when the man, the words and the music have faded away? Could someone who came forward in those circumstances not feel lost, cheated even, when the blanket of Billy Graham disappeared?'

'There is that danger,' he said. 'We are aware of it. There are mentally despairing people, coming forward, but they are only a fringe. Here, anyway, Christ can help; and if our counsellors feel that they need medical help, we get them psychiatric care.

'It's interesting that you should mention the choir, the hymn. When we came to London we were accused of using it to arouse emotion. So we dropped it. Then we were accused of arousing emotion by silence!'

'Is there not a danger,' I asked, 'that people will declare for Billy Graham and not for Christ?'

'He is conscious of that problem. We all are. Night after night he says: "You're not coming to me. I'm a sinner, just as you are." If we took him away, however, what would we publicize?'

'What George Wilson told me the Association was selling,' I suggested. 'The greatest product in the world.'

'You can hear that in any church on the corner,' said Dr Smythe. 'Here in Billy Graham is a man who has been called by God to evangelize. Look at it this way: I was converted as a boy of nineteen in 1931. In my early days I heard a preacher from North Carolina, holding tent meetings. He was a great man of God and a great preacher, but there were only between fifty and a hundred people in that tent. Do you know what went through my mind? I thought to myself: "When that fellow takes down his tent and leaves town, the man in the street won't even have known he has been there."

'An evangelist must be publicized and there is a legitimate way to do that. We feel we have the greatest message in the world. This humble man, Billy Graham, feels he must use every means of communication. Many times, mind you, he has insisted that we change the name of the organization, that we keep his picture off the material; but he must recognize, as we recognize, that for some reason we can't understand God has put His hand on Billy Graham for this century. God could do without any of us, but He chose to work through people and through some people in a special way. Billy was called to be an evangelist. I

believe God called some people round him to assist him. Back in the
early days, when there was only a handful of us, Billy would sit down
again and again and discuss with us his vision of what God had in mind
for him.'

What about his high-octane phrases? Billy is a doom or glory boy,
burning words in a continuous act of histrionic arson. It is true that he
has lowered his tone, tamed his gestures somewhat; but the message
remains extreme. Even when he is informing his audience that the end
of the world is nigh—which he does fairly frequently—he cannot leave
bad enough alone. He must go on: 'Everybody knows it. Everybody
feels it. It's in the air!'. When he speaks of America—which, he tells local
audiences, everybody knows is God's greatest, finest gift to the world—
he depicts it as a nation thrashed by the most dangerous clatter of crises
ever known. In the film he laced his commercial with this touch of
the terrors: 'If ever a series of telecasts was needed in America, it is
now!'

Does he really believe his theme or is it merely a legitimate artistic
device, designed to speed the process of saving souls? In an effort to find
the answer, I quoted to Dr Smythe a report of a Graham speech in
Pittsburgh a couple of years earlier. It appeared in the *Daily Mail* and it
certainly was an extravaganza.

'Britain,' he is recorded as having said, 'is on the brink of a parlia-
mentary dictatorship and will probably have a real dictatorship within
five years. If things don't change, America is heading the same way. The
only hope for the United States is for a sweeping spiritual commitment
by the country's citizens. They must have a personal faith in God.'

'What are his reasons for believing that Britain will have a dictatorship within five years?' I asked. 'Why does he think that America is in
the same danger?'

'I think we are heading towards dictatorship in America,' he told me.
'There are good dictators and bad dictators. Conditions are getting so
difficult that it may take dictatorship to control it. Our President has
more powers today than a President ever had.'

Out of deference, perhaps, to my adopted country, he made no
reference to Britain's fate. His answer indicated, however, that he—and
presumably therefore—Billy Graham believe all those wild words. I did
not dare ask which would come first—Fascism or Armageddon; but we
will be in right trouble if it is a photo-finish.

Rash he may be in his prophecies. When it comes to gauging the public mood, however, he is so subtle that he leaves himself open to the charge of kneeling before the altar of expediency. On the Vietnam issue, for instance, he was a hawk back in 1966. In his book, *Evangelist Inc.,** George Target quotes him as saying at the fourteenth annual Presidential prayer breakfast in Washington:

There are those who have tried to reduce Christ to the level of a genial and innocuous appeaser; but Jesus said: 'You are wrong—I have come as a firesetter and a sword-wielder' . . . He had made it clear to them that His coming, far from meaning peace, meant war . . . Those who hate tyranny and aggression will take sides when little nations suffer terror and aggression from those who seek to take their freedom from them . . . To preserve some things, love must destroy others.

In the *New York Times* magazine two years later, Ed Fisk, the Religion Editor, wrote: 'He has taken an ambivalent position on Vietnam; early in the war he called on the country to "get in with all we've got in Vietnam or get out" and now he professes uncertainty about everything except that it is "over-Americanized".' That, I think, sums up fairly accurately the shifting views of the American public on this issue; and Billy is right in there, shifting with them.

In 1953 in his radio sermon of the month on 'Labour, Christ and the Cross', he said of Senator Joseph McCarthy, who was blackmailing so many Americans at the time: 'I thank God for men who in the face of public denouncement and ridicule go loyally on in their work of exposing the pinks, the lavenders and the reds who have sought refuge beneath the wings of the American eagle and from that vantage point try in every subtle, undercover way to bring comfort, aid and help to the greatest enemy we have ever known, Communism.'

I quoted that chunk to Dr Smythe and asked: 'Would he say that today?'

He told me: 'I think he would use a different line today.'

In August 1966, he told an audience in the Astrodome, Houston, Texas: 'You go on campus and you see some guy on every campus and he usually has a beard. I'd like to shave a few of them.'

In his appeal for funds, dated October 1969, he wrote: 'We have just closed the Southern California Crusade . . . In many ways it was the deepest and most penetrating evangelistic crusade we have ever held . . . Most of the people attending were under twenty-five . . . Many of them

* Allen Lane The Penguin Press, 1968.

came with their long beards and girls in their miniskirts and hippie
dress.'

I quoted both those statements to Dr Smythe and, letting the hyper-
bole slide, asked him: 'Why has he changed his mind about beards? Is
he not contradicting himself?'

'I don't think it's a contradiction,' he said. 'I think he is being honest.
This mode of dress has become an accepted mode of dress among
certain elements.'

'Does that not make it a case of expediency?'

'I have never been conscious of Billy being expedient,' he said. 'I have
never known a man who hewed more to the line with a positive
message, rather than shift for reasons of expediency or otherwise.'

Here I could not agree with him; but there were more important
matters to discuss than beards. I said: 'In Mississippi poverty is so wide-
spread that thousands of black children are suffering from malnutrition.
In many cases it is doing permanent damage to their brains. In his
sermon at the Oregon crusade, Billy Graham said: "I've been in places
where really genuine, terrible poverty exists and we should do something about it in this rich country of ours." Why doesn't he do something about it?'

'He made a film with Sargent Shriver when he was head of the
poverty programme,' said Dr Smythe. 'He has toured these areas
with Shriver and has tried to stir the conscience of America on this
point.'

I said to Dr Smythe: 'There are Christian relief organizations
in these areas working to feed these children, to educate them, to
create employment for their parents by building co-operatives. They
need money badly to continue this work, let alone extend it. Billy
Graham could raise a million dollars if he spent one half-hour of his
television time telling the public of the terrible poverty he has seen.
Why doesn't he do it?'

'Anyone who has an axe to grind on some social issue wants him to
do that,' said Dr Smythe. 'But he can't do everything.'

'But he has seen this poverty. He has seen people hungry.'

'He feels these official agencies should handle the problem, the
existing government agencies set up to help.'

I found the three charges against Graham I had discussed with Dr
Smythe—emotion, exaggeration and expediency—particularly intriguing. The emotional approach, obviously, is reasonable, if it gives

lasting satisfaction to those in search of spiritual solace; but what of the others, who get no further than the well-dressed window? Are ten satisfied customers worth one who put his decision on the counter and learned a little later that the suit was skimpy and carried no guarantee?

There are, of course, records of those whose lives were changed. In his book *Those Who Came Forward*, Curtis Mitchell gives the case histories of fifteen people who were still practising Christians years after they had answered Billy Graham's call. He names them and their home towns. At the end of the book are fifty-nine anonymous letters, undated, but testimonies for all that. I found further evidence of those who had found that lasting satisfaction when I contacted Dr Maurice Wood, whom Dr Smythe had quoted to me in New York. He told me that six of his sixty theological students at Oak Hill College, London, had 'made their first committal to Christ at a Billy Graham crusade'.

He added: 'That is a regular occurrence, not just one year; and it is made more impressive by the fact that he has been here only twice—in 1954 and in 1966. It is not as if he came over annually. People say that his work is only a flash in the pan, but I travel a lot, interviewing those who wish to enter the ministry, and regularly I meet people who have been brought to it by Billy Graham. I have been so impressed, indeed, that recently a lecturer and I made a quick check around a number of theological colleges. We found 250 men and women who had been converted through Billy Graham's work and were studying so that they could serve God full-time.'

His statistics certainly were interesting. They were gathered, however, from the cloisters of dedicated Christians and therefore were not truly representative of the public at large. Seeking a wider field—a grass-roots view, perhaps—I spoke to the Rev. Raymond Lee, Vicar of St Mary's Church in Woking, Surrey, a fairly typical English suburban town with a population of just over 70,000.* He took 550 people to the 1966 Graham crusade in Earl's Court Stadium, London, about half of them regular members of his congregation and the remainder attached to it only loosely. From that total, twenty-one went forward to declare for Christ—two men, three women, two boys and fourteen teenage girls. Nine of the twenty-one did not attend church regularly before their declaration and, as I write, three of them are now active members.

* As I am one of them, I defy contradiction of that description!

Of those who remained loyal to the church, he said: 'The two men were of particular interest. One was a stockbroker and the other an estate agent. I would not describe either of them as men who are swayed easily by emotion. I believe that it was solely Billy Graham's preaching which compelled them to think seriously about the main issues facing the Christian faith. I do not attach so much significance to others who are with us still because I feel that they could have been won over by other agencies.

'Many of those who went forward, of course, went no further. The counsellors at the crusade sent me the name and address of a middle-aged woman who had declared and when I called on her she was quite upset because she felt she was wasting my time. She said to me: "My husband told me not to go. He said I could never resist buying from any salesman who called at the door and that I'd buy from Billy Graham, too. I told him not to be silly, but he was right. I don't know what came over me, but I went forward that night."

'When I visited the teenage girls, I found that the vast majority of them had not the foggiest idea why they had answered Billy Graham's call and they were very embarrassed about it.'

There, I felt, was a classic example of emotion without the starch of sense. I said to Raymond Lee: 'Do you think the experience did them any harm?'

'That would depend probably on the depth of their embarrassment,' he replied. 'If it was very deep, if they felt cheated or tricked, a barrier could be raised between them and the Church. On the other hand, their embarrassment could have been due to their age, part of their adolescence, rather than any failure on the part of Billy Graham. If that was the case, I imagine they got over it easily enough and probably laugh now when they look back on the affair.'

Raymond Lee is a man very close to the religious grass-roots, for he is deeply involved in parish work. He still regards himself as a supporter of Billy Graham and therefore his carefully considered reservations in relation to the value of the crusades have added weight. Here, in fact, is someone reporting his own experience rather than criticizing.

Other authorities who have studied the Graham scene, however, are frankly critical. The Scripture Union, a respected Bible Society, issued a report in the autumn of 1968, suggesting strongly that fifteen-year-olds should not be encouraged to go to vast crusade meetings. The authors came to the conclusion that these meetings produced only a small percentage of the total conversions to Christian belief, and went on:

We doubt whether this pattern will be as prominent in the seventies. Our questionnaires and interviews—in common with Press reports—reveal a declining confidence in this method among the Churches and their ministers. Dissatisfaction centres on the inadequate understanding of the inquirer about the nature of the appeal made by the evangelist and the limited counselling given afterwards. This seems particularly true of those responding in their teens.*

Will Billy Graham pay any attention to this warning and all the others which float around his handsome head? I doubt it. Nevertheless it might be a good idea if he were to curb his excitement over the numbers who answer his altar call, to tone down phrases like that which appears in his latest fund-raising letter: 'More people responded to the appeal to receive Christ in the ten days of the Southern Californian Crusade than in any other similar period in our ministry.' It would be more telling, perhaps, if he were to refer to them in his blurbs as inquirers, as he does, indeed, when he is off the stage and away from the limelight.

So much for emotion. How about this question of expediency? It is true that many Americans—some of them in high places—have changed their views radically on Joe McCarthy, Vietnam and even bearded hippies over the past few years. It could be that Billy has a nose that is particularly sensitive to public opinion. On the other hand, maybe he just changes his mind like the rest of us, though some may feel that a man upon whom God has laid His hand, to quote Dr Smythe, might have a greater insight than others and be more ready to plough a lonely furrow in an unpopular field.

It is his attitude to social problems, however, that I found most difficult to understand. He knows that there are children suffering from malnutrition in Mississippi. So do I, because I visited the Delta area, where poverty is particularly acute. He knows that he could raise large sums to help them if he spoke on television just once about their plight and it is difficult for me to understand how a man who has seen these conditions can refrain from doing so. Dr Smythe may talk about too many people with too many axes to grind, but personally I regard that excuse as inadequate.

Could he do more for these people? Would he be feeling the backlash

* *On the Other Side* (Scripture Union).

of his own fame? I found that there were many other clergymen who closed their eyes tightly at the first glimpse of social distress, sometimes for reasons of expediency, sometimes because they simply did not want to know. Their records are wretched compared with that of Graham at Selma and Montgomery, but because they are little men, few people notice them.

9: SOME ARE MORE EQUAL...

BY getting stuck in at Selma, Billy Graham not only set an example to the major Churches but, unwittingly, perhaps, challenged them on their attitude to social problems. Few clerics picked up the glove, however, for when it comes to ducking and weaving expediently in this nettle-strewn jousting arena, most of them make Graham appear like a clumsy apprentice. They will cheer the side of justice and hiss the villain, but when someone offers them a sword, they plunge deep into their clerical collars.

They are never slow to accuse their less orthodox brothers-in-God of exploiting the public by whipping up hysteria, swapping prayer cloths for love offerings and preaching the gospel as if the apostles were a vaudeville act. At another level, however, it could be argued that they, themselves, take money by false pretences on a massive scale.

Verbally they champion Christian morals and ethics. With a few outstanding exceptions, however, they fail to follow up their words with battle in the field. Their defence, of course, is that they are concerned with spiritual truths rather than social evils; but that is an argument which amateurs, like me, find difficult to follow. Racial discrimination has caused a major crisis in American life, not merely because it is immoral in itself, but because it deprives many people of adequate housing, education, work and food. Even if they could find sound reasons for remaining in their spiritual dug-outs while these social scandals explode in the world outside, how can they hide from the ancillary product of such circumstances—crime? Generally—though not always—what the law rules to be a criminal act, the Church regards as a sin. Surely all clergymen should feel it their duty to exorcise, not only with bell, book and candle, but with crusading action, the devil who causes the sin.

Instead they do little more than shout from distant pulpits: 'Devil, go home!' Naturally enough even the moderates among the black population, both secular and religious, feel slightly cynical about this lack of action on what seems to be so clearly a moral issue. Warren Marr II, Assistant Public Relations Officer of the National Association for the Advancement of Colored People, told me in New York: 'The hour when the people of this country are most segregated begins at eleven o'clock on Sunday mornings, when white folk go to white churches and black folk go to black churches.'

Dr Wyatt Tee Walker, Pastor of Canaan Baptist Church, New York and Second Vice-President of the Southern Christian Leadership Conference, which the late Dr Martin Luther King led so magnificently, went a good deal further. He told me: 'About seventy-five per cent of the white church in America has no sensitivity whatever about the nation's social dilemma. Of the remaining twenty-five per cent, all but a few do nothing except pass resolutions.'

I am glad that he mentioned the few. I met some of the men who refuse to take the insipid party line and I found their actions particularly impressive, set as they were against a backcloth of lassitude.

One was the Rev. John Fry of Chicago. Had he been a politician, a lawyer or a member of Mike Quille's Transport and General Workers' Union of America, he probably would be a national figure now, a David who squared up to the Goliaths of Mayor Richard J. Daley's police and showed them how to keep the peace, a task which they have not handled with any great dexterity in recent years.

He is, however, a white Presbyterian minister, plying his trade in and around the ghetto areas, and therefore few outside Chicago have heard of him. Had his battle concerned an esoteric theological point, it might have raised hackles in religious circles. Had he been fighting about the general level of stipends, his fellow-workers might have closed their ranks behind him, screaming bloody murder, and those of other denominations might have come out in sympathy. Instead it had to do with justice for black people, an issue which seldom makes the blood bubble in the veins of white clergy.

The authorities in Chicago may have been alarmed by the stand he took, but it could have come as no surprise to his congregation. Ever since this stocky man, who is only five feet tall, became Pastor of the First Presbyterian Church in the Woodlawn area in 1964, he has made his views very clear. Sunday after Sunday he has taken a newspaper as well as a Bible into the pulpit and related the text of one to the other. When he found what he felt was blatant injustice in his parish, he fought it as part of the job, like marriages and funerals.

The story began back in 1965, when members of the Woodlawn Boys' Club asked him if they could use the gym attached to his church because they had not got one of their own. He agreed and among those who came along were members of the Blackstone Rangers gang. That may sound a little ominous to outsiders with memories of other Chicago gangs; but, as John Fry explained to me, these groups form the only structure in which youngsters can find an outlet for their energies. Much of the area is what he calls 'a real gut slum, as tough as you'll find anywhere in the world'. Recreational facilities barely exist. Education is poor. Work is scarce and hope is dim. Gangs give them a sense of belonging in a situation in which nobody else seems to want them; and, as I walked those decrepit streets, I saw the names painted with aggressive pride on the walls: Rangers . . . Trixie Triggers . . . Disciples . . . Lone Tribe Midjets . . . Skulls.

John Fry accepted the Rangers into his gym without question. Then, according to *Tempo*, a vigorous bi-monthly newspaper published by the National Council of Churches, the police arrested seventy-five Rangers 'for no more apparent reason than that they were on the streets'.

'It was ridiculous,' said John Fry. 'The young people always gather in the church school yards because they've no other place to gather. About twenty were there and were arrested. Then the police started to arrest everyone in sight. Some of the guys were walking past the school yard on their way home from work. One fellow had spent all day at home and was on his way to the store to buy groceries for his mother. She didn't learn what had happened to him until the next day.'

What was behind this sudden swoop? John Fry said: 'The authorities felt there were going to be riots that summer. So they planned to stop them by arresting all the Rangers and keeping them in jail until the autumn. The school yard affair was the first step.'

Normally the plan would have worked. In Chicago, ten per cent of the bail bond must be produced in cash, a rare commodity in that gut slum. John Fry, however, astonished the authorities by scraping up enough of the stuff to bail out the Rangers. It cost him over $1,800, but it was the beginning of a long and worthwhile friendship, for the youngsters were just as amazed as were the police. Nobody had ever helped them in that way before.

It was, of course, only the beginning of the battle. There were more arrests. Somehow John Fry managed to find the money for more bail bonds; and so for months it went on until there was a happening which was extraordinary even by Chicago standards. John Fry arranged a meeting between police and gang leaders, which was akin to inviting the Pope and Bob Jones to meet at a cocktail party.

'The meeting took place right here at this table in this room,' he told me as we sat in the large, cluttered office that has become his campaign headquarters. 'I didn't sit in on it, but I knew from the start that these would be serious, extensive negotiations. There were not only men from the ordinary police force there, but representatives of the U.S. Treasury Department and Mayor Daley's private police force. The Rangers had quite a team against them, but they were wily enough themselves, very intelligent guys, though all of them were drop-outs from school.'

To probably everybody's surprise, the two teams agreed on a number of points, one of which was that there should be an end to unnecessary police harassment of gang members. The most important issue, however, was that of weapons, for in this explosive section of society, most gangs, the Rangers included, were armed. Those who were not, they maintained, were dead.

'The Rangers promised to give up their weapons and the police promised to provide them with protection against other gangs,' said Fry. 'But the boys would not trust the police with their guns. So both sides agreed to lock them in the church for thirty days and review the agreement together at the end of that period.

'They brought along their weapons and they were locked in a church safe. The only people who knew the combination were two elderly ladies on our staff. Even I didn't know it. At the end of the thirty days, however, it was palpably clear that the police had not kept even a syllable of their agreement. Everything they had promised to do, they had not done. The guns sat in the safe for three months. Then the police —at least one of whom had placed the weapons there—raided the church and confiscated them. They had to get one of the ladies over to open it for them, of course.'

Believing their agreement to be in tatters, the Rangers rearmed. Harassment became even more intense. By the end of that summer, about nine hundred of them were in jail on a variety of charges and John Fry was working almost full-time, raising money to get them out. At that stage the battle took a new turn.

The Woodlawn Organization, a body of voluntary social workers with which the church was associated, applied successfully to the Office of Economic Opportunity in Washington for a grant to help them rehabilitate young gangsters in the area. The local authorities, according to John Fry, were not pleased and soon retaliated.

'Investigators from the McClellan Committee, a permanent Government sub-committee, were in town investigating civil disorders,' he told me. 'The police showed them their file on the Blackstone Rangers and the committee men decided that they would investigate them, too.

'The next thing I was hauled before the sub-committee in Washington and found myself facing all sorts of charges, including one that I had passed murder messages for members of the Rangers. I had got together about fifty more or less expert witnesses of unquestioned integrity, but they were never called. None of the charges against me was substantiated, but by that time the damage was done. When television carries that sort of stuff for a week, people assume you are guilty and soon afterwards the Office of Economic Opportunity grant was withdrawn. That left us in very bad financial shape and all our major programmes had to be cut back.'

After the hearing, conditions worsened in Woodlawn. William R. Wineke, a member of John Fry's church, wrote in *Tempo*: 'Police frequently searched the church buildings with warrants and without warrants. Church staff members found themselves subjects of subtle harassment, frequent traffic tickets, "messed up" credit ratings and the like. In late 1968 a fire caused $15,000 damages to church offices. The Bomb and Arson squad of the police department said it had been ignited by blow torches, used by professional arsonists. After it was all over most of the records of the McClellan hearings had disappeared, including the letters from well-wishers and critics from throughout the country.'

When I quoted that report to John Fry, he said: 'Quite true. As a matter of fact they used our McClellan letters and records to start the fire.'

The important feature of the story, however, is not the raw relations between the police on one hand and John Fry and the Rangers on the other. It is his achievements in face of extreme and continuous pressure. Throughout those difficult years he never lost sight of the three positive objectives which he had set himself when first he became involved with the Rangers: to reduce existing very high levels of violence throughout the area; to establish the possibility of new relationships between the Blackstone Rangers and local institutions; and to provide creative options for the Rangers beyond automatic and needless violence.

Early in 1969 at his congregation's annual meeting he was able to report: 'The multi-faceted violence that plagued the area has been reduced to a minimum and by that is meant virtually to zero ... Attacks on private citizens, once a regular feature of the area's life, scarcely ever occur . . . On every occasion that major violence has broken out in Chicago—the riots of July 1968, the looting in the midst of the snow-storms in January 1967, the disorder following the murder of Dr King, April 1968, and the disorder during the Democratic National Convention—the Blackstone Rangers have remained cool and have used their organization to inhibit any other outbreaks of violence in their area.

'Moreover, the Rangers enjoy new relationships with individual Churches, the Chicago Theological Seminary, community organizations, the Black Consortium, Operation Breadbasket, businessmen and the Firman Neighborhood House.

'Finally, the Rangers now have economic, social and political options that did not exist thirty months ago. They are a famous and promising organization. Despite the considerable efforts made to discredit them in the public eye, the Rangers have maintained an impressive record of responsibility that discredits the attempt to discredit them . . . Each of the original objectives has been attained.'

Commenting on the report, William R. Wineke wrote in *Tempo*: 'The result is that the church is moving on to a new style of relationship. It is establishing a Legal Defense Fund which is attempting to raise $320,000 to provide a variety of legal services and community-building services. The church itself hopes to raise $100,000 of the total and contributions should be sent to it at 6400 South Kimbark, Chicago, Illinois, 60637.'

John Fry is proud of the progress that has been made, but sees nothing unusual about the major role he has played. When I mentioned it, he said simply: 'I've been involved with these kids and with their mothers, their fathers, their neighbours. Their brothers and sisters and some of their own children come to the church school.'

Of the changing pattern, he said: 'In the old days, having somewhere to play basket ball was about the biggest ambition the kids had. Now, if you ask them what they want, they say: "What we need is freedom." By that they mean economic freedom—jobs, education, housing. The Rangers—they're known as the Black P. Stone Nation now—are working towards those aims. They are in almost constant negotiation over the possibilities of new business, of bringing out community news-papers, of developing a system of community centres, which, of course, are political action fronts, really.'

He smiled suddenly. Then, casting his mind back to other days, he said: 'You know we never lost one dollar through guys jumping bail!'

One of their present objectives is to provide full-time staff as a support vessel for the Black P. Stone Nation group. I asked him whether Churches were helping in this or any other related field. With neither bitterness nor hesitation, he said: 'No. Most of them are afraid of the potential consequences, afraid of the city authorities. As a matter of fact, we have lost some of our own members because of the events over the past few years.'

'Were any of them replaced by Rangers?' I asked. 'Did any of the youngsters join the Church?'

He looked at me sharply, almost angrily and said: 'None of them have joined, but that's of no importance. That's not why I did what I did. I wasn't recruiting.'

The fact that no other Church has supported John Fry is depressing. Yet the story of his struggle has revealed hope for the future. Other pastors may not have rallied to him, but he found allies among the staff and students of the Chicago Theological Seminary. They have taken over now from John Fry, who is not relaxing, but concentrating on headstart classes, an excluded child programme and civic groups. Like Fry, they are having problems with the authorities, but they are not allowing these unpleasant diversions to interfere greatly with their objectives.

Bob Meyner, a member of the teaching staff, told me: 'Three years ago, when I came here, it was questionable whether white people could ever work in black communities. Black people felt that white workers were trying to manipulate them. The only answer open to us was to go in and seek to become a part of their efforts to get control of their own destiny, instead of going in with our plan, our agenda.

'So we got these three buildings in the North Kenwood area and decided that some students should live down there. Gradually we began to develop a style of responding to what the local people wanted to do, which was an education for us and for them. It began in a small way . . . talking, exchanging ideas, finding office space and so on. The Black P. Stone Nation boys, after their experience with the First Presbyterian Church, decided that the relationship with the seminary would be a good idea and they moved in.'

Craig Rennebohm, one of the students working in the area, said: 'There has been positive progress. The Black P. Stone Nation is no longer a gang, but an organization with written rules. Once they invariably confronted violence with violence. Now they are more likely to say: "Do you fight fire with fire or water?" They have a vision of what they want and they try to take responsible action in every situation, even if it means pulling away from confrontation.

'The important thing is that they are dictating their own needs, drawing up their own priorities. We work with them, particularly in the legal field, both criminal and civil. Once the problems were connected mainly with criminal charges. We had to find bail bond money, lawyers for the defence, even transport to see that their witnesses got to court when their trials came up. Now all of us, the Stones as well as the students, are learning other aspects of the law—about eviction, for instance. The law impinges on the ghetto in a lot of ways that it doesn't on the white community and we're learning from the Stones what we'd never learn from a course in social ethics. Soon we hope to have a couple of field officers to encourage this legal education and broaden it.'

Tim Leifer, another student working in the area, told me: 'The attitude in the area is changing. You hear a kid saying: "There's a Stone." Another kid will say: "No, he's not a Stone any more." He means that he's not a gangster. It's a reference to the rejection of violence. Once any white man who came into the area was robbed automatically. The Stones have stopped that and they are extending their area of influence.'

This progress has been achieved despite considerable police activity in the area. According to *Tempo*, which, perhaps I should stress again, is published by the National Council of Churches, there have been sixteen raids on the buildings since they were taken over by the Chicago Theological Seminary. More than forty-five Stones and one white CTS student have been arrested, but the police were not able to obtain a single conviction.

The white student was Craig Rennebohm, who told me with a grin: 'For nine months I had a charge of running a brothel hanging over my head. The idea behind all this activity, of course, was to discourage us from working in the area or at least to discredit us. In one of the early raids they came in with twenty-five police cars and surrounded the place. They arrested everyone in the house and charged us with having guns. After that they went running up and down the street with guns drawn, saying that they were looking for this Stone who was supposed to have killed someone. The charges were dropped, of course, but mud is inclined to stick. They have other unpleasant techniques, too. They pick up a Stone in his own territory, drive him to another, hostile zone, drop him out of the car and yell: "Black Stone!" That brings the enemy running and he's lucky if he gets away in one piece.'

The police raids on the Seminary houses have not been particularly gentle affairs. Bob Meyner told me: 'They've broken every window, the plumbing, the toilets, the bath tubs. We had to scrounge $3,000 to repair the damage and that wasn't easy. Since then two of the houses have been set on fire and are total losses.'

These heavy-handed raids have been recorded in *Tempo*, which in an attempt to be thoroughly fair reported, too, that there were police officers who tried to help. 'One officer,' it wrote, 'spent hours trying to find the home of a lost boy.' Acts of that nature take some of the rawness out of the air, but in spite of them, these theological students are attending a rough school. They are learning lessons which will last them a lifetime and they are paying for those lessons with a valuable contribution to a community that has been ignored for too long by the establishment. When they are ordained, other communities will benefit from their experience, for they will not be part of the seventy-five per cent that Dr Wyatt Walker says 'has no sensitivity whatsoever about the nation's social dilemma'.

Whether life for Chicago's minority groups is tougher than, say, life in New York's Harlem I do not know, but certainly it compares badly with the national picture. There are over 54,000 families—a total of 375,000 people—listed as below the official poverty level, which means that they are hungry most of the time. The black hungry outnumber the white hungry by five to two. Infant mortality in the ghettos is far higher than the national average and the unemployment figure is two per cent higher than the national average for black workers, which means that it is about ten per cent, compared with four per cent for all workers throughout the country. The gap between black and white wages, too, is higher than the national average and as an immediate consequence the health of black children suffers far more than that of whites. Dr Audrey Forbes, who runs a clinic in Chicago, reported that twenty-four per cent of Headstart children whom she studied suffered from iron deficiency anaemia. Among black and Puerto Rican children in the West Side centres, this figure ranges from forty-one per cent to forty-six per cent. Over sixty per cent of pre-schoolers and eighty-six per cent of students have dental problems; and a random survey revealed that 4,266 families were suffering from malnutrition.

It may be no coincidence, therefore, that one of the few Church organizations taking positive action on behalf of the black population has its headquarters in Chicago, though its influence is felt throughout the country. It is Project Equality and it has a simple creed: the Church dollar cannot be neutral. In other words Churches should buy goods and services only from those who offer equal opportunity in all aspects of employment.

The idea sprang from the National Catholic Conference for Inter-racial Justice which in 1965 launched the programme in two Roman Catholic Archdioceses—St Louis and Detroit. Today it embraces re-ligious institutions and bodies of all faiths—Baha'i, Eastern Orthodox, Jewish, Protestant and Unitarian Universalists; and their combined purchasing power is over $3,000,000,000, or about £850,000,000, a powerful weapon in the eyes of any financier.

Project Equality, however, does not wave it around its ecumenical head like a claymore. It uses a more gentle approach, based on the old-fashioned, but admirable thought that one should love one's fellow man. First its officers approach the local judicatory, a word they have coined to embrace the names given by various religious bodies to their denominational territories—jurisdiction, presbytery, diocese, conven-tion, conference and so on. If the judicatory should agree to participate, it is asked to send out a small commitment form, asking its suppliers to pledge that they will maintain policies that will promote equal employ-ment; that the policies will be communicated throughout the company and to the public—particularly to the minority community; that posi-tive steps will be taken to hire minority group people; that statistics on minority group employment, classifying the jobs, will be provided to the local Project Equality office; and that on request the firm will take part in discussions with Project Equality's employment specialists in an effort to assess and upgrade, where necessary, its fair employment practices.

When the signed commitment is returned, Project Equality sends the supplier a report form, asking for a head count of minority group employees and a breakdown by job classification. It requests him, also, to describe his equal-employment-opportunity programme and to out-line the steps he plans to take to fulfil it in the coming year. When that report has been filed, he becomes eligible to appear in the Project Equality Buyers' Guide, which is published annually and distributed to all churches, synagogues and religious institutions participating in the scheme.

It may be argued, of course—and it is, indeed—that Project Equality is unnecessary because under the Civil Rights Act of 1964, discrimination in employment is illegal; and further that it is duplicating Federal efforts to enforce that legislation. Recent statistics, however, reveal that the vigorous efforts of the Government's Equal Employment Opportunity Commission must be augmented by massive voluntary work, if the law is going to achieve its objects. Before the Commission got to work in 1965, the number of black people unemployed was twice that of the white figure. At the end of the year the ratio had worsened. By March 1967, 7·4 per cent of non-whites were unemployed, compared with 3·1 per cent of whites; and Dr Arthur M. Ross, commissioner of the U.S. Bureau of Labor Statistics has stated that the unemployment rate for Negroes will be four times that of whites by 1975, if non-white workers fail to gain access to skilled and white collar jobs at a much more rapid rate. The Equal Employment Opportunity Commission added weight to his words by reporting that only minimal gains had been made, despite concerted efforts by Federal, State and local agencies. Making the picture even more depressing is the fact that the number of black teenagers unemployed is something in the region of twenty per cent—one in five.

There are concrete examples which bring these figures to life. One large national manufacturing company with headquarters in Detroit, for instance, had 2,000 employees in 1966, most of them in salaried positions. Of these one per cent were drawn from minority groups which represented thirty per cent of the population. Another large company, employing 3,500 in Michigan, had only 123 minority group workers and of these only six held white-collar jobs.

The Churches have the power to change these figures because they rank second to the Federal Government in the total amount they spend on goods and services. Project Equality is trying to encourage them to do so, pointing out that they can scarcely act in a less moral manner than the State. The results, however, have not been as encouraging as they could be.

Admittedly Project Equality has expanded dramatically from its modest start in St Louis and Detroit in 1965. Today it has eighteen local offices, many with paid directors, in addition to its Chicago headquarters. Over 15,000 business firms, ranging from two-man shops to corporations hiring over 100,000, have pledged their support and the organization can point to some impressive successes. In one major mid-

West city it opened up 550 new jobs for minority groups and in another city employers who had agreed to participate hired 1,373 minority group members out of 1,628 new employees in one year.

Yet in a national context and set against the appalling black-white unemployment ratio, those successes are minor indeed; and unfortunately progress is being impeded not only by employers, but by the Churches themselves. The Rev. Herbert H. Mardis, the Project's Eastern Regional Field Director, told me in his New York Office: 'We find we are dealing with racism in the church. The Denominational Board gives us some annual findings, but that does not mean that all the churches have made commitments. The majority, in fact, do not return the form we send them. When we approach them again, they usually say something like: "We're one hundred per cent behind you, of course, but we don't want to get involved with business. We are concerned primarily, after all, with spiritual matters."

'Where Churches have co-operated, however, we have been able to make significant progress. If companies who pledge their support do not live up to their commitment, we write to them and tell them that they are no longer eligible for our buyers' guide. Here in New York that has brought some remarkable results, though inevitably, perhaps, with a programme of this nature, progress is slow because it takes time for people to hear about it. Nevertheless in the past fifteen months we have opened six new offices here on the East Coast.'

In Chicago, the Rev. Clyde Miller, National Director of Project Equality, confirmed what Herbert Mardis had to say about the reluctant Churches. In addition to pulling the old line about being concerned with spiritual matters only, they suggest heavily that the organization is trying to bring pressure by boycott on the business community. He told me: 'They say that the Church's role should be one of moral persuasion and that a boycott represents coercion; but we are not boycotting anyone. We are merely asking them to make a commitment. The "spiritual matters only" argument is not very convincing, either, because all Churches deal with firms and therefore deal with material matters. When they say "I'm one hundred per cent behind you, but..." they mean that they do not want to participate in the fight. We meet this opposition from people in the hierarchy and in high office—positive opposition. These are people who simply are not interested in the poor.

'There are times when we seem to be making progress, but I feel we have not done enough for two reasons. In the first place, we still have not been able to sell the idea to the religious organizations across the country. In California, for instance, we still get a very harsh reaction to the programme. Secondly, I don't think we've done enough with regard to the unemployment rate. For the minority communities it is still more than double that of the national average and as a result we have had depression level for some time in the ghettos.'

'What about the trade unions?' I said. 'Surely they are backing you.'

'In Chicago,' he said, 'most unions exclude blacks. The more enlightened ones may have about five per cent of them in their ranks. In the vast majority it would be ·001.'

It was incongruous to hear talk of depression levels in the days of moon-shots. I had heard, however, this theme expressed more than once. Billy Graham had said: 'I've been in places where really genuine, terrible poverty exists and we should do something about it in this rich country of ours.'

Wyatt Walker of the Southern Christian Leadership Council had told me: 'In the urban ghettos there are kids going to school without breakfast. They get no lunch. They exist on potato chips and a coke. That's real hunger.'

Warren Marr of the National Association for the Advancement of Colored People had said: 'Several official committees have visited Mississippi to investigate rumours of starvation. They have confirmed them. There are hundreds of thousands of black people there, suffering from malnutrition or on the verge of malnutrition.'

I had seen what a comparative handful of courageous Churchmen were doing about the depression level in the urban ghettos of the North. Having listened to Warren Marr, I decided that I would travel South to see whether their counterparts there were getting any more support from those who preached morals and ethics every Sunday.

10: GIVE US THIS DAY...

JUST about the time when Warren Marr was telling me how hundreds of thousands of black people were suffering from malnutrition in Mississippi, 2,600 white people were sitting down in Jackson, the State capital, to eat a $100-a-plate dinner in honour of Vice-President Spiro T. Agnew. When I arrived in the deep South, I soon learned that such stories of rags and riches are commonplace.

In Greenville, Mississippi, for instance, I was handed a Chamber of Commerce pamphlet which welcomed me to the city and, under the heading 'Kaleidoscope of Interests', it stated:

We are steadily adding to an already substantial payroll, but we remain essentially a farm market-river port on the banks of the mighty Mississippi and in the center of an incredibly fertile bottom-land . . .

Cotton, soy beans and pasture grasses grow thick and fast. Because we draw shoppers from a prosperous farming section, we have uncommonly smart shops . . . as important to us and probably more important to a visitor is the waterfront as a playground. We have a yacht club to service visiting boats . . . We boat, water-ski and fish by the hundreds in our lake and we invite you to enjoy it, too.

I could not accept the invitation because, among other engagements, I had an appointment with the Rev. Rims Barber, a Methodist Minister from Chicago, working with the Delta Ministry, an organization supported by the National Council of Churches of America and the World Council of Churches. An hour after I had read about the beautiful shops, the lush land, the yacht club, the fishing, the water-skiing, he was telling me: 'Two-thirds of the black kids in this Delta area suffer from malnutritional anaemia. If they should be under four or five years old, it can retard the growth of their brain cells. Generally the damage is not serious enough to cause them to be classified as retarded, but it can slow them down sufficiently to ensure that they won't get a job later. It lowers their resistance to pneumonia and tuberculosis, which means that the incidence of pulmonary diseases is high. A dollar a day can keep a person healthy here, but these people haven't got that sort of money.'

I had gone to Greenville to meet those who ran the Delta Ministry, for here is a fine monument to the action taken by the National Council of Churches. In 1964 the Council sent a handful of young preachers to the area to found a permanent mission. In *The Nation* magazine three years later, Victor Ullman, Assistant to the President of the University of Toledo, wrote that their programme was 'to teach words and numbers to illiterate adults and plantation children; to teach new skills to Negroes who had known only the use of the chopping ax and hoe; and to teach the meanings of citizenship to the largest group of native-born Americans ever denied the rights of citizenship'.

Originally the cause was supported by the National Council alone. Now well over half the budget of the Delta Ministry—described, incidentally, by John Bell Williams, Governor of Mississippi, as a group of 'pinks, punks and fellow-travellers'—comes from the World Council of Churches. Contributions have been received not only from the more prosperous nations, but from the emerging African Republics and from India, countries which remember, perhaps, how much their own missionaries welcomed aid from abroad.

This support, together with federal aid and a strong sense of purpose, has enabled the Ministry to broaden its base. Today it is fighting to make Mississippi a place fit for black Mississippians to live in, an object which it regards not only as elementary justice, but a means of easing pressures on the beleaguered ghettos of the North. If black people have an incentive to stay in the South, migration will slacken.

Significantly the Delta Ministry is not pursuing its aims with the aid of hand-outs alone, the charity of soup kitchens. It has positive programmes in the fields of hunger, education, housing, jobs and voting rights. It is helping black citizens to help themselves, to become involved in the community, to shape their own future; and here the Ministry itself has set an example. When it began, eighty per cent of the staff were white and from out of State. Now eighty per cent are black and from Mississippi.

The problems they face have grown substantially over the years and Warren Marr gave me one simple reason why they have grown. He said: 'The plantations, which have been the main source of employment for so long, are being mechanized. Black people are being thrown out of work and generally out of the shacks where they lived. In most cases they are untrained for any other job.'

Rims Barber translated that into terms of money, or lack of it. He said: 'There are 1,200,000 people in Mississippi and 900,000 of them are black. Of those, 500,000 fall below the poverty line set by the Federal Government. At a conservative estimate, more than 90 per cent of those in the Delta area are in that category.'

Mrs Thelma Barnes, Administrative Assistant to the Ministry, told me: 'In the rural areas you will see little ones with their bellies swollen by malnutrition. Often their parents can't send them to school because they've no food and no clothes.'

These statements have been confirmed by an independent and expert witness, Dr H. Jack Geiger, Director of the Tufts University Delta Health Centre in Bolivar County, which is in the Ministry's area. He told the U.S. Senate on 4 August 1969 that infant mortality in the county, often caused by a mother's malnutrition before the birth, was seventy per thousand live births, compared to the national average of 20·6. His examination of 344 black children showed that their development deteriorated seriously in the first three years of life, the period so critical to intellectual development. The medium family income of the 14,000 black families in Bolivar County was $900 a year. Studies showed that a family of four needed at least $1,200 for a minimum balanced diet.

He continued: 'Ninety per cent of the black homes, particularly in the rural and plantation areas, are unbelievably dilapidated; many are unfit for human habitation. More than ten per cent of the black children of school age at any given time are not in school usually because of lack of shoes and clothing . . . Some people try to survive on pecan nuts.'

The men and women of the Delta Ministry are fighting the problems of immediate hunger partly by distributing tons of food, partly by creating opportunities for work and partly by pressing the authorities to amend their food stamp scheme. Theoretically the scheme is sound enough. Those in need buy stamps and exchange them in stores for food worth several times the original investment. The problems arise when a family has little or nothing to invest and in the Delta that is often the case.

Mrs Barnes, who serves on a committee of the White House Conference on Food, Nutrition and Health, told me: 'In the Delta, families with incomes ranging from zero to 29·99 dollars a month were being charged twelve dollars a month for their stamps. We got the scale changed to fifty cents per person in the family up to six dollars. It still wasn't good enough, of course. A family with fifty-five dollars a month has only forty-three left when it buys its stamps. Rent is usually about thirty dollars and then there are gas bills, light bills and clothes to buy. Now we're fighting for free food stamps for those in dire need and a lower charge for others.'

Again on the food front, Delta Ministry officials found that many children were being denied their rights. The U.S. Department of

Agriculture introduced a policy that all school districts must sign papers that they will give free or reduced price lunches to children in need. Rims Barber told me: 'Many schools signed, but served no lunches. They didn't tell the children or the parents that they were eligible for them and they were able to get away with it because many of the parents were illiterate or semi-literate. So we told them about it. We involved them, got them to sign up for lunches and then the principal of the school just had to come up with something. The 149 districts in our area contain about 575,000 school kids. We estimate that they are serving about 150,000 lunches now, which is not enough; but before we got to work they were giving out no more than 50,000. We're still pressing them, of course, because our attitude is that everything a youngster touches when he goes to school should be free. If he gets a book, it should be free. If he gets a lunch, it should be free. Whatever he needs as a student is his right.'

Barber is in charge of the Ministry's educational programme, a tough assignment for many reasons. In the first place, education is not compulsory in Mississippi. Secondly he is in the middle of the battle over desegregation of schools. Affluent whites are demanding 'freedom of choice' and are hoping to achieve it by setting up private schools, even though the Supreme Court has ruled such tactics unconstitutional, where they perpetuate the dual school system. The parents, however, are being backed by Governor Wallace, who has advised them to stage 'sit-ins' until they get their choice. The Delta Ministry is fighting hard on many fronts here, peppering Washington with progress reports, supporting other active groups in the area, organizing parents and informing them of their rights. There have been legal actions. There have been boycotts. There have been victories, though always they have been hard-won.

Thirdly, Barber is concerned by the fact that many school boards are still controlled by owners and operators of large plantations. In a report to his Ministry, he wrote: 'It is alleged that a number of the members of these school boards are now or have been members of the Ku Klux Klan or the Citizens' Council. Thus the schools have remained in the control of those that view the Negro only as a necessary evil to be endured as cheap labor for their economic interests.'

A major cause of concern is the manner in which federal funds are being used by the Mississippi school authorities. The central Government gives $35,000,000 to the State for educational purposes, but Jake

Ayers, who became a Delta Ministry worker after he had been sacked from his previous job for his civil rights activities, told me: 'We investigated how those funds were being spent and we found that most of them were going into schools for the affluent. Black people and poor whites were not getting their rights because they didn't know what their rights were.'

Delta Ministry officials testified on their findings before a Senate committee and there was a Federal probe into the way the funds were being used. According to a Ministry bulletin, Mississippi State officials admitted that they had 'run a loose programme' and had not been concerned with following Federal guidelines. The Department of Health, Education and Welfare told them that they were required to follow those guidelines, but a further probe by the Ministry a month later revealed that there had been no substantial change in State policy.

Commenting on the situation, Rims Barber told me: 'The best people to break an authoritarian pattern are those who are being oppressed by it. We are organizing the community and the students and there is a growing sense of awareness, unity and identity. We're trying to centralize policy among the parents. We want them to know that the school is the servant, not the boss. We're getting them to take an interest in education, to understand what is going on so that they can begin to control their school system. We're arming them with facts, giving them ideas on how to operate, but it's not easy because not only are they poorly educated, but they have a psychological hang-up.

'The problem here, of course, is ninety per cent homegrown. The black school principals graduated from poor-ass black schools and went on to poor-ass black colleges, run by white State officials. They were taught just as much as those officials wanted them to know in what were no more than educational plantations run by white overlords for black underlords.'

The fruits of education, of course, will not be picked for a while. Of more immediate impact is the work the Delta Ministry is doing in the field of housing and jobs. Here it has managed to blend the two so that one helps the other to grow in a unique co-operative colony which they have named Freedom City.

It is a dream which began as a nightmare, when they tried to help more than a hundred families who had been thrown off the plantations. These people had nothing. First they occupied an unused Air Force base at Greenville until the military put them out. Then they built and lived

in a tent city until flooding put them out. They found temporary headquarters in Mount Beulah near Jackson and in 1966 they reached their
first stable base when the Delta Ministry managed to acquire 415 acres of
land.

On that land the displaced families lived in a barn and went hungry
because the Ministry could not afford food. Once a month some Northern churches sent food and they had meat bones for soup about as often.
The money they could raise or earn went into a milk fund for the
children. Though food was scarce, education was never ignored. There
and up and down the Delta, volunteers began to teach both children
and adults, often in abandoned shacks, sheds and garages, for at least
two hours from Monday through Friday.

That, however, was in 1966. Now the Delta Opportunities Corporation, founded by the Ministry, has got thirteen projects operating in
nine counties. They have educational and vocational training, building
activity, tuition support, day care and supportive services for displaced
farm workers. I visited one section of Freedom City—Freedom
Village outside Greenville—and saw eighty acres set aside for fifty
homes. Some had been built already and seven families had moved in.
The foundations of seven more were being laid and ready to serve them
were a health clinic and a community building where adult education
and vocational training classes were under way. There are plans for a
school and a shopping centre that will include a department store, a
restaurant, a beauty shop, a barber's shop, a supermarket and various
public service buildings. It is hoped to secure soon one or two small
industries, and to build a nursery, a pre-school unit and a home for
elderly people. A centre for nutrition classes is there already and will be
opened as soon as there is enough money to buy kitchen equipment.
Not only will it teach wives and daughters to get the best value from
the food they cook, but will provide all students at all classes with hot
meals at low cost.

Perhaps the most important aspect of the programme, however, was
the fact that the people themselves had built those houses and were
building more. Mrs Barnes, who showed me the development, said:
'They are owned co-operatively. Each family puts in so many hours on
other houses, when they have completed their own. That means they
are left to pay just for the cost of the building materials. When they
were put off the plantations, they were illiterate or semi-literate. Now
they have not only a basic education, but have learned brick-laying,

carpentry, plumbing and electrical work. The people who have moved in don't go to classes now because they've completed their courses and are working. We have a job placement programme and they're earning from $1·60 to $4 an hour, compared with plantation wages of $3 a day. They still work here at the week-ends, of course, helping to build other homes and in that way helping to pay for their own—putting in what we call "equity sweat".'

The smallest of the houses have two bedrooms; the largest, four. All have baths with hot and cold running water, and either central heating or dual wall heaters, depending on the size of the house. Indeed they are fine homes by any standards and dream homes compared with what their occupants knew and what so many still know.

On the way to Freedom Village I had driven past some of the dwellings that Dr Geiger of Tufts University had described as 'unfit for human habitation'. I had seen shacks with wilting walls and roofs, windows covered inadequately, but not inappropriately, with sackcloth, timbers cracked and warped. The only running water those hovels had ever known had come through the ceilings when it rained.

I received some further instruction on what those homes have meant to people a little later, when I read *This Land Is Our Land*, a booklet produced by the Delta Ministry. It told me what life was like before Freedom City.

There was the story of Mrs Willie Jane Eaton and her children, who were forced to leave the plantation where she had worked for twenty-two years because she had the bad sense to become immobilized by pregnancy. There was Mrs Savannah Williams, who had lived on a plantation all her life and was now able to send her children to school for the first time. There was Mr Clay Williams, who had been put off the plantation with his wife and four children and jailed by the owner when he went back for his belongings. There was Mr Arcola Butler, now learning to read and write after thirty-five years on one plantation. There was the woman who said: 'I came here because I was poor and I didn't have nothing. I've ten children and I couldn't make enough to get shoes for 'em to go to school'; and the father who said: 'You know we ain't dumb, even if we are poor.'

Freedom City began as a bootstring operation. Now it is receiving grants from the Federal Government and other sources, including the Ford Foundation, for its educational and housing programmes. Nevertheless, it wavers constantly on the edge of economic crisis, for on the land alone there is an annual loan repayment of 14,000 dollars a year, plus six per cent interest. In addition there are taxes, which increase every time a house is built.

Its psychological impact, however, cannot be measured in dollars. These Mississippians, who for generations have been taught that they owe their continued existence to the white master, know now that they can build and control their own lives. When I was there, over sixty of them had enrolled in the basic adult education and vocational training programme at Freedom Village alone. The Delta Opportunities Corporation was pressing home the self-help message by creating more co-operatives in which workers not only had an outlet for their newly developed skills, but a share in the profits, too.

The Mount Bayou Development Corporation, another Delta Ministry off-spin, has purchased land, begun an industrial park and started a brick factory which sells not only to commercial interests, but provides materials for the housing projects. Freedomcraft Wood Co-operative, which recently acquired ten heavy duty machines, produces toys and furniture. Freedom Farm Co-operative in Sunflower County has forty acres for vegetable farming and a further four for a housing and community centre project. Freedomcraft Candies, the latest co-operative, grew out of a heave-ho between Ministry officials and the authorities in the town of Edwards, who refused to do anything about a list of grievances presented on behalf of the black citizens, who made up seventy-five per cent of the population. Major complaints concerned lack of jobs and living wages. When nothing was done, the black families boycotted local businessmen and began working for themselves. Now they are producing and distributing on a nation-wide basis thoroughly Southern candies—Freedom Brittle and Southern Pralines. With a touch of mild irony, the factory workers line the containers with cotton straight from the fields.

Other co-ops produce leather goods—carrier bags, suede handbags, belts and so on. A contract has been signed with the Star National Manufacturing Company of Memphis, Tennessee, which produces floor waxes, window cleaning material and soap. DOC workers will bottle the products. DOC salesmen will distribute them; and the whole operation is quite a breakthrough because never before has the company allowed anyone to package its goods in small containers and sell them straight to the customer.

These developments create not only jobs, but a self-confidence that

has never before existed; and one of them—the Ceramics Co-operative
—has revealed a deep vein of talent that has never been mined. It began
in the summer of 1969 with five women apprentices who were taught
to produce both moulded and hand-made items. When I visited it a
few months later, it was selling to the commercial market which, in
view of the background to the enterprise and the atmosphere in
Greenville, was a remarkable achievement. The products had such a
graceful beauty that they had been exhibited in the Office of Economic
Opportunity in Washington and by the National Council of Churches
in New York. Even more impressive, perhaps, was the fact that they
were on display in Stein Mart, a large Greenville store, where they were
competing with products from much more sophisticated outfits. The
Rev. Henry L. Parker, the Ministry's Director of Interpretation, who
took me there, said: 'They plan to advertise our ceramics heavily. That
a white firm would buy from a black set-up like ours would have been
unthinkable in Mississippi five years ago.'

The women whose work was in that window had been hoeing and
picking their lives away until the plantation sacked them and the Delta
Ministry took them on and released their artistry. Self-help, self-
determination meant nothing to them; and, as Henry Parker said, there
are many more with talents which have yet to be tapped.

Another task at which the Delta Ministry has been hacking away
since its earliest days has been political education and now the results
are being felt throughout the State. In charge of this division is Joe
Harris, a twenty-four-year-old civil rights veteran who was fighting
for universal franchise before he was old enough to vote. That was in
1964, when the infamous literacy test was still in existence. Before a
citizen was put on the electoral register, he had to answer correctly
twenty-one questions, one of which concerned the interpretation of a
section of the Constitution. Writing in *The Nation*, Victor Ullman
described that question as one which no professor at 'Ole Miss' University could answer; and inevitably the examining circuit clerks failed
black people. The Voting Act of 1965 reduced the number of questions
to six and at last Negroes had a political potential.

Teaching them how to use that potential is Joe Harris's job. A slim,
cheerful young man with energy to spare, he told me: 'We're not concerned merely with getting people a vote. We must teach them what
the responsibilities of the candidates are, how to mark the ballot and
how elections should be conducted. In 1967 we put up the first black

candidate and in the municipal elections of 1969 we got eighty-one elected to public office. Now Mississippi is the State with the second highest number of black officials, which is quite something, considering the amount of time we've had.'

In 1966 only five per cent of black Mississippians were registered to vote. When I spoke to Joe Harris three years later there were sixty per cent and he was chasing up the remaining forty. 'Most of them work and live on plantations,' he said, 'and they're afraid for their jobs. We went on to the plantations in Sunflower County, campaigning, but the owners threw us off when they saw what we were doing.'

That was a minor inconvenience compared with other problems posed by powerful white supremists who do everything possible to impede black progress, particularly in the political arena. In the 1967 elections in Sunflower City the white election board agreed that Joe Harris could be present to help any black voters who were not sure how to mark their ballots. On election eve the agreement was rescinded and a white official, John S. Parker, was appointed to the task. He was a brother of a candidate, Alderman Joel T. Parker. After a later election, the Supreme Court was asked to rule on two cases—one involving the Governor, John Bell Williams—concerning voting rights. It found that Mississippi had passed laws that violated the rights of black voters and demanded that these laws should be submitted for individual review. The laws involved regulations for candidates qualifying for office, the holding of elections at large rather than by district, and the exclusion of independents from participating in primaries. The Court refused to order new elections, but its order will have an impact on future contests. A further example of obstacle-race electioneering occurred shortly before I arrived in Greenville. An election was held in Canton, despite the fact that the Supreme Court was considering a suit against the city for changing election practices. Four black candidates lost in a tough fight, but it was expected that the Court would order a new election.

Obstruction, naturally, is not confined to the political arena. Barriers are raised against most of the Delta Ministry's wide range of activities and sometimes opposition is violent, though Delta Ministry workers accept it all as an inevitable part of the job in their part of the country. It is true that they are seeking a revolution, but when I talked with Henry Parker, he made it quite clear that it was a radical change in the hearts of men he wanted, not violent upheaval at gunpoint. So there is no retaliation in kind.

A heavy-lidded man with a deep plush sense of humour, he has had a varied career in the Church. When I asked him about his background, he said: 'Well, first I was kicked out of South Carolina for trying to hold integrated services. Then I was in Michigan, where I was able to hold them. After that I worked in middle-class parishes with middle-class people who didn't want to get involved in the struggle. They were satisfied that the little they did was a lot; so I moved on to spend a year with a self-help project in Arkansas before coming here.'

'Why did you come to the Delta?'

After a moment's thought he grinned and said: 'I was invited in the first place, but I guess the real challenge was not knowing why I'd been invited and not knowing why I'd accepted. The mortality rate in this kind of ministry is about two years, but I've lasted a little longer than that.'

'What do you regard as your main job?'

'My job,' he said, 'is to bring about a whole society and we're working here in the most difficult field in the United States. We're not so much involved in hosings and beatings now as we are in housing projects, educational projects and long-term accomplishments. It takes time to see things in their proper perspective.

'Getting economic acceptance is a major problem. Here there is a mentality that believes it is bad to buy black goods. Because of history, however, it is absolutely essential for the black man to realize he's somebody because for a long time it has been pushed down his throat that he's nobody. Anyone with any real honest sense of conviction must try to move this situation into the right orbit and that's why I believe the Delta Ministry staff are God's divine agitators. What they're doing will become a motivating force which will move people to it, people who will do what is right.

'It's important, too, that it's all happening in Mississippi, though an outside force, the Delta Ministry, had to be the leverage of change. Mississippians, both black and white, were so ingrained with history that they would have found it well-nigh impossible to make that change. In certain areas in the South and even in the North, remember, a black man had to step off the pavement to let a white man pass. Laws don't change people's hearts. Words do . . . phrases like "black is beautiful", for instance. Those three words changed the whole mode of mind in black America. There was a time when we were all brain-washed to believe that white was superior; but not any more.'

'Are the local white Churches a help, a hindrance or neutral here?'

He shrugged, not so much in resignation, but as if they played little part in his plans. 'I opened a church once that was dedicated by the Archbishop of Canterbury,' he said. 'That wasn't in Mississippi, of course. Here I've been turned away from the biggest Baptist Church in Greenville.'

'You said that you were not so involved now with hosings and beatings. Does that mean there aren't so many?'

'No, I didn't mean that,' he said. 'I meant that we've got our priorities right. There are hosings and beatings and killings. We don't know how many black folk are dead in the South because sometimes they just disappear. Maybe they're in the Mississippi. Maybe they've taken a train North. We won't know until the Resurrection. Meanwhile we're keeping our sights on our targets—housing projects, educational projects, long-term accomplishments.'

'Are the police responsible for those hosings and beatings?'

'Not necessarily. It all goes back to the old thing that the white man thinks he has the freedom to treat a black man any way he pleases.'

I understood what he meant later, when I was handed a pamphlet that had been issued a couple of months earlier. Under the heading 'Emancipation Proclamation of the White Race', I read:

Be it known that the Republic of the United States of America is in a state of decay because of the rapid growth of Communism within the borders of Our Country which was nourished and promoted by President Franklin D. Roosevelt's 'New Deal'; President John Kennedy's 'New Frontier' and President Lyndon Johnson's 'Great Society'. From the aforementioned Presidential 'Communist Doctrine' was born the Infamous Communist Supreme Civil Rights for Negroes in 1954 as the Spearhead of Communism. The Tool of Communism was Earl Warren and his Unamerican Controlled U.S. Supreme Court with the help of the Unjust Justice Department controlled by the Kennedy Klan and the Infamous Johnson-Humphrey Freedom Destroyers . . .

After a few routine racist phrases about Northern Carpetbaggers and lowly citizens of England buying Black Savage Slaves it went on:

Further, the Negro Spearhead of Communism has been under the clever leadership of the National Association for the Advancement of the Communist Party and it's various cancerous arms and allies, including the Tax Free Financial Business, Political and Racist Roman Catholic Empire which is now rehearsing the 'Martin Luther Reformation Period' and the 'Spanish Inquisition Infamy'. Further, another ally is the Zionist Jews; 'Sons of Israel', whose banner is Marxism and Stalinism—Creators of Communism. Other allies are the Union Labor Racketeer Leaders, self declared Communists, Con Game Religious leaders, Power, Glory and Money seeking 'Price Tag Politicians' and Tax Evasion Foundations such as the Kennedy Klan, Ford and Rockefeller Foundations . . .

There followed several lines about the 'most Lawless, the most Immoral, the most Dishonest, the most Destructive, the most Vicious, the most Prejudiced and the most Ungrateful' black population before it went on:

Know All Men Because of the Aforementioned Truths—Proof and Facts the most Courageous and Patriotic Organisations in Our Country have voted, and have had their leaders meet in Secret Assembly to make a decision vital to the life and welfare of this country as well as the White Descendant of the White Patriots who worked, suffered and gave their Blood to Create the Great Republic of the United States. The Patriotic Organisations referred to above are seven (7) well trained, well organised, well tested, well prepared and extremely courageous orders of the Knights of the Ku Klux Klan who for years have been forced to work in 'Secret Underground' because of Tyrannical Communist interference.

Be it further known that on January 19th, 1970 the Birthday of Freedom, which includes, Freedom of Choice, Freedom from Black (Negro) Anarchy, Freedom from the 'Black Plague' and Reign of Terror, Freedom from American Communism and Russian Communist Workers, Freedom from Fear, Freedom from Injustice, Freedom from Federal Tyranny, Freedom of Private Business and Property Ownership and all other Freedoms guaranteed by the Constitution of the United States which has been desecrated by the Kennedy, Johnson and Earl Warren vermin.

Published in the name of the Judge of Judges, the Purety of the White Race, Freedom, Justice, States Rights, Free Enterprise, Capitalism, Truth, Loyalty, Patriotism, Law Enforcement and the Re-Birth of Our Nation, Pride and Glory of the American Flag and Our Loved and Adored Confederate Battle Flag which is our Freedom Banner . . . Published by—Knights of White Camellia, Ku Klux Klan and Affiliated Klan Groups.

Note: *Lawmen*: The 'Reign of Terror' has made this a country of Black Savage and Commy Control—Choose your side as this dam war against the White Race must end—Soon. *Patriotic White Men With Pride, Courage* and *Honor*:– Now is the time to be prepared. ORGANISE immediately neighborhood vigilante groups—Eternal Vigilance is the price of Freedom—&—Family Protection. WIN WITH WHITEY.

I grant that the tone is reminiscent of gang proclamations—or Gang Proclamations—drawn up by rather unpleasant small boys in a woodshed and that occasionally the spelling, punctuation and the spattering of capital letters suggest a similar source. Nevertheless, there is a document which cannot be taken lightly by anyone and particularly by the Delta Ministry staff. Rims Barber had mentioned the Klan to me. So had Mrs Thelma Barnes, who had said: 'It has been becoming more active since the question of desegregation has been raised. A Greenville school, which had been all white, had a bomb thrown at it when it admitted some black students.' Even Dr Walter Smythe, Billy Graham's Crusade Manager, who scarcely could be called a pink, a punk or a fellow-traveller, had told me: 'The Klan is making a comeback. It's a backlash to black militancy.' Credence was added to these observations when Joseph Williams, a former candidate for Supervisor in Yazoo County, found his home burned down following a black boycott.

Hostility from Ku Klux Klan elements is to be expected by bodies such as the Delta Ministry. Opposition from white Churchmen is less easy for an outsider to understand. I called, therefore, on the Rev. Dr Perry Claxton, the Baptist minister whose church had closed its doors to the Rev. Henry L. Parker; and the interview which followed was remarkable.

As soon as I mentioned all-white congregations, he asked: 'Have you been to South Africa yet? It's more oppressive still there.'

I told him that I had never been to South Africa and, as I was Irish, had never had any influence, imperialistic or otherwise, on its policies. With that we got back to Mississippi, though the conversation began to behave like a fish flapping in the bottom of a boat.

'The nigrahs prefer to have their own church,' he said. 'They'd never be happy in mine. We cut off their attendance because they were forcing the issue. A man comes here to disturb, to cause an incident. If he gets in, then he brings some more with him. Then they have a fellow come down to join the Church. We believe this is coercion by out-of-State people, by paid workers.'

'By whom are they paid?'

'The Delta Ministry is out to coerce, force and push. It won't work. We had five little pups and one was black and we had to take away the black pup. There's something bound up in human nature. We have nigrahs who are afraid of nigrahs because they mistreat them. Human nature is a vicious thing in some ways. No nigrah has ever asked to come to our church services. Only officials have—to try out a case.'

Clinging to the last point in that slippery speech, I asked: 'Is it not a legitimate case?'

'I don't think our people know whether it's legitimate or not,' he said. 'They just think this person is here to come here. Only two cases have come. One was the Rev. Parker with whom we have a very fine relationship. I didn't turn him away, personally. It was a vote of the Church. We operate here what we call a democratic policy. Every policy is voted on by the congregation and the majority voted for segregation. That was when the squeeze was put on. Until 1955 no nigrah had ever been turned away.'

'Did many turn up?'

'We had nigrahs who came to our funerals and weddings. They just didn't appear at worship services, except those who wanted to make a case. Our people didn't believe that was a legitimate purpose—just to break the practice of the Church. The second one who came was a young man from out of State, brought here in a Cadillac automobile with Northern State licence plates. He was on the payroll.'

'Whose payroll?'

'We've no evidence that he was paid, but after that he was a man of affluence and could buy good clothes; but we're not trying to jack up any evidence, not trying to make a case. This is a free country where you can do as you please. That applies to the Church, too.

'I've told my congregation that they've no right to turn anyone away so long as he's here to worship God and keeps the peace and doesn't disturb the worship of others. They don't agree. I'm not going to tell my congregation what to do. I have the right, of course, to give up the ministry, but I haven't come to that conclusion either.'

Changing direction suddenly, he said: 'Have you been long in Mississippi?'

I told him that I had been there for forty-eight hours. With a broad smile of understanding, he said: 'Well . . . maybe you haven't been long enough in the South to understand the minds of the people.'

'It's true that I haven't been here long,' I said, 'but, as I told you, I'm from Ireland. I grew up as a Protestant in the Republic of Ireland, which has a predominantly Roman Catholic population and always I was treated with tolerance and decency. Should one of my Roman Catholic fellow-countrymen from the South go to Northern Ireland, however, he keeps his head down in certain quarters because he may get a bullet between the eyes if he doesn't, as comparatively recent events have shown. That would happen, not because he was black, but because of his religion. I think, perhaps, that I understand the minds here a little better than most Europeans.'

It was quite a long speech, but Dr Claxton listened courteously. I think that he even accepted the point, for he got right back to our original theme. He said: 'In the South here a group of people comes up from slavery. There is that difference between slave and master. We don't argue the point of right and wrong. We know it's wrong. There are, however, social problems. Who do you let in your home? Who do your children associate with? There is the question of morals. One reason, I believe, that white people are appalled by the thought of sudden desegregation is that they would be mixing with undesirables, though I must stress that here I'm interpreting the minds of people, not giving my own opinion.'

'Who is an undesirable?'

'A person whose moral life is not up to the standards and conventions of the community. The people are the judges of what is moral and what is not. I believe their views are justified because we have criminal elements among our youth and the problem is growing. Anyway, the underprivileged, the uneducated man just doesn't have anything in common with the people in my congregation. He would be frozen out, whether they wanted this to happen or not.'

Hoping for a simpler answer to another simple question, I said: 'Can you give me any justification for the conduct of your congregation?'

'There is no justification for it from the point of view of Christian morality,' he said. 'It just doesn't work, desegregation, and it won't work until human nature changes.'

'Isn't it part of the Church's job to change human nature?'

'Yes, sir. You're exactly right, but to that extent we haven't succeeded. Christ had that same problem.'

'But Christ set an example.'

'We've no argument there. It's plain to the minister and it should be plain to the people. They simply believe that mixing won't work.'

'Why do they believe that, when they haven't tried it?'

'They have enough mixing with them in other ways. They meet them in the street. They work with them. They have business transactions with them. We've a closer contact with the nigrah than many people think. They come to our homes and work for us. They nurse our babies. We talk to them like we talk to our very special friends.'

'You allow undesirables to look after your babies?'

'Look . . . we don't have a foot to stand on scientifically,' he sighed, leaving me wondering what science had to do with undesirables and white babies. 'The social structure is wrong. When Paul was converted, they refused to accept him into the Church. Barabbas had to appeal to them to take him into the Church.'

'You have your Barabbases?'

'Yes, we have 'em.'

'They're having less success, perhaps?'

'You can't make these social changes overnight. In the North lots of people feel the way we feel, but they're hypocrites. Here we say where we stand. I believe in time it'll change, though I'm not trying to integrate the minds of people.'

'What is your Church doing to change men?'

'We're preaching the gospel of love, kindness and consideration.'

'And equality?'

'Yes, equality, though it's true that the congregation isn't responding. In the Baptist ministry we're not committed purely to the social gospel. We preach that Christ came to this earth and died for the sins of men and that the Bible is the word of God and that there is a salvation and a hell. The root of all our problems is sin. We don't believe you can save the world by equality. We believe that one should embrace Christ and emulate His works.'

'If Christ came to Greenville tomorrow,' I said, 'what would He think of your congregation which denies a man membership of the Church because he is black?'

'Go back to the old Testament,' he said. 'Noah had three sons and one was black. The Bible says it was because he did something wrong and was made a servant. I believe all men are born equal, but nature doesn't give them equality.'

'That's not really an answer to my question,' I said. 'I asked what Christ would think of your congregation for denying membership of the Church to a man because he is black.'

'It worries a lot of my members,' he said. 'They're wrestling with the problem. One day nigrahs may be received more warmly here than anywhere else in the United States. Why, for instance, are we not having riots and all the problems that are happening in other parts of the United States?'

I thought of Selma, of Montgomery, of a balcony in Memphis where another clergyman had been murdered; but I said nothing because I knew these memories would not change the mind of the man before me. Anyway, he was still talking, telling me: 'We have a maid, a good, Christian, nigrah girl. She wants to come in and watch a certain TV programme. We say: "Come in and sit down." She comes in, but she won't sit down. She uses the back door. We've never told her she couldn't eat at table with us, but she'd be shy about it, feel uncomfortable about it. She'd prefer to stand.'

I made one last attempt to establish contact. I said: 'Isn't it wrong that her mind should be conditioned in this way?'

'It is wrong,' he said, 'but there may be homes where she wouldn't be able to watch that TV programme.'

His mind, too, was conditioned, of course, and would remain that way. So would many others. Yet here and there a few have broken through the walls of what some call prejudice and others call the Southern heritage. There is the Rev. Larry Wood, Associate Minister of the First Presbyterian Church in Greenville, an honest man and often an unhappy man. He was born, raised and educated in Mississippi and he told me: 'I was as prejudiced as the next boy at school and it didn't help when I went to a Church-supported college in South Carolina. Then I moved to a seminary in Atlanta, which may not sound much better, but there I was exposed to professors and students who were struggling with the problem of racial justice. I learned a great deal there.

'Our Church has an open-door policy, which means that black people will not be turned away. The local governing body agreed on that policy in 1961 in face of great opposition from the congregation. It doesn't mean that we've an abundance of black people worshipping there, of course. In fact none of them has ever applied for membership, though I think they would be received, if they did. Yet the local body wouldn't allow a black minister to preach in the church.

'I wonder sometimes what I can do, but I haven't many options. I can leave and be a nine days' wonder, or I can stay and work as part of a sustained effort to bring about the social and theological changes that are necessary. Change is possible. The open-door policy, for instance, was a great victory and it came about through sustained dialogue. Some of my friends believe that the only way to get change is by having continuous crisis, by standing up and demanding change. I feel there is a place for crisis and a place for dialogue, too.

'In one Presbyterian church here the minister resigned when a coloured woman from Chicago was denied membership. What would I have done? I probably wouldn't have resigned, but I respect his right to say: "This is wrong".'

'What justification do they offer for turning away a black person?'

'They say that God didn't intend black birds and blue birds to live in the same nest,' he said. 'They talk about social discrepancies, too, but I think it boils down to the fact that they're not honest with themselves or with their God.

'People ask me what I do most in my ministry. Do you know what I tell them? I say that I cry a lot. It's the shame of it. They have this inborn thing; and if I hadn't left Mississippi, I'd be the same. My own parents have this inborn feeling. My father made sacrifices for me. He's a man who has suffered for his principles. He is the most Christian man I know —except on this question of race. I'm going home for a family reunion this Thanksgiving and I know there'll be tears because of my views.'

Then, chasing away the thought with a story of hope, he told me of a local black community which told the white power structure in a school: 'We want equality for our children—or else!' The fifty whites present agreed to their demands.

'They didn't like the way those black people spoke,' he said, 'but they knew they were right. They met and agreed that no matter what the pressures, they'd get rid of injustice in the school. The leaders were members of my Church. They had a lot to lose. Their brothers in the white community might ostracize them and there would be threats from the Ku Klux Klan; but they did it. Maybe some were afraid of a black boycott, of course. I believe, however, that most acted because they thought the cause was just. I've been here for three years now and I've seen minds opening.'

'What about the young?' I asked. 'Is there hope there?'

'They're from affluent families and their parents can bring great influence on them,' he said. 'In spite of that, I've heard them express themselves on race in language that would shock and anger and frustrate their parents. They haven't faced up to the problem yet, but when they do, I think they'll handle it a heck of a lot better than their elders.

'I think there's going to be a parting of the ways in the white Protestant Church in the next two years with one side sticking to theology and the other going ahead on social matters. It will be a time of brother against brother and it will lead to a lot of tears.'

He has my sympathy because every day and particularly every

Sunday he faces a conflict. He preaches not only in a white church, he told me, but in a black church, too. He baptizes black babies, marries black couples, buries black dead. Yet when Henry Parker asked him to march in memory of Dr Martin Luther King, he had to say: 'I'm in sympathy with you, but if I march down the main street, my usefulness is over.' Then on Race Relations Sunday he preached to his white congregation on the theme: 'Level Ground before the Cross.'

The Delta Ministry fights with different weapons and fights magnificently. Are there no white auxiliaries willing to help them in this hostile territory? Is the Church as a whole doing all it can to solve social problems in the South, in the ghettos, wherever it finds them? Is it practising what it preaches? When I put those questions to Dr Wyatt Tee Walker of the Southern Christian Leadership Conference, I got some blunt and depressing answers.

'The white Church in America,' he told me, 'has become decadent and irrelevant because of its avaricious pursuit of wealth. It is closing its eyes to the malnutrition, the hunger, the discrimination. What can it do? It can solve the racial problem by taking the money it has laid up in investments and putting it to work on programmes which impinge directly on the dilemmas of the blacks in the urban ghettos and the South. That money could help black congregations get loans for day centres, recreation facilities, multi-purpose health centres, whatever we need.

'The National Council of Churches is not too bad, but it lacks muscle. The only thing that will make the white Church as a whole change will be the threat of losing their material possessions. White Churchmen are afraid of losing their creature comforts. White preachers live very comfortable lives. Followers of Christ must be willing to be nailed to the cross, to be hungry, to be ostracized, to be unpopular.'

Can money swing the battle and, if so, why do the Churches not dig more deeply into their pockets? I took those questions to the Rev. Charles S. Spivey, Jnr., Executive Director of the National Council of Church's Department of Social Justice, and he agreed that the Church as a whole could give more financial aid.

'We are powerless, however, to change a system which the people don't want to see changed,' he said. 'The minority groups are saying with one voice now that they no longer intend to accept money with all kinds of strings attached to it. That could mean that money would be made available to groups like the Black Economic Development

Conference and few, if any, white Churches would be willing to give
it to an organization like that because they think, rightly or wrongly,
that its purpose is to destroy the American system.

'The whole issue of hunger, around which there should be basic concern in the Churches, has brought only limited response, of course,
because the Protestant ethic supports the premise that he who doesn't
work doesn't eat. They take no interest in the unemployable. They
regard them as excess baggage, instead of accepting the fact that food,
shelter, education and health care are fundamental rights of every
human being, not gifts to be bestowed. You would think, for instance,
that Churches would be most active in helping minority groups to
organize and secure political influence in a community. Large sections
of the New York population, however, are violently opposed to the
black or Puerto Rican communities having any say even in how their
education should be administered. The amount of help they get from
the Churches is minimal. Indeed, the weight of the Churches, Catholic,
Protestant and Jewish, is all in favour of maintaining the system.

'There should be a reallocation of resources, wise use of investment
funds and property for constructive programmes. They should open up
their own structures, change their own employment pattern. We have
a Board of Missions which has no minority members. Most of the
minority people employed by the Church are in jobs related to minority
problems. Why?'

'How wealthy is the Church?' I asked. 'How big is the financial gun
they could fire, if they felt like pulling the trigger?'

'I don't think there is a single record anywhere which will show
accurately the resources of the Churches, either Protestant or Catholic,'
he told me. 'You can get figures on bank balances, income, investments
and the value of real estate, but they're all speculation.'

Certainly all Church authorities hold the cards very close to their
surplices when the subject of money crops up, a fact which embarrasses
some clergymen and angers others. Before his cruel death in the desert,
Dr James A. Pike, a staff member of the Center for the Study of Democratic Institutions in Santa Barbara, California, and a former Episcopal
Bishop, wrote in *Playboy* magazine: 'There is no atomic secret that is
more heavily veiled in mystery than the wealth of American Churches
today.'

In an attempt to lift the veil, he gave his own personal view that the
visible wealth, the real estate of U.S. religious bodies, was worth

$79·5 billion. As a billion in the United States is a thousand million,* that should look something like $79,500,000,000 in figures, or more than £35,000,000,000, though it is quite likely that I may have dropped a nought here or misplaced a comma there, for, as my bank manager keeps insisting, I am no figure juggler. It will be gathered, however, that a heap of money is involved and Bishop Pike broke those astronomical figures down further. The Roman Catholic Church, he estimated, had the lion's—or should I say the lamb's?—share with about $44,500,000,000; the Protestants and others, including the Eastern Orthodox, Buddhists, Moslems and the Mormons, $28,000,000,000; and the Jewish religious bodies a pittance of $7,000,000,000. In addition, he wrote, all Churches had a 'vast amount of invested endowments or businesses operated for income on which they paid no taxes'. Warning that they would have 'economic power beside which all other corporations and even the Government itself will be comparatively impotent' if they continued to accumulate wealth, he commented: 'Many of the Churches are presently in danger of gaining the whole world and losing their own souls.' Their businesses, he said, included a nightclub, banks, a laundry, office buildings, radio and TV stations, more than a hundred steamships of one company and stocks in oil companies.

Making the situation even less tasteful is the fact that some of the larger Churches are inclined to look down their ecclesiastical noses at their smaller, less orthodox brethren in God for earning a commercial penny here and there. They smile with patronizing disapproval, for instance, at the Cathedral of Tomorrow in Akron, Ohio, which is reported to own not only a shopping centre, an electronics company, a plastics and wire plant and an apartment complex, but the Real Form Girdle Company of New York. As the late Bishop Pike pointed out in *Playboy*, however, they, themselves, do more than dabble. According to *Church and State*, the magazine of an organization called Americans United for Separation of Church and State, the Jesuit Order founded the Di Georgio Fruit Company of San Francisco and the Trappist Monks of the Abbey of Gethsemane in Kentucky offer for sale a wide variety of cheeses, hams, Canadian bacon, beef sausage sticks and a delicacy they call 'Gethsemane Fruit Cake'. The Catholic diocese of Austin, Texas, it states, owns the Newton Asphalt Company, which occupies

* In Britain it is a million million and readers, therefore, should watch those carpet-bagging Yankees next time they are cashing travellers' cheques in New York.

about seven acres in an industrial park area. The Christian Brothers, a Catholic Order, produce wine in California. They had tax-exempt status until 1961, when they lost it in a court case initiated by Americans United and agreed to pay $3·4 million in back taxes.

Another group singled out by Americans United is the Southern Baptist Annuity Board which, it claims, owns one of the largest American textile mills—Burlington Mills of North Carolina—and other properties which it has leased back to nationwide concerns such as Bemis Bags, the Borden Company, Dunlop, Firestone, Fruehauf, Huttig, Rath, Reynolds Metals, Mobile, Textron, Westinghouse, Hertz, Newberry, Burroughs, Mack Trucks and others. *Church and State* quoted Dr R. Alton Reed, executive secretary of the Annuity Board, as saying that full property taxes were paid on all holdings and that the Board was the agency which handled the retirement funds of pastors and denominational employees.

Leasing back, incidentally, is a popular ploy which has attracted Government scrutiny. A Church buys a business at a price higher than its market value. It then leases it to a company made up principally of the original owners and charges them an annual rent. The rent is exempt from taxes, seeing as how the money is going to a religious body and that makes the Church happy, the original company gets more than it could have expected elsewhere for its property and that makes it happy. The operation is called wittily a 'bootstrap sale', for the property, in effect, buys itself. The percentage of rent which normally would be handed to the tax man helps to pay the purchase instalments.

Church and State points out, of course, that all this wealth seldom is held by the local Churches, many of which face hard financial struggles. A further irony, it points out, is that a parishioner of a struggling Church may find himself in business competition with its hierarchy, which has a tax advantage over him.

Christianity Today, a conservative Protestant fortnightly magazine, estimated in 1967 that the Church real estate was worth a little more than the late Bishop Pike had suggested—$80 billion (and please don't expect me to get into that nought business again). Dr Martin A. Larson, author of *Church Wealth and Business Income*, agreed with the Bishop's figure, having analysed the tax rolls in fourteen U.S. States. It is interesting to note that the assessed valuation of New York City, including its five boroughs of Manhattan, the Bronx, Queens, Kings (Brooklyn) and Richmond (Staten Island) is a mere 47 billion 399 million dollars, substantially less than the estimated value of Church property. The value of this Church land, of course, increases year by year, as one Church near New Britain, Connecticut, found to its benefit. In 1939 it bought 121 acres of land. It buried one body there, which was enough to make a cemetery out of it. Twenty-seven years later there was still but one body there, but the value of the land had increased many times. So the church sold 111 acres to the city, keeping only ten of God's little acres and thus making a high profit that was exempt from capital gains tax.

In downtown Chicago, the Methodist Church owns the Chicago Temple, a twenty-two-storey building. Several of the lower floors are used for worship and other purposes related to the Church. The other floors are rented for commercial use. The Methodists, admittedly, pay a property tax on the commercial portion of the building, but no federal income tax on the $250,000 they receive in rents every year. There are, of course, other examples of Church property wealth, but I see little point in going on and on and on.

What about offerings? According to figures gathered by the National Council of Churches and published in their *Year Book of American Churches* for 1969, they totalled $3,612,671,698. Only sixty-two denominations made returns to the Council, however, and notable omissions included the Jewish synagogues, with 6,000,000 members, the Mormons with nearly 2,000,000 and the Roman Catholic Church, whose membership of 47,000,000 far outstrips that of any other denomination in America. What the actual amount received is nobody knows, but in 1968 Mortimer Caplin made an intelligent estimate on a CBS television programme, with the title 'The Business of Religion'. He was interviewed not merely because he was a prominent Washington tax attorney, but because he was Commissioner of Internal Revenue in 1962, when the Internal Service conducted a statistical analysis of the income tax returns of individuals. As people can claim tax deductions for money donated to churches, he was able to fashion a reasonable yardstick; he gauged from it that in 1962 donations totalled 4·6 billion dollars. By 1968, he estimated, that figure would have been in the region of 7·5 or 8 billion, if gifts from corporations and foundations were included.

According to *Christianity Today*, the American Association of Fund Raising Council estimated that offerings in 1967 were about 6·5 billion dollars, a figure which strengthens Mortimer Caplin's thought about the following year. The magazine commented with some acid: 'Despite Churchmen's vociferous expression of concern for people everywhere, it is doubtful that much more than one per cent of total church income finds its way into foreign economies. All available figures indicate that the vast portion of the money is pumped back into affluent American society.'

Lump it all together—investments, real estate, offerings—and what would we get? Again there can be only intelligent guesses. Robert J. Regan, who investigated the empire for United Press International, said, for instance: 'If you insist upon a ball park figure, counting real property, securities and other investments of all U.S. religious bodies, I'd plump for one hundred billion dollars.' I am not quite sure whether he counted offerings as well, but what is eight billion when the century has been reached? Figures of this magnitude are bewildering, anyway, and I think the CBS investigators put the whole business into fair perspective when they reported that the gross revenue of Churches is greater than the after-tax income of General Motors, American Telephone and Telegraph, Standard Oil, Ford, Texaco and Sears-Roebuck combined.

The reason that the Delta Ministry cannot afford kitchen equipment for its nutritional centre could be, perhaps, because starving children make little impact on stock markets. They have not gained the whole world or any part of it.

11: MORMONS, MONEY AND MARRIAGE

FOR sheer efficiency of operation, said Mark Twain a while back, the Church of Jesus Christ of Latter-day Saints was equalled only by the Prussian Army. If he were alive today, I feel that he would revise his view. Those aloof, élite militarists have had their starch softened a couple of times since; but the Saints go marching on.

Known more familiarly as the Mormons, they have grown large and rich faster, probably, than any other religion in the world. They have survived vicious persecution in the past and still meet it in some parts of the world today. They were hounded for their polygamous practices until they publicly renounced them in 1890, but still face up patiently to the backlash of ridicule today. Even more embarrassing is the fact that a handful of dissident Mormons refuse to accept the Church's ban on a multiplicity of wives and have been excommunicated for their beliefs. I met some of these spiritual and temporal outlaws and found both men and women thoroughly happy. I shall report on them later.

First, however, it is necessary to measure the mettle of the Church itself. Obviously it is a stout organization that can survive so many slings and arrows in a comparatively short history. In an attempt to gauge its strength, therefore, let us hold our collective noses for a moment, plunge into an ocean of statistics and scramble out before we drown. Cold figures give me an attack of the vapours, but duty is duty.

In 1951, when David O. McKay* became President of the Church at the age of seventy-seven, there were 1,416,731 members. Five years later there were 1,823,661. By the end of 1969 there were 3,035,000. In that seventeen-year period the number of wards (roughly parishes) and stakes (just as roughly dioceses) more than doubled.

Nor has this amazing expansion been confined to their homeland, the United States, where they have their battle headquarters in Salt Lake City, Utah. Their missionary soldiers, clean-cut, clean-limbed, clean-minded and exceptionally clean-shaven to a man, have produced results just as dramatic throughout the world, even unto the British Isles, where some of the natives still believe that America is no more than a chewing-gum mine. Just after the Second World War, Britain had about a thousand Mormons. By 1963 there were 35,000. Seven years later they were 86,000 strong, attending 213 chapels, which have mushroomed all over the country and continue to do so at the rate of about fifteen a year. When I asked Dr. W. Dean Benlap, a Salt Lake

* David O. McKay died in 1970, and was succeeded by Joseph Fielding Smith.

citizen and at the time Mission President in London, how that remarkable success had been achieved, he said simply: 'Through intense proselytizing. The number of missionaries here has increased from about three hundred in 1945 to 1,200 in 1970.'

Most of these young men are from the United States and in their early twenties. That they all pay their own expenses is a sign of their dedication, but the depth of their faith is but one reason for the healthy state of Mormon affairs, and, perhaps, not the most important. Mark Twain was close to the heart of the matter, as usual, when he spoke of their sheer efficiency, which has made them both powerful and wealthy. They more or less own the State of Utah, which is fair enough, indeed, because they invented it, taking over a heap of desert, trimmed with the Rocky Mountains, back in 1847, making it flower with their sweat and gathering the honey which has been flowing in increasing quantities ever since.

How thick and sweet is it today? The Mormons do not scatter their financial statements like consolidated confetti. In Salt Lake City, the head of their information service, Henry A. Smith, told me with candour, that in fact: 'We haven't issued a financial report since 1951. They never gave any information about our income anyway, only about our expenditure.'

That year they spent on administration, stakes and wards, missionary work, temples, building, schools, welfare work, hospitals and whatever, $40,252,000, but that, I gathered, gave little indication of their real wealth and certainly kept none of their accountants awake at night, wondering how the electricity bill was to be paid.

Life magazine estimated in 1956 that their U.S. assets alone were $160,000,000, but, when I quoted that figure to Henry Smith, he did not seem very impressed. He replied: 'Church money is given back to members in some form or another, as funds for the building of chapels, for instance, or for education. We don't hold any great financial reserves. When you consider, however, all the property the Church owns, the chapels, the temples, farms and other assets, $160,000,000 would seem to be a very low figure. A new chapel is built every working day of the year.'

Coming in at a different angle, I said: 'A Mayor of Salt Lake City has been quoted as saying that the Mormon Church receives a million dollars a day on tithing alone. Would that be true?'

'I've no idea what the income of the Church is,' he told me, 'because, close as I've been to it over the years, I've never asked and nobody has ever told me. To get the Church's income, you'd have to find accurately the number of people who pay tithing. That is ten per cent of a member's income—ten per cent of the gross, by the way, before any expenses are deducted, for our tithing comes off the top. I doubt if you would find that half pay an honest tithing. Perhaps thirty-five to forty per cent would make a contribution which doesn't come anywhere near to being a tenth of their income.'

Even on the basis of that estimate, the figure which the Mayor was quoted as giving—and which, I understand, he denied very soon afterwards—would seem as conservative as *Time* magazine's guess about the Mormon assets. Most Mormons are middle-class, industrious and therefore reasonably well-heeled because material success is regarded as a sign that God approves of their efforts. In the United States alone there are 2,028,000 of them. Let us assume that their average income is 10,000 dollars a year; and that sixty per cent of them make an honest tithing of 1,000 dollars a year. That would work out at $1,216,800,000 a year, or over $3,300,000 a day. If even fifty per cent of the Mormons in the rest of the world gave two dollars a week, that figure would be topped up to an international total in the region of $3,500,000 a day.*

With scalding reluctance I shall return at a later stage to dig up some more intimate details from this field of lucre. To make any sense of it all, however, I must try first to untangle the highly complex history and beliefs of this remarkable organization. It was founded on 6 April 1830, by Joseph Smith, junior, son of New England parents who were farming without much success in Palmyra, ten miles from Rochester in New York State. At that time revivalists were blasting the area, shattering eardrums in a style that would make Billy Graham sound like a Trappist monk. Wild sects in bizarre clothes jostled for souls in a frenetic religious free-for-all. At least two self-styled prophets claimed to be Jesus Christ, one of them a handsome woman by the name of Jemima Wilkinson, who assured her spell-bound audiences that she would never die. Pulverized from all sides by these spiritual salvoes, some people changed their faith as often as they changed their clothes; but not Joseph Smith Jnr.

Though he was only fourteen years old and had had little schooling, he was intelligent and articulate, a handsome lad with a lively, probing

* If the mathematics seem suspect, please write to the Saints, not to me. They have computers.

mind. Having listened to the discord of so many salvation songs, he acted more logically than most. He went into the woods near Palmyra, knelt down and asked God which church he should join, a simple question which got a simple answer. He wrote later: 'I saw a pillar of light exactly over my head, above the brightness of the sun, which descended gradually until it fell upon me. I saw two Personages, whose brightness and glory defy all description, standing above me in the air. One of them spake unto me, calling me by name, and said, pointing to the other: 'This is My Beloved Son. Hear Him!'

He was told that he must join none of the sects. 'The personage who addressed me,' he wrote, 'said all their creeds were an abomination in His sight; that those professors were all corrupt; that "they draw near to me with their lips, but their hearts are far from me; they teach for doctrines the commandments of men, having a form of godliness, but they deny the power thereof."'

That was in the spring of 1820. The personages, he said, were God and Jesus Christ; and, while Jemima Wilkinson might have disputed the claim, he accepted the message. Three and a half years later another heavenly being, who gave his name as Moroni, appeared to Joseph and revealed the existence of a record engraved on metal plates hidden in a hill called Cumorah, not far from the Smith home. Those records, he was told, contained the sacred and secular history of a people who were ancestors of some of the American Indians in the period from 600 BC to AD 421. He was directed to the plates, which, he wrote, were gold, and with divine aid translated them into what was to become the Book of Mormon.

It told of two separate peoples who had come to America. The first were the Jaredites, who fled from the tower of Babel in 2,500 BC to the new world in eight water-tight barges which were driven by a following wind. It seems that they spent as much time under the water as on top of it and the journey lasted three hundred and forty-four days. Light was provided by heavenly stones, but fresh air came to them in more mundane fashion. The Lord told them to make a hole in the bottom of the barges and in the top. Whenever they were in need of air, they were to remove the plug from whichever part of the barges happened to be above the water at the time. Noah-fashion, they brought a pair of every animal, also birds, fish and a swarm of bees, which must have been a rather hazardous cargo, what with the barges twirling in the ocean. As it turned out, however, the journey, undertaken in such difficult circumstances, was not too successful. Soon after they arrived in America, the Jaredites quarrelled among themselves and nearly all were killed.

The second people were lead from Jerusalem just before its destruction in 600 BC. At their head was Lehi, who died and was succeeded by his son, Nephi. His leadership was contested by his older brothers, Laman and Lemuel, and the tribe killed him. For that and for their conduct generally, the Book of Mormon states, God darkened their skin, thus making them the ancestors of the North American Indians. Battles rolled on between the Nephites and the Lamanites until AD 400, when the Nephites were wiped out. Before that happened, however, Mormon, one of the last of the Nephites, buried the historical plates and it was his son, Moroni, said to be literally the last of his tribe, who returned to tell Joseph Smith where they were.

The Mormons believe that Christ visited America and referred to this when He said, according to the Gospel of St John: 'And other sheep I have, which are not of this fold; them also I must bring and they shall hear my voice: and there shall be one fold and one shepherd.' They accept the general Christian belief that He will return, but are more precise about the spot that He has chosen for his reappearance. It is the city of Independence, Missouri, they say, and one of their articles of faith states: 'We believe in the literal gathering of Israel and in the restoration of the Ten Tribes; that Zion will be built upon this continent; that Christ will reign personally upon the earth; and that the earth will be renewed and receive its paradisaical glory.'

They maintain, too, that there was a pre-existence before the world was made and that there are four kingdoms awaiting us. From the bottom up they are: the Kingdom of Darkness, reserved for Satan, his angels and earthlings who become Sons of Perfidy by their conduct here—'liars and sorcerers and adulterers and whoremongers and whosoever loves and makes a lie'; the Telestial Kingdom, for those who have sinned, but not sufficiently to be perfidious, those who failed to accept the gospel of Jesus Christ and went away from righteousness; the Terrestrial Kingdom, for those who are righteous, but died without acknowledging Jesus Christ as saviour, honourable people, in other words, who were not of a religious or spiritual nature; and finally the Celestial Kingdom, the abode of the followers of Christ, who grasped His doctrine. This, in fact, means Mormons. In the Celestial Kingdom will be three internal degrees of glory, the highest of which is a state of exaltation in which those who qualify will find themselves Gods, living in the presence of their heavenly Father.

This Celestial Kingdom, they say, will have many features in common with life on Earth. God, the Father, will live in a house, as will all others who join him. Their wives will not only cook, sew and keep their homes tidy, but will continue to bear children by the old-fashioned, earthly method of sexual intercourse, for one of the purposes of those who reach this state of exaltation will be to produce new souls for this and other worlds. Henry Smith—who, I would like to mention at this point, was a courteous and patient informant for me throughout my stay in Salt Lake City—told me: 'We believe that God has a wife. We believe that we have a Father in Heaven and that it is a matter of logic that we should have a Mother, too. It is a physical thing.'

Some Mormons to whom I spoke hold that Christ was married, while He was on earth. They reason that He came here as a man and could not experience the full state of manhood without a wife. When I asked Henry Smith about that point, he said: 'I have heard the question discussed in Sunday school classes, though we don't have any more knowledge about it than anyone else. It would seem, however, to be a logical conclusion in the eyes of the Church.'

According to Mormon records, Joseph Smith had visits from more heavenly personalities than many an old Testament prophet. In the spring of 1829 he was walking in the woods with Oliver Cowdery, who was transcribing the Book of Mormon at his dictation. As they knelt in prayer, John the Baptist appeared to them, conferred on them the Hebraic priesthood and told them to baptise each other. Later, after he had promised that three men would see the golden plates, he took Cowdery, David Whitmer and Martin Harris into the woods and an angel appeared to them. When the first Mormon Temple was dedicated at Kirtland, near Cleveland, Ohio, Smith and Cowdery claimed that they saw not only God, but, in what appears to have been fairly rapid succession, Moses, Elias and Elijah, too. Joseph wrote later that the Temple was filled with angels and that many saw glorious visions.

In addition to these events, he claimed to be receiving revelations from God not infrequently. Through these and a series of visions, he produced what he said were lost books of the Bible, which included a section of St John; the Book of Moses, said to be a conversation between God and the ancient prophet, omitted from the Old Testament because of the wickedness of the Hebrews; and the history of Enoch. He also translated what he said was the Book of Abraham from papyri which his mother purchased for him, along with four Egyptian mummies, from a traveller called Michael Chandler. The arrival of a man with mummies on Joseph Smith's doorstep is not as unlikely as it may seem, for at the time there was unlicensed looting of Egyptian tombs and many sarcophagi reached America. His translation of the papyri has not been accepted by any acknowledged expert on the subject, a fact which worries a few Mormons. Joseph, at any rate, continued to have revelations, which ultimately were gathered together in *Doctrine and Covenants* which, with the Book of Mormon and the Bible, is in the house of every good Saint. Since then it has been accepted that all Presidents of the Church have this link with God and that the affairs of the Church, therefore, are shaped by constant and direct divine decree. Individual Mormons, too, claim to receive revelations, though they cover a limited field only. Henry Smith told me: 'I can receive revelations to direct me and my family. They would come through prayer, fasting and extreme humility, seeking to know the mind of God. When it comes, there is no doubt about it. The feeling is definite.'

Joseph Smith certainly had no doubts and soon he was convincing others of his mission as a prophet. When the Church was founded, it had just six members. Within a month it had made forty converts. The following January, in response to yet another revelation, they moved to Kirtland, where he met Brigham Young, who was to be his successor, and in a remarkably short time the number of members had risen to two thousand. It was there that a further revelation told him to choose Twelve Apostles, a hierarchy which is part of the Church still.

Trouble, however, was never very far away. Soon after the Kirtland Temple had been dedicated, Joseph was instructed by revelation to open a bank with a stock not less than four million dollars. He did so and the bank began issuing its own bills. Unfortunately it had little more than spiritual backing and those of little faith grew very angry when they could not get their money. On 22 December 1937, Brigham Young had to leave town to escape his creditors. On 12 January 1938 he was followed by Joseph Smith, who in turn was followed by what Mormon historians have described as 'human blood-hounds, armed and thirsty for their lives'.

Despite this setback, membership continued to increase. A thousand followed him from Kirtland, as he drove west to Caldwell County, Missouri. Soon they numbered eight to ten thousand. As they travelled, they clashed violently with anti-Mormon elements and it seems clear that some sections of the Mormon band had organized themselves into an efficient fighting force. There was a series of holy and unholy wars which ended in November 1838, with Joseph, his brother, Hyrum and a number of other Mormon leaders chained in Richmond Jail, charged with treason, murder, arson, burglary, robbery, larceny and perjury. In a way, however, they were lucky, for the General in charge of the troops to whom they had surrendered had been in favour of executing them by firing squad after a court-martial held the previous night.

The conditions in the jail were appalling, but in the time they spent there before and after their preliminary trial, public feeling against the Mormons eased, as news of the opposition's atrocities began to circulate. By early 1839 he and Hyrum were free again, not through the mercy of any Judge, but because they had managed to feed a jug of whisky, sweetened with honey to their guard. As a further sweetener, they gave him a bribe of $800 and with that they were out.

He crossed into the State of Illinois and there he showed that he was not only a man of irrepressible character, but of extraordinary vision, too. At a bend in the Mississippi he halted his followers, gazed down from a hill on the lowlands beneath him and decided to build a city there. 'It is a beautiful site,' he said, 'and it shall be called Nauvoo, which means in Hebrew a beautiful plantation.'

He built his city. It flourished and soon it was the largest on the frontier with a population of between fifteen and twenty thousand, much larger than Chicago at the time. From there he sent Brigham Young and many of the Twelve Apostles to England in search of converts. Young set out with $13.50 in his pocket and landed with about seventy-five cents; but it was a wise investment both spiritually and otherwise. He found England in the grip of a depression and the Government urging people to emigrate to America. Disillusioned with both Church and State, eight thousand of them embraced Mormonism and set out for Nauvoo.

The Church seemed to have found a home. Trouble, however, was never very far from Joseph Smith and in the early 1840s he was right in the middle of battle again. Rumours that the Mormon leaders were practising polygamy began whispering, then whistling around the city and the State of Illinois. They were, in fact, true. A schism in the Church aggravated an ugly state of affairs even further, particularly when those who left Smith's banner supported the stories. Finally the Nauvoo

Expositor printed affidavits by three of the dissenters, testifying that they had seen or heard a revelation that granted every man the privilege of marrying ten virgins and forgave him all sins except the shedding of innocent blood. For good measure, the *Expositor* included a few stern words about Smith's adventures in real estate, which had been worrying quite a few people.

A weak man might have retreated in face of these charges. Joseph Smith, however, was never weak even in his early days before he had gathered any support. Now he was Mayor of Nauvoo and its founding father, a man with several thousand supporters. He declared the *Expositor* a civic nuisance and ordered it to be tried by the City Council, which found that it was libellous and must be destroyed. The newspaper office was wrecked and every issue burned, an unwise and violent move that signalled the beginning of the physical end of Joseph Smith.

When Governor Thomas Ford of Illinois learned of the burning of the *Expositor*, he went at once to the nearby town of Carthage. There he learned that the militia were about to launch an attack on Nauvoo. Joseph, after considerable hesitation, gave himself up for trial with his brother Hyrum and a handful of Church elders. They were charged with riot and remanded in custody.

Governor Ford visited him in Carthage Jail and announced that he was going to Nauvoo to address the Mormons. As soon as he had left town, militia from Warsaw, a town that always had been jealous of Nauvoo, stormed the jail and shot both Joseph and Hyrum Smith dead.

To many outsiders it seemed that the Church would die with them. Apart altogether from the violence of their non-Mormon enemies, the loss of the prophet inflamed the internal dissension. Brigham Young announced that they must move west. Emma, Joseph Smith's wife, refused to go and denounced 'the tyrants who have seized on the government of the Mormon Church'. Others, including Joseph's brother, William, sided with her and with Young's rivals, creating a bitter cleavage which culminated some years later in the establishment of the Reorganized Church of Jesus Christ of Latter-day Saints. It still lives with its headquarters in Independence, Missouri, where all good Mormons in either camp believe that Christ will reappear; but it is a weak body compared with that in Salt Lake City. The Year Book of American Churches gives its membership as only 169,248.

This bitter squabbling inside and outside the Church was overshadowed, however, by what has become an epic in American history:

the trek of the pioneers to the Valley of the Great Salt Lake. The trek began in 1847 under Brigham Young, now Smith's successor as President of the Church. Thousands left Nauvoo and pushed west. Some rode in wagons drawn by oxen. Others—about three thousand of them—could not afford oxen and they pulled their goods with them in handcarts. Casualties were heavy. Many froze to death; but the Saints, men, women and children, many straight from comfortable, urban lives, kept marching on, covering between twelve and twenty miles a day. Just over three months later, at the mouth of a canyon, Young halted them. Looking down on a fertile valley, an expanse of marsh and the shimmer of the Great Salt Lake, he said: 'This is the place where I, in a vision, saw the ark of the Lord resting. This is the place whereon we will plant the soles of our feet and where the Lord will place his name among his people.'

He spoke not only with a fine sense of theatre, but of purpose, too. By noon the following day five acres of potatoes had been planted and watered. Slowly a splendidly planned city—designed years earlier, it is said, by Smith, but executed with the energetic genius of Young—began to rise. The grace of Salt Lake City today with its broad, tree-lined streets, its elegant buildings, its solid, comfortable prosperity, is a monument to the pair of them.

About fifty per cent of the population are Mormons, though in the State of Utah, particularly the more rural areas, the percentage is considerably higher. Quantity, however, is not so important. The Mormons run the place, not so much because of nepotism, but because of what Mark Twain described so accurately as their sheer efficiency. Henry Smith told me: 'The Church owns a number of businesses and properties, the Temple Square Hotel, for instance, the Beneficial Life Insurance Company and Bonneville International, which is a holding company for the Church-owned radio and television station. Apart from our stations here in Salt Lake City, we have a short wave station in New York, one of the most powerful in the world, TV and radio stations in Seattle and a radio station in Kansas, though they are not used specially for propaganda purposes. *The Deseret News,** one of the two daily newspapers here, is owned totally by the Church and it has a big commercial printing plant outside the city as well. Contrary to public

---

* Before it became the State of Utah, the Mormons named their territory Deseret, the Book of Mormon word for the honeybee, carried by the Jaredites to America in their remarkable barges.

opinion, we have no stock in the Union Pacific, though Elder Harold B. Lee, one of the Twelve Apostles, is a director of that company. We owned three banks at one time—Zion Savings Bank, First National Bank of Utah and the Finance and Trust Bank. These were joined together in one banking system, the Zion First National Bank, but the Church sold it to private interests about eight years ago. Two of the men who took part in it are members, but one is not. Some of the church officials are on the Board of Directors, but only as individuals.

'Real estate? We own Temple Square and the Church's administrative block. For its own protection the Church has tried to purchase what property it can adjacent to these blocks. It owns the building in which we are sitting now, the Deseret Book Company and two whole blocks in the centre of the city. Other than that we're not in the real estate business, though we own some in Hawaii because we bought a big sugar ranch there a few years ago. We have a big ranch in Florida, but it is in the process of being sold.

'Why are we selling? Obviously we don't go into the purchase of real estate just for its own sake. There are circumstances when it would be advisable to buy and others when it would be better to sell. The money, I presume, goes back into securities. Most of our funds, however, are put into the development and growth of the Church. Right now we have three multi-million dollar temples under construction, two in Utah and one in Washington, D.C. We are constructing, too, a new comprehensive headquarters here, a high-rise building that will cost thirty million dollars.

'Taxes? We claim relief only on Church premises—temples, chapels and property used for welfare purposes. We pay taxes on all our profit-making businesses and properties.'

The physical signs of this affluence are not confined to the United States. Magnificent Mormon buildings are dotted throughout the world. There are temples in Canada, New Zealand, Switzerland and in England, where the Saints built one on thirty-two acres in Lingfield, Surrey, which they bought from Sir Winston Churchill. He kept race horses there. The Mormons keep the faith. In addition, they have many chapels, the most elaborate, perhaps, being that in Kensington. It is reported to have cost $792,000. In addition to its admirable religious facilities, it has a basketball court, a kitchen with electric potato peelers and a sound-proof room—known as the cry gallery—for restless infants who might disturb the services. It was opened in February 1961, to the sweet sound of hymns from the Mormons' International Singing Mothers' Chorus. Soon afterwards the Church announced that it was embarking on a $24,000,000 building programme in England.

Despite those awe-inspiring financial figures, not all Mormons are rich and the Church has a remarkable welfare system, based on the doctrine which teaches: 'Care for your own.' Henry Smith told me: 'It began on a modest scale during the depression. The Church has always been opposed to dole, believing that there should be opportunities for work and for helping to rehabilitate people so that they can become gainfully employed. That help and the opportunity to work comes from what we call the bishop's storehouse. The bishop of each ward decides who needs help and who is worthy of it. He then makes out an order for food, clothing or whatever is needed and the family collects it from the storehouse. Those who are too sick or too old to collect their goods have them delivered in plain vans so that there will be no embarrassment.'

Then he took me to Welfare Square in Salt Lake City, the biggest bishop's storehouse in the world, a city within a city. This amazing complex contains every possible item that a family might need and, as I was led around its overflowing shelves, he told me: 'This is the only supermarket in the world where money is no good. To produce what you see here, every stake—diocese—is given a production budget. They establish various projects to supply it. When I was a stake president, for instance, we established a dairy farm. Another stake might have a beef project or a soap factory. A stake in Kansas produces gelatine products and another in Texas provides peanut butter. Most of our orange juice comes from stakes in California. What we can't produce economically ourselves—electric light bulbs, toilet paper and so on—we buy commercially with money raised for the purpose by stakes in highly urbanized areas, like New York or London.

'We're all expected to work on these projects. In my stake, for instance, we have an eighty-acre farm. My bishop will say: "We need so many men to work on the sugar beet or to cut the hay, perhaps.' When I've a few hours to spare, I go. Those who get help work, too, of course, both here in Welfare Square and on projects.'

There are roughly a hundred bishops' storehouses and a fleet of trucks carries goods from one to another on an exchange basis, Californian orange juice, for instance, being swapped for flour and canned vegetables in Utah and Idaho. The Salt Lake City storehouse is unique not only because of its size, but because of its magnificent equipment. There is ultra-modern plant for making canned milk, powdered milk, butter and cheese. There are canning facilities, used not only for the programme, but by groups who wish to can for their homes in accordance with their elders' advice that they should lay aside a year's supply of food for an emergency. There are two huge grain elevators, built by voluntary labour and extensive storage cellars. The programme—indeed, produces virtually everything, even fuel, for in South Utah it owns a coal-mine.

The storehouses are basically for the benefit of Mormons. In emergencies, however, the President of the Church can give instructions for aid to be sent to areas outside the Church. This President McKay did, a recent example being the dispatch of blankets and food to Chile after an earthquake. Church members have first claim, of course, and in 1967 alone over 16,001,446 pounds of food, 5,795 tons of coal and 1,199,993 items of household supplies, including clothes, were distributed. Hospitalization and cash for medical, burial and other expenses cost the scheme $3,072,693 that year. Over 81,000 people were helped and 4,018 were found jobs. To keep this massive machine in motion, those not in need themselves donated 599,159 man-hours of work.

The average Mormon, however, has no need to seek help from the programme, for his religion imbues him with a spiritual urge to be industrious. Prosperity, as I have said, is a sign that he is favoured by God and the Saints' wives encourage them to acquire these material signs of divine blessing. They will point, indeed, to the worldly success of their leaders and that certainly cannot be denied, though a share of it comes from Church-owned businesses.

President David O. McKay, for instance, was at ninety-five years of age President and a director of Deseret Farms of Florida, Inc., which has a capital of $18,100,000; Board Chairman of the Utah-Idaho Sugar Company, capital, $11,865,415; President and director of Zion Securities Corporation, capital, $10,000,000; a director of the Utah Hotel Company, capital $1,500,000; a director of Bonneville International Corporation, which deals in radio and television management with a capital of $12,075,167; a director of the Zion Co-operative Mercantile Institution, a chain store with a capital of $7,046,040; and a director of KSL, Inc., the radio and television station in Salt Lake City, with a capital of $246,933.

Two senior members of the Church, Hugh B. Brown and N. Eldon Tanner are directors of these highly valuable concerns. Robert L. Simpson of the Church's Presiding Bishopric, is a director of the Deseret Book Company, capital, $1,000,000, the Zion Securities Corporation and the Zion Co-operative Mercantile Institution. Mark E. Petersen, one of the Twelve Apostles, is President and a director of the Deseret News Publishing Corporation, capital $10,000,000 and Vice-President and a director of the Newspaper Agency Corporation, capital, $10,000. Thomas S. Monson, another Apostle, is a director of the Deseret News Publishing Corporation and of the Deseret Book Company. Marion G. Romney, Apostle; Franklin D. Richards, an Assistant to the Apostles; and John H. Vandenberg, a member of the Presiding Bishopric, are all directors of the Zion Securities Corporation. LeGrand Richards, Apostle, is a director of both the Utah Hotel Company and the Zion Co-operative Mercantile Institution. Victor Brown, a member of the Presiding Bishopric, is a director of the Utah Hotel Co. Delbert L. Stapley, Apostle, is a director of the Zion Co-operative Mercantile Institution. Gordon B. Hinckley, Apostle, is a director of the Deseret News Publishing Company. The late President's son, David Lawrence McKay, is treasurer of Deseret Farms of Florida, Inc., and a director of both the Utah-Idaho Sugar Company and the Zion Utah Bancorporation, capital $4,919,451.

No details are given of the directors' fees which the brethren receive. The records of insurance companies, however, are more revealing and in this context those of the Beneficial Life Insurance Company are of particular interest, as the Saints own it. From the records I learned that the late President McKay, Chairman of the Board, received $13,400 for his services in 1968. Hugh B. Brown and N. Eldon Tanner, the Vice-Chairmen, were paid $9,200 each. Joseph Fielding Smith, David O. McKay's successor as President of the Church and Howard W. Hunter, an Apostle, received $6,200 each as Board members. Other directors are Spencer W. Kimball, Apostle, and Victor L. Brown, a member of the Presiding Bishopric, who got $5,000; Harold B. Lee, Marion G. Romney, Ezra Taft Benson,* LeGrand Richards, Gordon B. Hinckley and Thomas L. Monson, Apostles all, $1,400; Victor L. Brown, John H. Vandenberg and Robert L. Simpson, members of the Presiding Bishopric all, $1,400; and Marion D. Hanks, an Assistant to the Twelve,

---

* A prolific writer, whose books may be bought from the John Birch Society, which has a branch and a bookshop in Salt Lake City.

$800, the sum being below the average presumably because he served on the board only from 1 June that year.

It is unlikely that any of those in the long roll of honour I have just quoted ever will need to seek help from Welfare Square; and with that comforting thought, let us scurry from the fleshpots to more spiritual plains. There the practising Mormon, as opposed to those who have strayed, thus earning themselves the nickname of Jack Mormons, exudes a confidence that arouses envy in some and irritation in a few who feel that it verges on smugness. Their confidence is understandable, however, because they have been taught that they have transport to celestial bliss. They can be forgiven, perhaps, if their smiles seem a trifle patronizing when they are faced with those who can hope for no more than a second or third-class spiritual landing-base, if, indeed, they should be lucky enough to catch the plane.

Nevertheless there are two points of conversation which make them uneasy, not only with outsiders, but among themselves. One is the rusty, multi-edged sword of polygamy, which they prefer to call plural or celestial marriage, and the other is the fact that Negroes cannot hold the priesthood, which normally is conferred on every adult male Mormon in good standing with the Church. When I raised these questions in one Saintly home, my urbane host became so agitated that he dropped a cup, whereupon I dropped the conversation.

The whole question of the Mormon church and polygamy is confusing not only for those outside the faith of Joseph Smith, but for some who embrace it, too. Those who never got beyond Section Forty-Two of *Doctrine and Covenants,* the book which the Saints believe contains God's revelations to their prophet, might wonder how it ever became an issue in the first place. That Section is described in the preamble as 'a revelation given to Joseph Smith, the Prophet, at Kirtland, Ohio, February 9, 1831, in the presence of twelve Elders, and in fulfilment of the Lord's promise previously made'. Verse twenty-two states: 'Thou shalt love thy wife with all thy heart and shalt cleave unto her and none else.'

Section 131 may not be acceptable to unbelievers in Mormon doctrine, but at least it is clear and consistent. Introduced as 'instructions by Joseph Smith, the Prophet, given at Ramus, Illinois, May 16 and 17, 1843', it states: 'In the celestial glory there are three heavens or degrees; and in order to obtain the highest, a man must enter this order of the priesthood (meaning the new and everlasting covenant of marriage); and if he does not, he cannot obtain it. He may enter into the other, but that is the end of his kingdom; he cannot have an increase.'

That, to my untheological mind, means that no man can obtain the highest degree of Celestial heaven—the status of a God, according to the Mormons—unless married according to the new and everlasting covenant. Bachelors, therefore, are in trouble.

Section 132 explains this new and everlasting covenant, at which point some minds begin to grope nervously in a spiritual fog. The explanatory note at the beginning states that it is a 'revelation given through Joseph Smith, the Prophet, at Nauvoo, Illinois, recorded July 12, 1843, relating to the new and everlasting covenant, including the eternity of the marriage covenant, as also plurality of wives'. The first verse makes it clear that Joseph, who regarded himself as a prophet of the Lord, had been contemplating the lives of his predecessors, Abraham, Isaac, Jacob, Moses, David and Solomon, all of whom, he had noted, had had 'many wives and concubines'. Wondering whether this state of multiple marriage and concubinage applied to latter-day prophets, he had asked the Lord.

In reply, the Lord explained at some length what he meant by marriage. It was not simply a matter of a couple being united until death them do part. It was an everlasting union that had to be sealed by His law, which at that time, he added, His servant, Joseph Smith, had the power to administer on earth. Those marriages would last for ever and those who married outside God's law could look forward only to be ministering angels, never Gods.

He went on to state that Abraham, Isaac, Jacob, Moses, David and Solomon had many wives and concubines at His command and in accordance with His law. He told how Sarah, Abraham's first wife, had given her husband Hagar, the Egyptian maid, and went on: 'And why did she do it? Because this was the law and from Hagar sprang many people. This, therefore, was fulfilling, among other things, the promises. Was Abraham, therefore, under condemnation? Verily I say unto you, Nay; for I, the Lord, commanded it.' He then made it quite clear that Joseph Smith not only should have more than one wife, but must have them, if he were to keep the law of God. He stated: 'And again, as pertaining to the law of the priesthood—if any man espouse a virgin, and desire to espouse another, and the first give her consent, and if he espouse the second, and they are virgins, and have vowed to no other man, then he is justified; he cannot commit adultery for they are given unto him; for he cannot commit adultery with that that belongeth unto him and no one else.'

He explained further that any girl who entered into such a marriage after she had been with another man, would have committed adultery and would be destroyed. All in all, it seemed a very anti-feminist revelation, for a little later on he took the muscle out of the line which said that the first wife must give her consent to a second marriage. In verse sixty-four, Joseph Smith records Him as saying: 'And again, verily, verily, I say unto you, if any man have a wife, who holds the keys of this power, and he teaches unto her the law of my priesthood, as pertaining to these things, then she shall believe and administer unto him, or she shall be destroyed.' In other words, if she should refuse her consent, she has no hope.

The message was not merely general, but personal, not just a rule for all mankind, but a direct instruction to Joseph's wife, Emma. The revelation stated: 'And let mine handmaid, Emma Smith, receive all those that have been given unto my servant, Joseph, and who are virtuous and pure before me . . . And I command mine handmaid, Emma Smith, to abide and cleave unto my servant Joseph and to none else. But if she will not abide this commandment she shall be destroyed, saith the Lord; for I am the Lord thy God, and will destroy her if she abide not in my law.'

All good Mormons insist, of course, that there was no question of lust involved, for that would cancel out the whole point of the operation. Plural or celestial marriages, they say, were sealed so that man could multiply and replenish the earth and, to quote from verse sixty-three of Section 132, 'for their exaltation in the eternal worlds that they may bear the souls of men; for herein is the work of my Father continued that he may be glorified'.

Apart from the seeming contradiction of the earlier revelation that Mormons should love their wives and cleave unto none else, Section 132 seemed clear enough. Man could have more than one wife, provided they were virgins when he married them and provided the ceremony was in accordance with the laws of God which were, of course, the laws of the Mormon Church. If a woman refused to accept those laws, she was damned. Joseph Smith, however, was slow to announce the Lord's will to the world.

It is said that he received the revelation as early as 1831. It was not until around 1840, however, that he began sharing it with his immediate associates. Fawn M. Brodie in her biography of Smith,★ wrote: 'The men who were taken into the system at this early period—Hyrum Smith, Brigham Young, Heber Kimball, William Clayton, Willard Richards and Benjamin F. Johnson—after an initial period of shock and spiritual torment, were won over with very little argument. Joseph's brother Don Carlos, fought polygamy before his death in 1841. "Any man," he said to Ebenezer Robinson in June that year, "who will preach and practise spiritual wifery will go to hell, no matter if it is my brother, Joseph."'

Why did the prophet hesitate? Joseph W. Musser, himself the descendant of polygamous unions, wrote in *Celestial or Plural Marriage*, which he published himself in Salt Lake City in 1942:

The Revelation, while not reduced to writing until July 12, 1843, was received as early as 1831. The Prophet was taught the law at that time and later he was commanded to enter into the principle and establish it. This he did, himself taking twenty-seven plural wives . . . The principle was taught to those of his associates in the Priesthood whom the Prophet felt to trust, it not being deemed wise to attempt to publicize the law at that time among a people not prepared to receive it. As it was, the public, aroused by intimations of the fact, became fiendishly hostile, resulting in the martyrdom of Joseph and Hyrum Smith, June 27, 1844. Satan not only aroused his followers to acts of atrociousness against the Saints, but prompted the enactment of laws—wholly unconstitutional in their character—prohibiting this form of marriage. Under Satan's gospel monogamy is the marriage system with bachelorhood the ideal and sexual promiscuity the rule.

That last thought, of course, was one of the stronger arguments put forward by the Mormons. They pointed to monogamous society which, they claimed, was rife with promiscuity and adultery, whereas their homes were pure and blessed. Many of the plural wives accepted this philosophy, adding to it the fact that they were destined for exaltation because they were sealed for ever to their husbands by Temple rites. Some felt that it was better to have part of a true Saint—particularly if he were the Prophet himself—than all of an unbeliever. Orson Hyde, one of the earliest Apostles of Joseph Smith, staunchly supported all these arguments and went even further, suggesting that Jesus Christ practised polygamy and that it was one reason why he was crucified. Christ was married at Cana of Galilee,' he was reported as having said.

★ *No Man Knows My History* (Alfred A. Knopf, New York).

'Mary, Martha and others were his wives and he begat children.'
Brigham Young announced that Adam was God and a polygamist, that
Eve was his celestial wife before they came to Earth, and that Jesus'
mother was another of his wives. Adam, he said, created Jesus 'by the
process known to nature—just as men now create children.' The Father
and the Son, he went on, looked exactly alike, except that God was
older.* Young is credited with having had at least seventy wives. It
should be pointed out, however, that there remains argument about the
number of celestial marriages in which he and Joseph Smith were
sealed. Some undoubtedly took place after they had died, the ceremony
taking place by proxy. In other cases, Young married women to give
them a home and security, but may not have been their husband in a
physical sense.

Whatever the views of Mormon men and some of the women at the
time, one person was distinctly unhappy about the idea; and that was
Emma Smith, the prophet's wife, though reports vary about the depth
of her disapproval. Joseph, it seems, told her about the revelation before
it was committed to paper. At first she was shocked by the idea. By the
spring of 1843, she had accepted it reluctantly, but nagged him a good
deal about it. It was then that Hyrum Smith persuaded his brother to
commit the revelation to paper. When he had done so, Hyrum brought
it—against the advice of Joseph, who knew his wife a little better than
did his brother—to Emma, thinking that she would understand all, forgive all and accept all. When he returned to Joseph, he reported that
never in all his life had he been so abused by a woman; and the prophet
replied: 'I told you you didn't know her as well as I did!'

Other reports say that she remained violently opposed to the idea
until her death and that on one occasion she flung a pregnant wife of
Joseph's out into the snow. It seems more likely, however, that she
accepted the inevitable though not always with good grace. Henry
Smith told me, indeed: 'Emma didn't approve of plural marriage.
Nevertheless, she was well aware of the revelation for ten or twelve
years before the prophet died. There was no apparent break in their
relationship because they continued to have children in that period.'

Non-Mormons, of course, condemned the practice vociferously.
When the Saints publicly acknowledged their belief in plural marriage
in 1852, splendidly exaggerated stories of wild orgies in Utah circulated.

* *The Lion of the Lord*, a biography of Brigham Young by Stanley P. Hirshon
(Alfred A. Knopf, New York).

At that stage, however, they must have felt safe enough in their own, far-Western territory, though one of their leaders, Heber Chase Kimball, said prophetically at the time of the announcement: 'The cat is out of the bag and that's not all. This cat is going to have kittens and that's not all. Those kittens are going to have cats.'

He was right. Plural marriage continued in Utah with the blessing and encouragement of Brigham Young. There were some bitter clashes with the Federal authorities. Mormons were arrested and imprisoned for 'lewd and lascivious cohabitation'. Others were fined heavily and had their lands confiscated. More went underground to escape from U.S. Marshals and a cruel blow to the Saints was the confiscation by the government of all Church property, including Temple Square. By 1890, after the death of Brigham Young and of his successor, John Taylor, it was reckoned that over 1,300 men and women had been jailed for plural marriage and the Mormon leaders decided that something would have to be done. In September of that year, Taylor's successor as President issued a manifesto which stated:

Press dispatches having been sent for political purposes from Salt Lake City, which have been widely published, to the effect that the Utah Commission, in their recent report to the Secretary of the Interior, allege that plural marriages are still being solemnized and that forty or more such marriages have been contracted in Utah since last July or during the past year, also that in public discourses the leaders of the Church have taught, encouraged and urged the continuance of the practice of polygamy, I, therefore, as President of the Church of Jesus Christ of Latter-day Saints, do hereby in the most solemn manner declare that these charges are false. We are not teaching polygamy or plural marriage, nor permitting any person to enter into its practice, and I deny that either forty or any other number of plural marriages have during the period been solemnized in our Temples or in any other place in the Territory.

One case has been reported in which the parties allege that the marriage was performed in the Endowment House in Salt Lake City in the spring of 1889, but I have not been able to learn who performed the ceremony; whatever was done in this matter was without my knowledge. In consequence of this alleged occurrence the Endowment House was, by my instructions, taken down without delay.

Inasmuch as laws have been enacted by Congress forbidding plural marriages, which laws have been pronounced constitutional by the court of last resort, I hereby declare my intention to submit to those laws and to use my influence with the members of the Church over which I preside to have them do likewise.

There is nothing in my teachings to the Church or in those of my associates, during the time specified, which can be reasonably construed to inculcate or encourage polygamy; and when any Elder of the Church has used language which appeared to convey any such teaching, he has been promptly reproved. And I now publicly declare that my advice to the Latter-day Saints is to refrain from contracting any marriage forbidden by the law of the land.

In earlier days he had spoken much differently, supporting to the hilt the principles of Joseph Smith. His manifesto, however, was approved unanimously by a Church conference two weeks later. Soon afterwards all the confiscated land was returned and in 1896 Utah entered the Union to become one of the United States of America.

How did he justify such an about-face theologically? Henry Smith told me: 'One of the doctrines of the Church is that we are subject to kings, magistrates and rulers in honouring and sustaining the law. When the law of the land was such that polygamy was no longer possible, the only thing the Church could do was to conform. In announcing the manifesto, the Church didn't deny the doctrine of plurality. It denied the practice.'

'Was the manifesto the result of a revelation,' I asked, 'or was it merely a policy statement by the President?'

'The President inquired of the Lord, asking what the position should be,' he told me, 'and the Lord announced that the Church should obey the laws of the land.'

The Lord also said, according to Joseph Smith in the famous plural marriage revelation: 'Everything that is in the world, whether it be ordained of men, by thrones, or principalities, or powers, or things of name, whatsoever they may be, that are not by me or by my word, saith the Lord, shall be thrown down, and shall not remain after men are dead, neither in nor after the resurrection, saith the Lord your God.' Those who oppose the ending of plural marriage—and there are quite a few of them in Salt Lake City—deny that President Woodruff's manifesto was the result of a revelation and quote that part of the revelation to Joseph Smith in support of their arguments. 'If it were a revelation,' one of them told me, 'it would mean that God had changed His mind or that He had admitted that he had made a mistake. We prefer to think that manifesto was issued so that Mormons could get their land back and Utah could become a member of the Union.'

The manifesto is printed at the end of *Doctrine and Covenants*. Its opponents find significance in the fact that it is not described there as a revelation, merely as an 'official declaration'; and the Church itself admits that not all have accepted that ruling of 1890. Henry Smith told me: 'There are a few groups who do not accept the present leaders and their teachings on this matter. As rapidly as they can be found, they are excommunicated. Some are sincere in their beliefs and some are just immoral, using the plural marriage revelation as an excuse. How strong are they? There is no way of determining their membership because they have no public structure as we have. They have no temples, though undoubtedly there is some form of organization. I have heard of a small colony in Short Creek on the Mexico-Arizona border. It is a small group of buildings and a small chapel, but when I drove through it a while back I saw no more than fifteen or twenty houses. I doubt if there would be three hundred people in the community.'

I had heard reports of other rebels in Colorado City, for instance, on the Arizona-Utah border, and in Davis County, Utah. It was in Salt Lake City itself, however, that I met my first two supporters of plural marriage and I must say that both they and their wives were charming, straightforward people. They told me that there were more polygamists in the State capital than anywhere else, presumably because it is a fair-sized city and it is easier to keep a secret there than it would be in a rural district.

Currently neither of them is legally polygamist, though that, they assured me, was no fault of their own. The first, a well-built, cheerful civil servant, told me: 'I was born and raised in the Church and believed that the manifesto was a revelation until 1952. Then I was taken into the library one day by this man, who showed me newspaper stories about Mormons who had been found guilty of polygamy nine years and more after the manifesto. I studied the records and the documents and I became a convert. I was excommunicated in 1959. By that time my wife had eight children—five girls and two boys. She was completely against plural marriage. Then I met the girl who was to be my second wife and we were married in the autumn of 1962. My wife had begun divorce proceedings earlier, but it wasn't final until the following spring; so I actually had two wives for a few months.

'Now I have seven children by my second wife—four boys and three girls, the youngest only a few months old. They're the pride of my life and I hope to have at least fifty children, a hundred, if possible. If I had the wives, it would be easy, but finding a good woman, a woman who holds the same views as my second wife and myself, is difficult . . . as difficult as finding the Pearl of Great Price.'

I met his seven children by his second wife. They were charming, exceptionally handsome and obviously very happy. His home was comfortably furnished and his second wife was as happy as her children. I thought, however, of the financial burden and asked him how he managed to afford to keep two homes.

The question seemed to surprise him. He said: 'Afford it? I never consider that. To think whether I could afford another wife would be like asking myself whether I could afford another child. I'd never stop having children because I couldn't afford them and it's the same with plural marriage. I expect to have children as long as humanly possible and I know that the Lord will always provide.'

His wife beamed at him and said: 'The Lord will increase the man who increases his family.' Obviously she was one hundred per cent behind him in his ambition to marry again and again and again. I asked him, nevertheless, whether he felt there might be jealousy with plural wives.

'There is trouble in some cases,' he said, 'but it is rare. Good men who marry good women never have any trouble. The lustful man, however, will suffer. If he marries just for his personal pleasure and not because he wants to have children, he will fall, as sure as I'm sitting on this couch. I've heard good men say that they've had less trouble in plural marriage than they've had in monogamy because in monogamy, the woman tries to rule.'

'Do the children of your two wives ever meet?'

'They meet as often as my first wife allows,' he said. 'They get on very well together. As a matter of fact my eldest daughter works in the same office as my second wife and they are good friends. I'm sorry about my first wife divorcing me, of course, but the Church forced her hand. They told her they would excommunicate her, if she didn't get a divorce. They tried the same tactics with my second wife, but she told them: "He's the father of my children. He's the one I chose. It's a woman's right to choose the man she wants."

'We polygamists still consider ourselves Mormons, of course, even though we have been excommunicated. We meet in small groups, but we don't have a church. If we had a church, someone would probably destroy it. We meet in houses, but we don't have big congregations.'

'If you marry again,' I said, 'aren't you afraid that you may be arrested and jailed?'

'I've no fear of being put in jail,' he said. 'It would merely convince

me that I was right. I don't enjoy going to jail, but the threat of it
wouldn't stop me from marrying again. As a matter of fact I've been in
already, though not directly for polygamy. My first wife said that I
couldn't visit the children. So I told her I wouldn't give her any money.
I was sentenced to thirty days and she got a restraining order that I
wouldn't talk to the children about religion.

'Many have gone to jail. In 1944 they arrested fifty men and three
women and marched them handcuffed down the main street of Salt
Lake City. The trial lasted a long time and finally they put fifteen men
in prison, most of them from Salt Lake City. One was sent to prison for
twenty-two months and three others for three years. There's a man not
far from here who has spent six and a half years in a penitentiary and
his only crime was that he had three or four wives—I can't remember
the exact number. He went to jail twice and no other man has stayed
there longer since the Church was organized.

'They arrested five men in 1955. He was among them. If they get
him a third time, he'll get fifteen years, what they call life. I knew one of
the other men very well. He spent four years inside. A third man was
lucky. He had been in jail before, but that time a quirk of fate helped
him. They arrested the wrong woman—his first wife, who had done
nothing illegal in the eyes of the law. I think myself that the Lord had a
hand in it. Certainly I don't think that anyone could accuse those men
of marrying more than one wife for lust. They proved that they had
the courage of their convictions, that they were prepared to suffer for
their spiritual beliefs. Thousands of people, however, will wink at sin,
at adultery, but they won't stand for what we call righteousness. Yet
over the years 1,300 people have spent a combined total of five hundred
years in prison in defence of their right to marry more than once.
They've paid together over a million dollars in fines.'

'Who performs the marriage ceremony?' I asked. 'Surely the
Church makes that difficult?'

'That has been made possible by John Taylor, who was the third
President of the Church,' he told me. 'He was in prison with Joseph
Smith and his brother when they were killed and was shot five times
himself. In 1886 the Saviour appeared to him and reminded him that
the principle of plural marriage would never die. After that revelation,
he prophesied that the manifesto would be produced, but said that he
would have his arm and his tongue pulled out before he signed it. When
eventually it came, however, he was dead.

'He instructed a number of men to keep this principle alive. Before they died, he said, they were to ordain others who would perform plural marriage ceremonies. The last one he ordained was Joseph W. Musser in 1886 and he ordained the men I follow. The marriage, of course, should take place in the Temple, but in these circumstances it can be performed anywhere. Brigham Young taught that.'

My second witness in favour of plural marriage had only one wife and it was she who told me: 'Every night we go down on our knees and pray that the Lord will send along a good girl for him to marry.' He nodded in total agreement and said: 'If I become worthy I will have the privilege of other wives. I am praying and working for that day.

'There are many in this valley, you see, who are living in lust and sin—living a lie, in fact. They hunt for women and they date them and they carry on just as people outside the Church do, courting and so on which is outside the law of the gospel. They act as if they were single men despite the fact that they hold the priesthood in the Church.'

'What do you think of the manifesto?'

'When I was first converted to the Church seventeen years ago,' said his wife, 'I believed it. But I don't believe it any longer.'

Her husband said: 'I've studied extensively over the past five years with the aid of fasting and prayer in the hope that I would get a spiritual testimony that the manifesto was a revelation. The instruction which I got, however, was that it was not binding on the Church. President John Taylor, of course, said that it came from the lower regions, from Satan.'

'Where do you worship?'

'We have one little chapel,' he said. 'About fifty per cent of us are excommunicated, including my wife and myself. We stay together and we try to keep our mouths shut. I am very close to brothers who have ten or twelve wives and over sixty children. They can support those children more easily than men living in monogamy with only one, two or three children. They are good men, these polygamists, and the Lord blesses them with beautiful families. The purpose of having these children is to bring forth our seed and has nothing to do with gratifying the physical desires of our body. Anything which is a matter of pure sex is wrong.'

'Do the wives live under one roof?'

'Usually they don't,' he told me. 'Each sister has a right to her own home.'

'Do they get on well together?'

'If I am led by Lucifer,' he replied, 'the union obviously has not the blessing of the priesthood and so the families will live in contention and bickering. If, on the other hand, a man lives according to the laws, his family will be blessed. I have seen both sides.'

His wife added: 'I have never seen a people with a greater love and understanding than those who have had plural marriages. There is a fullness of heart and a proudness of mind.'

'Do you think plural marriage will ever be accepted by the country, by law?'

He shook his head and said: 'On the contrary, I think persecution will get worse. President McKay is a kind man, a tolerant man, and I do not think he wants to see us persecuted. When he dies, however, there may be a President with more harsh views. He could encourage the authorities to launch an all-out drive against us. We are prepared for that.'

The sincerity of these people is obvious, the depth of their conviction impressive. They are but a handful, of course, but there must be few members within the Church who have not had qualms about this issue, because it is one for which Saints of only a couple of generations ago fought and suffered. The question of race, which is another major subject of debate both within and without the Church, is different. The pioneers took it for granted that Negroes were inferior for at the time that attitude was general, not only in America, but throughout the white world. To them it seemed quite natural that God should withhold the priesthood from Negroes. A growing number of Saints today, however, are deeply concerned about this ruling, particularly in view of the fact that their leaders insist that it can be changed only by a revelation from God. The pioneers felt that they were being remarkably liberal, allowing Negroes to be members of the Church, to be baptized in it and confirmed—and they were, too, compared with some of the Churches in the Southern States today. Many a modern Mormon, however, feels guilty about the denial of the priesthood because to a Saint it is of vital, of eternal, importance. All male Mormons are expected to become lay priests because only thus can they achieve a state of exaltation in the Celestial Kingdom. Those who are not priests can enter the Kingdom, but only as servants. They cannot help in the task of producing souls. They cannot be Gods.

Why? In Salt Lake City I was given three reasons and none of them seemed to reflect the spirit which imbued Joseph Smith when he wrote the second of the Church's thirteen Articles of Faith, which, presumably, were inspired by God. It reads: 'We believe that men will be punished for their own sins and not for Adam's transgressions.' All three reasons for withholding the priesthood from Negroes stem from the transgressions of their ancestors; and I shall try to report them in chronological order.

The first reason dates back to pre-existence. God, I was given to understand, called the whole family together and announced His plan to make the earth and populate it. That started a discussion about who should return to heaven, how and why. Lucifer stepped forward and said, in effect; 'Leave it to me. I'll see that everyone gets back, though, mind you, I'll want the credit for it.'

Jesus then said: 'I think that we should give everyone the right to choose their own destiny, to prove themselves worthy. The praise, of course, Father, will be yours.'

With that, apparently, the ructions started. There was war in heaven. One-third of those present supported Lucifer. One-third supported Christ. The remaining third are said to have hung back a bit, not quite sure which side they should take. Eventually God, the Father, settled the issue by throwing Lucifer and his adherents out. Jesus and his followers were praised suitably, but those in the middle came in for some divine displeasure. They were, I suppose, what the pollsters of today would call the 'don't knows' and because they could not make up their minds on what seemed to the Divinity a perfectly simple issue, He punished them by making them black.

The second reason, as even casual Sunday school pupils will have guessed, probably, was the murder of Abel by Cain. For that dastardly act, God cursed him and put a mark on him so that all would know him for what he was. The mark, of course, was a black skin. To make matters worse, or perhaps I should say to explain the crime, Cain in the pre-existence was a 'don't know', according to some Mormon theologists, though personally I thought that he would have arrived on earth black, if that were the case.

The third reason involves Ham, the son of Noah. According to the Book of Genesis, he found his father lying drunk and naked. He ran and told his two brothers about it, treating the matter lightly, which certainly was unfair because his father was over six hundred years old at the time. His brothers showed more sympathy and covered Noah with a garment. When Noah awoke, he was so angry with Ham that he cursed him and made him a servant or, as Orson Hyde, an Apostle of the Mormon Church, said in 1845, 'put the curse of slavery on him'. He married a descendant of Cain, thus, according to John Taylor, third President of the Church, 'preserving the Negro lineage through the flood'. Why did God wish to preserve this lineage? Again the answer comes from John Taylor: 'So that the devil might be properly represented upon the Earth.'

It is true that attitudes have mellowed since John Taylor's day. Henry Smith, for instance, told me: 'We believe that some day Negroes will hold the priesthood, though President McKay says that it will not happen until a revelation comes from the Lord to permit that change in doctrine. An analogous situation, perhaps, is the issue of polygamy. Even the manifesto was not accepted until it came as a revelation of the Lord.

'The doctrine, of course, has nothing to do with the Negroes' rights in this life. The Church believes in civil rights as much as any other organization and has issued a statement to that effect. We believe that the Negro should be given equal opportunity on earth, but at the present moment he is not equal in heaven.'

He gave me a copy of the statement, which read:

During recent months, both in Salt Lake City and across the nation, considerable interest has been expressed in the position of the Church of Jesus Christ of Latter-day Saints on the matter of civil rights. We would like it to be known that there is in this Church no doctrine, belief or practice that is intended to deny the enjoyment of full civil rights by any person regardless of race, color or creed.

We say again, as we have said many times before, that we believe that all men are the children of the same God, and that it is a moral evil for any person or group of persons to deny any human being the right to gainful employment, to full educational opportunity, and to every privilege of citizenship, just as it is a moral evil to deny him the right to worship according to the dictates of his own conscience.

We have consistently and persistently upheld the Constitution of the United States, and as far as we are concerned this means upholding the constitutional rights of every citizen of the United States.

We call upon all men, everywhere, both within and outside the Church, to commit themselves to the establishment of full civil equality for all of God's children. Anything less than this defeats our high ideals of the brotherhood of man.

That statement was signed by Hugh B. Brown, First Counsellor of the First Presidency, which is encouraging because Wallace Turner, author of *The Mormon Establishment* and a highly respected member of the *New York Times* staff, wrote of him: 'Every scrap of information I've gathered about Mormons and Negroes points to Hugh Brown as the liberal voice at the top of the Church. I suspect that . . . he hoped the change was to come.'

Another liberal voice is that of Dr Sterling M. McMurrin, a Mormon doctor, who is Professor of Philosophy and Dean of the Graduate School at the University of Utah and a former United States Commissioner of Education. In a speech to the Salt Lake City Chapter of the National Association for the Advancement of Colored People, he made the following incisive points which, so far as I know, have not been answered yet by any responsible Mormon leader:

For any Church to deny full religious fellowship to an individual on grounds related essentially to his race or color is an almost unbelievable moral deficiency that deserves the most rigorous condemnation. For a Church that less than a century ago was aggressively committed to the achievement of social justice to have receded so far from the frontiers of social morality, while at the same time its political power and influence have materially increased, is nothing less than a major tragedy.

It is difficult to understand how people who are otherwise typically intelligent and moral can believe and defend such crude immoral nonsense, but it is nothing new for religion to be a perpetrator of both nonsense and immorality.

The main charge that must be leveled against the Church is that at a crucial moment in American and world history, when the movement towards equality of opportunity, the destruction of racial hatred and prejudice and the legal guarantee of civil rights are central issues in moral thought and action, it has persistently refused to raise its voice loud and clear, not only to its own people, but to the nation and the world in defence and advocacy of principles and policies that are obviously essential to the achievement of social righteousness and justice. It has failed to use its considerable influence and economic and political power, in the State of Utah its overwhelming political influence and power, to further the cause of justice for Negroes and other minorities. I find this entirely reprehensible, as I believe that the destruction of injustice and the establishment of justice are a primary moral responsibility of any church.

In its early decades the Mormon Church was alive with social, moral reform . . . Now it is quiescent and conservative and has lost much of its capacity to dream new dreams and chart new paths. It honors its prophets and pioneers of the past, but has lost the art of prophecy and pioneering for the future.

He ends on a note of sombre optimism;

I firmly believe that the time will come when the Mormon people for the most part have abandoned their crude superstitions about Negroes—their children will force them to—and when the Church will have a new vision of universal brotherhood and social justice. When that time comes, those who can remember will remember with sadness and moral embarrassment the day when their Church could have done great things to hasten the achievement of the good society, but failed. I am confident that such a day will come, but I am one of the disenchanted and am now quite sure that when it comes, I won't be around.

There are, unfortunately, other voices. Mark E. Petersen, one of the Twelve Apostles, is quoted as saying: 'I think the Lord segregated the Negro and who is man to change that segregation?' Ezra Taft Benson, a former Agriculture Secretary in the Government, seems to have given a fine impersonation of that well-known comedian, Billy James Hargis, for the Mormon-owned *Deseret News* reported him as saying in 1963: 'Civil rights legislation . . . is part of the pattern for the Communist take-over of America.' He could become President of the Church. The Lord could tell him that Negroes must be offered the priesthood, which, I imagine, would surprise him.

That, however, does not appear likely, despite several references in *Doctrine and Covenants* to the equality of man. Writing in the *New York Times* of the possibility of change, Wallace Turner, who has studied the church so thoroughly, mirrored the mood of Dr McMurrin. He wrote:

David O. McKay is the most liberal Latter-day Saints President in sight for a long time to come. Yet he made it plain in 1964 that he felt it unlikely that any revelation would come that would lift from Negroes their historic disability in LDS doctrine and practice. He was in Oakland, California, in November, 1964 . . . then the question was asked directly in the proper words to discover whether the prophet, seer and chief revelator thought doctrine on Negroes would be changed to allow them to hold the priesthood. He said: 'Not while you and I are here.'

Yet orthodox Saints, snug in the protective clothing of their faith, still react with injured surprise when the more liberal elements greet cynically those brave words of Hugh B. Brown on civil rights. They do not discriminate on earth, they say, only in heaven and then it is Lucifer's fault, or Cain's fault, or Ham's fault, or Ham's black wife's fault, or God's fault. This argument, I feel, might carry more weight, however, if they were to back these words with actions, if, for instance, they were to open their bishop's storehouse to the starving in the Southern States, for that, surely, is an emergency worthy of their attention.

There are other matters which cause some uneasiness among Mormons and bewilderment among non-Mormons. One of them is Joseph's translation of the papyri which became the Book of Abraham. Leading Egyptologists who have examined facsimiles of these papyri have dismissed them as ordinary funeral documents, which had little to do with Abraham and were found in thousands of Egyptian graves. Even Mormon experts have their doubts about them. One of them, Dee Jay Nelson, an international authority, is reported as saying: 'I have been swamped lately by letters and long-distance telephone calls from troubled people. Almost every one of them asks if I really believe that the Book of Abraham is untrue and each seems almost pleadingly eager for me to defend it. To each I have had to say that I do not believe it.'

To such criticism, Dr Hugh Nibley, a faculty member of the Church's Brigham Young University, replied: 'Today nobody claims that Joseph Smith got his information through ordinary scholarly channels.'

Another matter of some embarrassment to the more cautious Church leaders is the enthusiasm with which some members claim that the Book of Mormon is being borne out by archaeological research. It has been suggested, indeed, that non-Mormon archaeologists have used it as a guide and The Bureau of American Ethnology of the Smithsonian Institution in Washington has received so many inquiries on that point that they have prepared a statement for the benefit of all future callers. It stresses that the Institution has never used the Book of Mormon in any way as a scientific guide and adds: 'Smithsonian archaeologists see no connection between the archaeology of the New World and the sub-ject-matter of the book. The physical type of the American Indian is basically Mongoloid, being most closely related to that of the peoples of eastern, central and north-eastern Asia . . . Extensive archaeological researches in Southern Mexico and Central America clearly indicate that the civilizations of these regions developed locally from simple beginnings without the aid of outside stimulus . . . We know of no authentic cases of ancient Egyptian or Hebrew writings having been found in the New World. Reports of findings of Egyptian influence in the Mexican and Central American areas have been published in news-papers and magazines from time to time, but thus far no reputable

Egyptologist has been able to discover any relationship between Mexican remains and those in Egypt.' In a personal letter to an inquirer, William C. Sturtevant, Acting Director of the Institution, wrote: 'No present reputable scientific ethnologist or archaeologist holds that any part of the Indians may have come from Jewish descent. All reputable archaeological work, recent and other, detracts from the "Jewish origin" theory. There is no known family resemblance between Hebrew or Egyptian or any other language of western Asia, Europe and Africa on the one hand and any aboriginal New World language.'

Even Mormon archaeologists and anthropologists urge caution among their co-religionists who make over-extravagant claims about scientific backing for the Book. Dr Ross T. Christensen of the Saints' Brigham Young University, wrote in the Newsletter of the University Archaeological Society: 'The statement that the Book of Mormon has already been proved by archaeology is misleading. The truth of the matter is that we are only now beginning to see even the outlines of the archaeological time periods which could compare with those of the Book of Mormon. How, then, can the matter have been settled once and for all? That such an idea could exist indicates the ignorance of many of our people with regard to what is going on in the historical and anthropological sciences.'

The Mormon attitudes not only to alcohol and tobacco, but to tea, coffee and even Coca cola also can be the cause of mild embarrassment to some members. According to *The Word of Wisdom*, given to Joseph Smith in revelation, the Lord advised strongly against wine, strong drink, tobacco and hot drinks. According to Fawn Brodie, this revelation was stimulated by Emma Smith, who complained bitterly about the condition of the room above her kitchen after Joseph and his Elders had been meeting there. 'The first thing they did,' Emma said, 'was to light their pipes and, while smoking, talk about the great things of the kingdom and spit all over the floor.'

At first *The Word of Wisdom* was accepted merely as good advice. In 1836, however, total abstinence became obligatory for all Saints and eventually tea, coffee and tobacco also became the mark of the un-righteous. In later years 'coke' was frowned upon because it had a caffeine content. Hot drinks were bad, according to the revelation, because the Lord said they 'are not for the body or the belly'. He added that flesh of beasts and of the fowls in the air should be used only sparingly—'only in times of winter, or of cold or famine'—but that last

admonishment is not followed very rigorously by the average Mormon
today.

On drink, however, the Church was and is adamant. Yet Joseph
Smith himself did not take the regulations too seriously. Even after the
Church had made its ruling in 1836, he continued to enjoy wine, though
for the Communion service, water had been substituted. In those days,
few questioned his occasional lapses, some indeed welcoming his cheerful acceptance of human frailty; but today there is less tolerance. One
ex-Mormon told me: 'When I was a child, I believed that anyone who
was a non-Mormon smoked and drank. I was brought up feeling
superior to others, as if we had invented morality.'

Certainly the rigid rules are not ignored by the non-Mormon world.
When United Airlines were advertising a Red Carpet service to the
Mormon Pavilion at the New York World's Fair, they changed their
copy text to avoid offence. The advertisement for non-Mormons read:
'Welcome aboard! We'll have the coffee waiting and a delicious breakfast, too.' For the Saints, it read: 'Welcome aboard! We'll have a
delicious breakfast waiting for you.'

The Saints, in fact, are winning, despite their problems, big or small.
More and more dedicated young missionaries are fanning out through
five continents, though in Africa they confine their attentions to the
white South Africans. Every minute of their lives is dominated by their
faith, because this is not a Sundays-only religion. They even carry a book
which leads them through every step from the moment they first knock
on a door until a conversion is completed. I have a copy and I must say
that it reads rather like the manual of an encyclopaedia salesman. Based
on the experiences of a hypothetical Elder A and Elder B, it contains
such phrases as: 'Here Elder B breaks in spontaneously . . .;' 'Elder A
gives a "sparkling preview" of the Godhead Lesson;' 'As Elder B finishes
this sentence, he is already getting down on his knees, taking it for
granted that the Bradys will follow suit. They will;' 'Elder A, bubbling
with enthusiasm, pulls out his visual aid cards;' 'Elder B breaks in
naturally;' 'This part of the discussion by Elder B should be given in a
spiritual manner and with a reverent, natural enthusiasm,' and 'It would
be well for Elder B to get eye-to-eye contact, remembering that the
opportunity to bear this testimony is one of the prime objects of the
lesson plan.'

Scattered through the texts are catchy sales phrases to guide the
missionaries: 'Smile and be cheerful! They'll want you to return!' 'It is

unwise to become involved in a needless discussion about the Holy
Ghost. Keep it plain and positive;' 'Our time is short. Don't wear out
our welcome. Get to the point. Don't stray from the plan. And be
cheerful!' 'Smile. Keep it simple, enthusiastic and keep to the plan. It's
faster that way. They should be in a cheerful, spiritual mood when we
leave.'

They keep it simple. There is no mention of the history of polygamy,
no mention of Negroes and the priesthood, no mention until late in the
book of tithing—'The Lord hasn't asked us to give Him all we have,
but He has asked us to return only a small part of what He has given us.
Is that too much for the Lord to ask?' They stick to the plan and, while
cynics may smile, it works. The Church is growing so fast, in fact, that
there is no mathematical argument to refute its leaders' claim that by
the year 2,000 it will have 10,000,000 members.

12: THE END OF THE WORLD IS NIGH

THE average housewife regards the Jehovah's Witnesses as a serious threat to domestic time and motion. They arrive on her doorstep unannounced, strangle all her excuses at birth and pummel her with prophecies about the hereafter, while she is battling to cope with the here now. If all the hot dinners reported to have been spoiled in that fashion were laid plate to plate, they might not stretch to eternity, but they would make a massive burnt offering.

Such a judgement, however, is facile, moulded, perhaps, by the wrath of hungry husbands. The Witnesses merely want to save the world before it ends in a few years' time, a task which they regard as more important than washing dishes, wiping tiny noses or stewing steak. I must say, too, that the rank and file of this much-abused movement are gregarious, cheerful and happy people, saddened only by the fact that so few seem to accept the importance of the simple message they bear.

Fortuitously for me, they met in London for their international assembly as I began my research for this book; and so for a couple of days I swam in a sea of over 82,000 of them. The gathering was held in Wembley Stadium, better known for less spiritual activities, and while I was there I was treated with the utmost kindness, gentle courtesy and genuine friendliness by every Witness I met. They answered my questions with a buoyant confidence, making no attempt to force their views into my notebook. Though they are strict non-smokers, they did not frown when I produced a cigarette, and they merely asked me gently not to smoke while I was in the arena itself, for the proceedings there, they said, were of a religious nature. That may seem a small point, but it showed a tolerance which was missing later, when I interviewed other people of other persuasions and equally rigid views on the sin of nicotine. Naturally I respected their wishes and so found myself gazing down on the famous turf without a cigarette in my hand, an experience unique for me and, I imagine, for Wembley, too.

All my early impressions of the Witnesses at that gathering, indeed, were pleasant. They had come from all parts of the world. Pigmentation meant nothing, for here were a people thoroughly and naturally integregated, calling each other brother or sister and meaning it. It was only when I entered the arena to hear their President, Nathan H. Knorr, deliver his address that a touch of winter entered the holiday atmosphere.

Facing out on to the board that in different circumstances carried the names of runners in greyhound races, he belted his audience with slabs of the Old Testament, haranguing them about their responsibilities, their duties, their need for even greater loyalty to God. They loved it and they applauded it.

Then, with an intolerance so splendidly lacking outside the arena, he swung into action against the churches. 'Adultery, homosexuality and fornication are condemned by God,' he thundered. 'Yet a Presbyterian Minister is advocating sex outside marriage as a positive good . . . and in Holland two men were married by a Roman Catholic priest!' Here there was more applause and an even greater ovation greeted the commercial which followed: 'We are pleased to announce the release of a new book *Is The Bible Really the Word of God?* You can get four copies for $1.08.' Momentarily puzzled about what made the spectators clap so wildly and so indiscriminately, I reached for a cigarette and left the arena.

The answer was simple. Nathan Knorr, who, appropriately enough, I suppose, was born in Bethlehem, Pennsylvania, in 1905, was their President and could do little wrong. The churches had turned away from the Bible and could do little good. Books, magazines, pamphlets and tracts were the main weapons in the battle the Witnesses were fighting all over the world and new additions to the armoury were always welcome. To give some idea of their fire-power, their 1970 Year Book reports that in 1969, their printing presses at their Brooklyn head-quarters produced 268,324,140 Bibles, books, booklets, magazines, convention reports, advertising leaflets, calendars, tracts and miscellaneous printed items, using 15,800 tons of paper in the process, enough, probably, to wrap up the world and post it to Paradise.

All those billions of words, of course, would lose much of their power if the men distributing them were not so thoroughly dedicated, willing to face not only snubs and often humiliation, but sometimes physical punishment. That dedication is all the more remarkable because, like the Mormons, their doctrine has been dented on a number of occasions by ugly, though undeniable, facts and is regarded by many as rather bizarre. They believe, for instance, that the world, as we know it, will end very soon, probably in the mid-1970s. Armageddon will bring appalling destruction and all agencies of imperfect man—his governments, his armies, even Mayor Richard J. Daley in Chicago—will disappear. All but the very wicked will be resurrected and a world government, which may include such veteran personalities as Daniel, of lion's den fame, will take over under guidance from heaven.

Of all the people who ever lived, 144,000 will go to heaven, where they will be close associates of God. The rest will remain to face one more test, for, as the millennium after Armageddon draws to its close, Satan will be set among earthlings again. Those who succumb to him will be destroyed. The remainder will have earned 'a life of eternity in perfection on Earth'. There is no hell, just a first death and second death. The first is the grave from which the vast majority will be resurrected. The second is annihilation for those who intelligently and persistently have disobeyed God's laws. Adam, I was told, will not be resurrected, for, as a perfect man, he knew what he was doing and certainly could blame nobody else. Judas has not much hope, either. 'God created people for a purpose,' I was told. 'If they don't fulfil that purpose, He just disposes of them. So the world will be full of righteous people.'

To minds unschooled in the ways of the Witnesses, the practical application of these theories would seem to involve immense physical problems. Already there is considerable concern—and rightly so—about population explosions. If those who have lived before come back, where are we going to put them? The Witnesses, however, have the answers, as I discovered when I called at their headquarters in Brooklyn and spoke with their spokesman there, Ulysses V. Glass.

'There will be no trouble finding space for everybody,' he assured me. 'You could take every single person who ever lived and fit them into the State of Texas.* Then there are the unclaimed territories of South America and Africa. Anyway, we don't know what Jehovah God will do after Armageddon. There is every indication that the world changed at the time of the flood, that vast oceans came. It is equally possible that vast tracts of land will appear.'

'Will procreation continue?' I asked. 'Is that not a worry?'

'It probably will go on in a very limited way among those who survive, but it will cease eventually,' he told me. 'Adam and Eve, remember, were told merely to fill the Earth, not to continue indefinitely.' Later in London another spokesman added an exp'anatory addendum to that. He said: 'You will have younger people surviving anyway and in the nature of things they will have families.'

How about the 144,000? Ulysses V. Glass told me: 'We feel the number

* I might have known those Texans would get in on the act!

may have been completed already, though some may have been unfaithful and will have been replaced. They are taken from among men and women who work on earth and that work must be done in integrity. If they have committed some act of immorality and have not repented, they will have lost out, like Judas.'

How do they know how many places have been filled? In London I was told: 'Every year we have what we call the Lord's memorial supper. Only those who have been chosen for heaven partake of the symbolic loaf and wine. In 1948 376,393 attended the supper and 25,395 partook. In 1968, 2,719,860 attended and only 10,368 partook. We call them the anointed remnant and, as they die on this earth, their numbers decrease at the supper.'

How do people know they have been chosen? 'It is a personal conviction,' I was told. 'It is something that cannot be proved. A man cannot prove, for instance, that he loves his wife. He just knows it. We say that God's holy spirit is working in their minds.'

I did not ask any Witnesses whether they had been chosen, for I felt, indeed, that it would be like asking a man whether he loved his wife, probing into his private affairs. I did raise the question, however, of whether personal mistakes could be made and I was told: 'It is possible, but unlikely. Always there is close self-scrutiny. It would be very strange, for instance, if a person were to claim that he was anointed, when he knew his life was not in full accord with the fundamental Bible principles. Jehovah God, however, judges how far a person is genuinely mistaken and how far he has acted from wrong motives. Precisely why they are chosen, of course, we do not know.'

What will their heavenly lives be like? Ulysses V. Glass told me: 'Heavenly life is beyond man's conception. Jehovah God is represented as having white hair, but we know that he is not like a man. Man could not look at Him. We can't even look at an atomic explosion and Jehovah God is the source of all power. The Scriptures indicate that He has a central place and gathered around him will be the 144,000 and certain exalted spirit creatures with special responsibility. These creatures have form of some sort, identity and personality, but what form is impossible to say. The 144,000 are known as Jehovah God's Little Flock and those who survive on Earth after Armageddon are known as "The Great Crowd".'

Whether destined to be members of the 'Little Flock' or 'The Great Crowd'—nicknamed the Jonadabs—Witnesses have strict rules which ensure that they will never make the mistake of confusing divine authority with that wielded by man. They do not vote, for they have elected to serve God alone. They do not stand up for any national anthem or salute any flag, for these are but earthly symbols and to honour them would verge on idolatry. They will not serve in any army, for there is only one just cause and that is the cause of the Lord. Inevitably these beliefs, to which they adhere firmly, have got them into serious trouble in most parts of the world from Paris to Pittsburgh to Peking, from New York to Newcastle to Novosibirsk. Thousands of Witnesses have been imprisoned throughout their history and throughout the world. More than six thousand died in Nazi concentration camps.

Their courage and dedication is seen by many as misguided; but to others it is obviously an inspiration, for the number of Witnesses has grown rapidly since the organization was founded in 1870. Forty years ago membership throughout the world was less than 100,000. By 1958 it was about 1,500,000. By 1969 it was over 2,700,000; and that remarkable expansion has happened despite shatteringly bad publicity, some of it true, some of it false and a fair share of it concerning the movement's founder, Charles Taze Russell, who was born in Pittsburgh to Scottish-Irish parents in 1852 and died sixty-four years later.

Unlike Joseph Smith, he had no truck with heavenly visitations or fireside chats with God, preferring to seek all the truth he needed in the Bible. Again unlike Joseph Smith, he was wealthy and a more than competent businessman. His father ran a draper's store, which was in a modest enough way until young Charles went into partnership with him at the age of fifteen. By the time the lad was in his early twenties, he had helped to expand it into a chain of stores. Had he stayed in business, he probably would have become a national tycoon, for, when he sold his business interests to devote all his time to religion, he netted a quarter of a million dollars. Before he died, he had founded the Witnesses' publishing house, which was to become the largest of its kind in the world; moved his headquarters from Pittsburgh to Brooklyn, founded branches not only throughout the United States, but in Britain, too, toured the world many times and made a film, *The Photo-Drama of Creation*, at a cost of $300,000 and at a time when many moguls in the entertainment world were dismissing movies as a passing fad. To spread the word, he had travelled over a million miles, preached more than 30,000 sermons, written millions of words and dictated letters at the rate of a thousand a month.

The quality of these achievements has been and remains the subject of vociferous debate, but its quantity cannot be denied. It had made little impression, however, on his native Pittsburgh, which scarcely mentions him in its official records, perhaps because of the scandalous stories which buzzed around his head. It has been alleged, too, that the Witnesses themselves have published no biography of him for the same reason, but they deny that story, stating: 'Were we to give the honour and credit to Pastor Russell, we would be saying that the works and success were his; but Jehovah's Witnesses believe that it is God's spirit that guides and directs His people.'

It is inevitable, of course, that fact and fiction, slander and truth, should wash around the heads of powerful personalities, as Joseph Smith would be the first to confirm if he were still around. I found myself wading through both while studying the Witnesses and therefore I sought out Ulysses V. Glass in an effort to disentangle one from the other.

First I raised the question of his scholarship, which had been disputed, for he went to school for only seven years. 'Pastor Russell,' I said, 'is reported to have written extensively about the correct meaning of various Greek and Hebrew words in the Scriptures, yet he spoke neither language. Is that true?'

'He read extensively about Greek and Hebrew words,' said Ulysses V. Glass, 'but he spoke no Greek or Hebrew. He studied many Bibles, however, and relied on dictionaries and concordances.'

'It is alleged,' I said, 'that he offered for sale what he called "Miracle Wheat", saying that it gave five times the yield of ordinary wheat, and charged customers $60 a bushel or a dollar a pound. It is said, too, that the Department of Agriculture tested it and found its yield to be only average; that he sued for libel when that charge was published, lost and had to refund the money to all buyers.'

'Actually Pastor Russell was not selling the wheat,' explained Ulysses V. Glass. 'It was donated to the organization by people who wished to further the work. Any money received for it was for that purpose and it was advertised in one of our publications. As far as misrepresentation is concerned, I have seen evidence that representatives of the Department of Agriculture made that claim about its high yield and actually sold it themselves.'

'He was accused, also, of sponsoring a cancer cure which analysis showed to be nothing but a caustic paste of zinc chloride, which was not only useless, but could be positively harmful.'

'There was something about that in one of our magazines, *The Watch Tower*,' he told me, 'but so far as I know it was never offered for sale.'

I then broached an even more delicate subject. According to some biographies I had read, the Pastor had not been free entirely from the sins of the flesh. One quoted him as saying with a high degree of poetry: 'I'm like a jellyfish . . . I float here and I float there. I touch this one and that one and if one responds, I take her to me and, if not, I float to others . . .' Another section stated: 'His course of conduct towards his wife evidences such insistent egotism and extravagant self-praise that . . . it would render the life of any sensitive Christian woman an intolerable burden.' Certainly nobody disputed the fact that they had had their troubles and had separated.

When I asked Ulysses V. Glass about domestic upheavals, he said: 'There was a court case and the verdict went against him. He was very harshly treated, but then even Jesus was accused of being a glutton and a wine bibber. She never accused him of being unfaithful. In fact, when she was questioned, she said that she did not believe her husband was guilty of infidelity.'

That was confirmed in *Jehovah's Witnesses in the Divine Purpose*, a book given to me by Ulysses V. Glass and which for the sake of tidiness will be called hereinafter *The Divine Purpose*. The author's name is not given, but it tells with the obvious authority of the organization how Mrs Russell, a brilliant, well-educated woman, had been lecturing on her husband's behalf with such success that she sought a stronger voice in the direction of *The Watch Tower*, of which she was Associate Editor. Simultaneously she was a director, secretary and treasurer of the Watch Tower Tract Society,* the corporation which controlled the affairs of the Witnesses and was, therefore, quite a power around the place. That power, however, was curtailed abruptly in 1893 and of that event the author of *The Divine Purpose* wrote:

When Mrs Russell realized that no article of hers would be accepted for publication unless it was consistent with the Scriptural views expressed in *The Watch Tower*, she became greatly disturbed and her growing resentment led her

* Now the Watch Tower Bible and Tract Society.

eventually to sever her relationship with the Society and also with her husband. This forced Russell to provide a separate home for her, which he did, providing financially for her support.

Years later, in 1906, after due court proceedings, her separation was declared legal and she was awarded a court settlement against Russell for several thousand dollars. Because of certain statements made in this trial, opposers of Pastor Russell have endeavored ever since to make it appear that he was an immoral man and hence not qualified for the position which he had now attained in the religious field. However the court record is clear that such charges are false. Reporting on this point later, it was stated: 'That Mrs Russell herself did not believe and never has believed that her husband was guilty of immoral conduct is shown by the (court) record in this case where her own counsel (on page 10) asked Mrs Russell this question: "You don't mean that your husband was guilty of adultery?" Ans: "No".'

The person who delved into that court report and who is quoted by the author of *The Divine Purpose* was Joseph Franklin Rutherford, Russell's successor as President. The quotation crops up in a book which he wrote under the title, *A Great Battle in the Ecclesiastical Heavens*, though whether the case of Russell *v.* Russell was part of that battle I do not know, for I have not read it. I was surprised to note, however, that Joseph Franklin Rutherford, an eminent Supreme Court lawyer and one-time District Judge, seemed to have fallen for the old illogicality that all mammals are whales because all whales are mammals. All adultery is immorality, but, as any jellyfish will tell you, all immorality is not adultery.

Whether Pastor Russell was pristine pure or a lascivious lecher in private, however, should have little bearing on his public and professional abilities as a theologian. In that region he ran into seas almost as rough as those which for one reason or another, obviously swirled around his homestead; and the elements at the heart of the storm were not of minor importance, either, because they concerned the end of the world. According to *The Divine Purpose*, he preached a sermon in 1881 about 'the blessings of the Kingdom and pictured the happy conditions that would be brought about by Christ's thousand-year reign'. It proved a popular theme and, recording this encouraging public reaction, the account goes on: 'It was necessary for him to go deeper into this matter and talk to them about the time that these things would take place. This he did, pointing to 1914.'

He was a courageous man, for in fact he was forecasting that the world, as it was known then, would end on that date, with Armageddon and that Christ's millennium would begin. Since then, for fairly obvious reasons, the Witnesses have tried to hedge his bet retrospectively for him and in *The Divine Purpose* he is quoted as saying in 1912: 'There surely is room for slight differences of opinion on this subject and it behoves us to grant each other the widest latitude.' That, however, was no more than a mild saver and it was nullified somewhat by the Pastor himself, for he went on to say that he had interpreted what the Scriptures had to say on the matter and the prophecies therein still read the same to him.

Certainly there was an upheaval in 1914, a world war, indeed, but no Armageddon, no 'happy conditions that would be brought about by Christ's thousand-year reign'. When I raised that point with the patient Ulysses V. Glass, he remained as loyal as possible to his past-President, but admitted with generous candour that mistakes had been made. He told me: 'We now believe that God's Kingdom was set up in heaven in 1914 and that this was the beginning of the end of the world as we know it. We had thought that it would carry on into Armageddon and that was the mistake we made. It was due to lack of clarification of prophecy. We now realize that all systems on earth were not to end at that time. We see many things now that make it clear that other things had to happen first. We telescoped too much time. We still believe the same things about 1914 as we always did, but the things which we expected in 1914 didn't happen as we thought they would. We expected more to happen immediately after 1914.'

My thimbleful of Christian theology had left me with the impression that Jesus had become King after the resurrection and I was glad to learn from expert Witnesses later that many others, who should know better, shared my view of the teachings on that point. Pastor Russell and his followers disagreed, however. They maintained, and their successors still maintain, that Jesus had to wait until God saw fit to establish the Kingdom or, as a London spokesman of the Witnesses put it, until 'He turned His attention to earthly matters and decided that it was time for something to be done about them'. He added: 'Things have got much worse since 1914. This is a consequence of the setting up of the King-dom. When it happened, the devil and all his angels were thrown out of heaven and came to earth. Satan, remember, was the angel who turned himself into a devil. It is generally assumed that he was turned out of heaven immediately, but the Bible doesn't say that. He couldn't have been in hell because there is no hell.'

If you are having difficulty with that argument, do not worry. I have seen Witnesses trumping each other with text after text, while they have debated it. One fact which stands out clearly, however, is that Pastor Russell boobed, which is no great disgrace because he never claimed to be infallible. Nevertheless, it should have made him a little more cagey the next time he felt a prophecy coming on, but unfortunately the experience seems to have taught him little. Some time afterwards he went even further, bringing forth an even more startling prediction and backing it with the hard cash of the Watch Tower Tract Society. He announced that the Princes of the Old Testament, Abel, Abraham, Noah, Isaac, Jacob and David, were coming to live on earth—in San Diego, California, to be geographically precise—and gave instructions that a mansion should be acquired so that they could live in a style which suited their station. The Society officials did as they were bid and the house was named 'The House of Princes'. Pastor Russell lived in it himself for a while and was quoted as saying: 'I've landscaped the place with palms and olive trees so that King David and these Princes of the Universe will feel at home.' It was said that he had the deeds made out in the names of the Princes, though I doubt, somehow, whether Californian law officers would have accepted that. When I asked Ulysses V. Glass about the affair, he said: 'It is true that the President anticipated the arrival of the prophets. He was wrong.'

Russell, I suppose, could be excused for having a second fling at the future after what generous friends might call a near miss over 1914. When he was so wildly off target over 1925, however, I would have thought that the Witnesses would have kept their dates to themselves and stuck to the safer, if less spectacular, line about the end of the world being nigh; but not a bit of it. Like amateur gamblers, playing it double or quits, they had yet another throw. According to two books written by ex-Witnesses, the new date for Armageddon is 1975. Headquarters staff in Brooklyn refuse to be quite as precise as that, but nevertheless they stick their collective necks out far enough to receive a woeful belt from the chopper if they come unstuck for a third time. Ulysses V. Glass told me cautiously: 'We are not predicting Armageddon in 1975. The Bible shows, however, that it will mark the end of man's 6,000 years on earth, dating from Adam. There could be an error of calculation in chronology, but still we feel that it will be in the mid-seventies, though here again, of course, we could be wrong. Nevertheless, our calculations show that by the mid-seventies man will have been on earth for 6,000 years. It is significant that God made the earth in six days. Jesus still has 1,000 years of peaceful reign to come. So, if man has lived 6,000 years and the time of his reign is very near, it would seem likely that it would begin then.'

At the Wembley Stadium gathering, I was handed a statement which was more positive. It read: 'Re-checking Bible chronology reveals that six millenniums of mankind's life on earth will end in the mid-seventies. Thus the seventh millennium from man's creation by Jehovah God will begin within less than ten years. This statement of fact also identifies Jehovah's Witnesses today, doesn't it? The Bible tells us that this coming thousand years will be a peaceful time for this earth and its inhabitants. A time of rest from all warfare and violence. A time when all weapons of warfare will be beaten into implements of peace, used in cultivating this earth. Indeed the entire earth will be cultivated into an everlasting paradise filled with liberated, perfect humans.'

That statement made no reference to Armageddon, to the horror before the peace. Ulysses V. Glass told me, however: 'We tell people that the world is going to die, just as Noah told them.' A London spokesman said: 'The Bible speaks of Armageddon as a terrible time of destruction, a great tribulation such as the world has not known since it was made.' *The Watch Tower* warned: 'Make no mistake by treating this war as a light or trivial thing. Satan will use every conceivable method to destroy the remnant of Zion . . .'

Altogether the picture painted of Armageddon by the Witnesses, particularly by some of those who call from house to house, is calculated to horrify those who hear it for the first time and believe it. The Witnesses, therefore, bear a grave responsibility and none of those to whom I spoke seemed to realize it. They feel confident about their own future, but not all have their faith. For that reason their horrific tales of the fate of the world have brought misery to a number of families.

On 22 November 1968, for instance, the *Daily Mail* reported:

A wife was driven round the bend by her husband's predictions that the end of the world was nigh, a Judge said yesterday.

Three or four times a week he told her everyone would perish unless they became members of the Jehovah's Witnesses. His wife, 32-year-old Adrienne Locke, was not a Jehovah's Witness, but a Girl Guide mistress. Before she went to meetings her husband warned her not to salute the flag because this amounted to idolatry. He disapproved of his family celebrating birthdays, Christmas, Easter and Guy Fawkes in the traditional ways.

It all added up to cruelty, said Mrs Justice Lane in the Divorce Court in London. She granted Mrs Locke of Malden Road, Staplehurst, Kent, a decree nisi against her 36-year-old husband, Roger.

The Judge said the couple were happy for the first year of their marriage. Then Mr Locke joined the sect and gradually his beliefs ruined his wife's health and wrecked the marriage.

He told her that the world was going to end in five years. Only 144,000 Jehovah's Witnesses would be saved. The rest of the world—the goats—would meet their end in utter destruction.

Mrs Locke did not believe his predictions, said the Judge, but when he pointed to earthquakes, train crashes and disasters such as Aberfan, she began to get unnerved.

Her biggest worry was her husband's refusal to consent to a blood transfusion, should either of their children ever need one.

Although he did not expressly forbid his family to celebrate Christmas, he managed to spoil their enjoyment of it. He refused to let his children be baptized in the Church of England faith and was sarcastic about his wife's religious beliefs. He turned religious TV programmes off, stopped his children singing carols at school and told his son that the religion he was being taught at school was wrong.

At first his wife tried to share his beliefs, but her reason revolted against some of them. She changed from being a healthy, light-hearted woman into someone who was worried, depressed and unhappy and unable to cope with life.

In 1966, after nine years of marriage, she left home with her children. Mr Locke wrote, saying: 'I don't understand why you've gone.' Even now Mr Locke of Surrender Road, Staplehurst, wanted her back.

On 22 July 1969, the *Daily Mirror* reported:

The Shepperd family was a happy one—until the day a Jehovah's Witness called. His preaching split the family, said Mr Justice Stirling in the Divorce Court.

John Shepperd began telling his three small children that they had only ten years to live. He told them that the day of Armageddon would come within that time and that the 'angels will destroy the earth'.

He was 44. His 38-year-old wife stood up to him and there was, said Mr Justice Stirling, a head-on clash. Her husband's fanaticism led to other rows. Again and again his wife told him that the Witnesses' beliefs were nonsense, but he refused to listen to her and in 1964 she warned him that he was breaking up the family. She warned him again in 1966, again in 1967, again in 1968.

He granted Mrs Shepperd of Chestnut Copse, Oxted, Surrey, a decree for cruelty, although Mr Shepperd of the same address denied it.

The Judge said: 'From the time he was indoctrinated I consider he was guilty of infamous conduct. If it had continued indefinitely, there would have been a real danger to Mrs Shepperd's health.'

They were married for nine years.

On a B.B.C. television programme in August 1969 about the Witnesses, called Until Armageddon', a wife told Esther Rantzen, the reporter who did much of the research:

My husband is not the same man I married . . . Since becoming a Witness, he keeps seeing signs in the newspapers, keeps talking about Armageddon . . . 'There's been an earthquake in Peru. That's a sign! And there's another one . . . a plane crash!' It was frightening the children . . . The literature had quite frightful pictures of houses and buildings toppling down. He often came off the train and went straight to a meeting. Then there were meetings at each other's houses. He was like a lodger and I was like the landlady . . . Then there was the question of their opposition to blood transfusion . . . A child or a mother can die through lack of it and all the family stand around and say: 'Good old Mum! She's dying for Jehovah.' I told my husband I was considering a divorce and all he said was: 'I've got to go to a meeting . . .'

On 20 April 1967 the *Daily Telegraph* reported:

A happily married mother of three killed herself after developing a 'religious obsession', following repeated visits to her home by Jehovah's Witnesses, Mr James Bullin, the Isle of Wight Coroner, said yesterday. Mrs Sylvia Adams, 26, of Warwick Place, Leamington Spa, threw herself under a train near Sandown on Sunday.

In her pocket was a note written in religious terms. Her husband, Mr John Adams, told the inquest at Ryde that he persuaded her to break with the Witnesses, but they gave her a *Watch Tower* leaflet, foretelling the end of the world and she became 'frightened and brooded', developed insomnia and lost weight.

On 2 July 1969 the *Daily Mail* reported:

Mrs Alice Couch, suffering from depression, was told by two Jehovah's Witnesses that the world would end in eight years, an inquest heard yesterday.

Next day Mrs Couch, 56, was found dead in bed from an overdose of drugs.

Her son, Mr John Couch, told the inquest at Hammersmith, London, W., that his mother had been living with his grandmother—her mother—in Myrtle Road, Hammersmith, since her husband died last year.

She had been very depressed and had a lot of setbacks, but finally seemed to be improving. Then, when the Jehovah's Witnesses—two young men—called, she talked with them for nearly two hours.

Mr Couch, of Clymping Dene, Feltham, Middlesex, said: 'My grandmotl·er told me that the Witnesses told my mother she would meet everyone else in 1977, when the world was going to end.'

Coroner Dr John Burton: 'This must have stirred things up a lot.'

Mr Couch: 'Yes. It was the final straw.'

The coroner recorded a verdict that Mrs Couch killed herself while suffering from depression. He said the visit from the Jehovah's Witnesses appeared to have been well meant, 'but, if you knock on someone's door, you don't know the state of their health'.

Last night Mr David Sibrey of the Jehovah's Witnesses News Service, said: 'We have not heard anything about this case. Our belief is that the current world system, not the world itself, must end. And we do not give a specific time, like eight years, for this. I can't imagine any of our people saying everyone will be dead in eight years.'

I asked Ulysses V. Glass for his comments on families who had been split by the preaching of Jehovah's Witnesses. He said: 'Jesus himself said that would happen. He said that father would be set against son, mother against daughter.'

I then asked him about those who had killed themselves because they had understood Jehovah's Witnesses to have said that the world was going to end shortly. He said: 'We baptize 120,000 people a year. How many records do you have of people committing suicide? What do you want to happen to the 120,000 who are baptized? Should we forget them because one or two are mentally disturbed? If we quit going from door to door, those 120,000 would not have been baptized. I don't believe that people in their right minds will commit suicide. I believe they will have a resurrection and then will have a real opportunity of accepting what is offered because they won't be mentally sick.'

'Is it not dangerous, telling people that the world as we know it will end in a few years?' I asked. 'Could that not be misinterpreted?'

'It could be misinterpreted,' he said. 'If we go too far, we could run into problems, like we did in 1925.'

It occurred to me that already too many others had run into problems. In the space of two years in England alone, where a quarter of the world's population of Witnesses lives, one couple was on the verge of divorce, two had divorced already and two mothers had committed suicide. Those were cases which had been mentioned in the newspapers or on television and it seemed reasonable to assume that they represented only a sliver of the sadness which the Witnesses' prophecy must have caused. I wondered, too, what the leaders would say, if their latest forecast should be proved as inaccurate as its predecessors. For those whose cases I have quoted, apologies would come a little late.

I must stress that I am not criticizing the sincerity of those who call from door to door. They are the friendly people whom I met at Wembley Stadium and I am sure that, as individuals, they would wish harm to nobody. It is absolutely reasonable, too, that their religion should mean more to them than anything or anybody, for they believe in it implicitly and want to share it. Nevertheless, tragedies have followed their visits. People have killed themselves. If these Witnesses have delivered their message correctly—which some of their leading spokesmen seem to doubt—then their message must be wrong. If they have delivered it incorrectly, then it is time for those who run the organization to reconsider its training programme and to restrain members from preaching to the public until they know precisely what they are doing and what they are saying. They are dealing with human beings, some of whom can be highly strung, nervous, depressed or, as Ulysses V. Glass said to me, mentally disturbed. It simply is not good enough to weigh the number of converts against the number of suicides.

One reason for these instances of crassly clumsy proselytizing, though it is no excuse in my view, is the fact that Jehovah's Witnesses frown upon education. Ulysses V. Glass told me: 'We don't disapprove of higher education, but it doesn't centre its interest on the Bible. All the sciences support the theory of evolution, for instance, and that is contrary to biblical teachings. The primary reason for the position we take on education, of course, is that we don't think it is absolutely necessary for those who expect to be ministers and we encourage people to take up the ministry full-time. We believe that this world system is going to go down in just a short time, anyway; so why should we encourage them to prepare for it? They would be better off preparing themselves for God's work.'

That view was borne out by Esther Rantzen's television programme, on which, incidentally, the Witnesses refused to appear. They told her that no member could take part in a presentation which included those who had been disfellowshipped, excommunicated. In fact there were no disfellowshipped Witnesses on the programme, only those who had left voluntarily. That, however, made no difference to the attitude of the Watch Tower hierarchy. She raised the question of education and one ex-Witness said: 'I was told there was no point in studying because

Jesus Christ was coming in the near future.' Another said: 'Being a Witness cost me my career. They persuaded me to stop my "A" level studies.'

As a result of that policy, many of the door-to-door preachers are academically unsophisticated. It seems clear that on occasions they say too much to the wrong people and bring fear into their lives. On other occasions, according to Esther Rantzen's programme (which bore the stamp of thorough research), they say too little. Until a person is committed deeply, they make no mention of such controversial matters as the fact that Witnesses refuse blood transfusions.

They take this stand because it says in Genesis: 'Every moving thing that liveth shall be meat for you; even as the green herb have I given you all things. But flesh with the life thereof, which is the blood thereof, shall ye not eat.' They interpret that as a ban on the consumption of blood in any way. They eat meat because in the vast majority of cases it has been properly bled after slaughter, but they would refuse chickens which had been killed by strangulation and rabbits, for instance, that had been snared. To take blood by transfusion is regarded as eating it and therefore they refuse it not only for themselves, but for their children. According to medical evidence given at inquests, children have died where a transfusion could have saved them and, as a result, both in Britain and America, doctors sometimes seek court orders so that they may give a transfusion without the permission of the parents.

The Scriptures, however, are not the only basis for the Witnesses' arguments against transfusion. They maintain that doctors give transfusions too freely; that there are occasions when they can be harmful; and that they do not seek other methods which would be just as good, if not better. When I asked Ulysses V. Glass, for instance, to confirm that parents who are Jehovah's Witnesses would allow their children to die rather than permit them to have a transfusion, he said: 'In the vast majority of cases the child would not die, if the doctor would do all the things that are available to him.'

'What happens to parents who allow transfusions in these cases?'

'We exclude them from the congregation. God may forgive them, of course, but if He doesn't, they will not be resurrected.'

'What happens to the child?'

'That is up to God. He probably would not hold the child responsible, unless, of course, it was at an age at which it could understand.'

'Is the parent thinking of his own spiritual future or that of the child?'

'His own. The Bible makes the parent responsible. The parent gave that child life and the parent will have to answer to God for it.'

What about transplants? In London I was told: 'We regard it as tantamount to cannibalism. All the trouble over transplants has been over rejection. No human body wants to accept flesh or substance from any other human body and the same applies to blood from another person. It's a foreign body.'

That is a matter of opinion—of violent debate, indeed—and the Witnesses, I suppose, are entitled to make their own decisions when it is their own lives that are at stake. I cannot understand, however, how divine merit can be earned by a person who places another life in jeopardy for the good of his own soul. Even more difficult to accept is the idea of a mother and father sacrificing their own child's chances to enhance their own spiritual future. I suggest, therefore, that Witnesses have an imperative duty to make their views and their arguments on these points clear to potential members in the early stages of the conversion course, even if it should mean the end of the lesson.

Their policy with regard to blood transfusion and, to a lesser extent, education, of course, has earned them severe public criticism. Yet in spite of that, in spite of the appallingly bad press which they have had since the rumbustious days of Charles Taze Russell, they have continued to expand, not only numerically, but economically. Their London headquarters cost over $720,000. In Brooklyn they own large chunks of extremely valuable property and, when I was there, they had just bought Squibb's factory, which was renovated only four years earlier at a cost of $2,000,000. Local residents will be glad to hear that they intend to start the factory's famous public clock again.

That gesture to both sentiment and utility is more than counter-balanced, however, by the behaviour of some Witnesses when they acquired some other Brooklyn property at Clark Street. It reveals a dedication to their cause which permits nothing to stand in the way of salvation, but it shows, too, that charity and tolerance are not conspicuous in the lives of some of these soul-savers. According to the *Brooklyn Heights Press*, tenants at One Clark Street had to file more than one complaint with the Rent Control Commission against their landlord, the Watch Tower Bible and Tract Society, charging that its agents had posted offensive religious material in the hallways of the building. The report continued:

Last Friday, said Seymour Holland, a tenant, on the even of the Jewish high holy day, large illustrated religious calendars were placed in the public halls of the building which together with other literature espoused the theme that respective religions of the various tenants in the building were false and should be assaulted.

Mr Holland said that he asked the Witnesses to remove the offending material, but they refused. 'I did so myself on the premise no one's religious beliefs should be forced upon another.' The landlord retaliated by immediately reposting the material, he said.

'The religious issue here is a recent one,' Mr Holland said. 'What has happened is that the Jehovah's Witnesses have been harassing us in an effort to oust us from current rent-controlled apartments for a long time. They have tried various tactics, including the installation of mechanical equipment and compressors directly under the apartments of tenants. Garbage cans are dragged deafeningly through the halls at all hours. Our building has been converted into a dormitory for more than one hundred printing factory workers. All this has proved quite successful—more than half the original tenants have fled in horror,' he said.

'The latest effort represents an escalation in their continuing pattern of harassment tactics by openly inviting assault on the religious beliefs of the tenants in a manner which is calculated to insult and offend. And in the public halls. And on every floor of the building.'

The tenants of One Clark Street will draw little comfort, I suppose, from the fact that the Jehovah's Witnesses lash out at most religions without discrimination. The words I quoted from President Knorr early in the chapter were mild compared with those in their magazines, their chief target being the Roman Catholic Church; and what happened in One Clark Street did not strike Ulysses V. Glass as of any great importance.

'We bought that property for expansion,' he told me. 'When we told the tenants we wanted to expand, they wouldn't move. It is true that some of our people put up calendars in the lobby. They showed pictures of the Jews coming out of Jerusalem, but they weren't put up to antagonize.'

'But they did antagonize,' I said, 'and these people pay rent.'

'It was probably a small thing to do,' he said, 'but those people don't belong there. They've been given official notice to get out. It's our home. I don't think, however, that the calendars were put up for reasons of spite.'

I doubt if the local residents would agree with him there. What interested me even more, however, was where the Witnesses get the money to buy up such large chunks of New York. When I raised the question, I found that their attitude to money seemed very idealistic indeed.

'There is no tithing,' I was told. 'We never take up a collection. Did you ever hear of Christ passing the plate around, when he was on earth? There is simply a box in the back of the local Kingdom Halls, where the Witnesses worship, and people put into it what they like.'

Yet there seems to be a strange form of ambiguity about this question of money. A year after he had formed The Watch Tower Society, Charles Taze Russell wrote in its magazine: 'We never solicit donations. Those who possess this world's goods and are wholly consecrated need only to know how they can use it. Donations to this fund should be specified.'

To me that means: 'We don't ask for your money, but send us some.' That impression was reinforced when I discussed the matter with Ulysses V. Glass. 'All contributions are voluntary,' he said. 'When it comes to buying property, we always pay cash. We don't go to banks. We just write letters to the congregations, when we need money for some project, and all those who want to give or lend can do so. They consider it a privilege to help God's work. In the very first issue of *Watch Tower* magazine, Charles Taze Russell said: "If this work is of God, it will prosper. We will never ask anyone for money." I don't know any other religious organization which operates that way.'

For some reason that I cannot understand, they believe that they never ask for money, but merely tell the faithful when they need it. The point does not seem to worry the faithful, however, for they always send it and quickly, too. They do not even seem interested in what happens to it, because, when I asked Ulysses V. Glass the tatty old question about balance sheets and financial statements, he told me: 'Our income and assets are not published because it is something which our people accept. The work costs money, of course, because we must have buildings and we must buy paper. We are very cautious, however, when it comes to spending. We economize by planning carefully and doing as much as we can ourselves—making our own ink, for instance. We own three farms, which provide us with food, for that is the most economical way of doing so.'

He was referring there to the administrative staffs who live in what the Witnesses call Bethel Homes and certainly those people do not spend money on themselves. In the United States all those who live in get the same amount, from President Nathan Knorr right down to the cleaners. It is $14 a month, plus their keep, plus an unextravagant clothing allowance. In Britain they get the equivalent in sterling—£5 16s 0d a month. I gather that they simply do not worry about money, but live together, as one of them put it, like one big happy family. Ulysses V. Glass told me: 'All the directors of the society, including the President, live here. So does every worker in our side of the operation—cleaners, printers, clerks and so on. We all eat at the same table and we all have our own rooms. Only those couples with children live out.'

There are a few full-time ministers, who get $50—about £20—a month and must pay their own travelling expenses. They augment their meagre income by selling the literature which cascades from Brooklyn and which they get at a special rate. Occasionally someone in the congregation will give them a little help, but generally their lives are happily frugal. They are expected to put in at least 150 hours a month, which is fifty more than the unpaid ministers, who include about half the total membership and who must support themselves and their families by doing part-time work, for religion is their main business.

There, indeed, is the final paradox. The organization is extremely wealthy, but those who work for it are extremely poor. Most of the money is ploughed back into the printing presses, the property and the other instruments which they use to win recruits to fight in the Battle of Armageddon, but only pennies go into the preachers' pockets. The rules are strict, but the members are loyal. Those who break away insist that they were brainwashed, but they still glance back, sometimes wistfully, sometimes a little fearfully. When Esther Rantzen asked one ex-Witness whether he felt completely free from the organization's influence, he said: 'I don't know. At the back of my mind there's always a doubt, always a feeling that maybe they're right after all. I can tell you this: if I suddenly saw the sky filled with chariots, I wouldn't be surprised.'

I do not believe in the teachings of Jehovah's Witnesses. I do not approve of some of those teachings. I deplore their constant, acid attacks on the religious beliefs of other people. Yet I must report that their behaviour is governed by absolute faith and a deep sense of duty to which no financial strings, no material rewards are attached. The reason they do not subscribe to a policy of live-and-let-live is because to them it would mean live-and-let-die when the world is hit by that Great Tribulation in the middle seventies. Even if they should be wrong about it once again, I am quite sure that they will search their hearts, their scriptures and their chronology charts for an explanation. They will find one. They will believe in it implicitly. They will continue knocking at door after door, smiling, talking and refusing to go away even when the smoke is pouring from the ovens and the chops are charred.

13: THE QUIET ONES

I had covered many miles and many sects. I had been shown guaranteed, pre-shrunk, pre-packaged faith in svelte, sin-free wrappings, ready for distribution around the world through courtesy of radio, television, tapes, discs, glossy magazines and love offerings. I had watched Christian soldiers, self-styled and otherwise, in many different uniforms, blanket-bombing with their spiritual defoliant to expose a million devils, spraying indiscriminately their very own, personalized, sanctified napalm that would cauterize evil, no matter how cunningly it was camouflaged, no matter how loudly it protested its purity.

I had met men so sure of their products that they smiled sad smiles at the thought of all the firms next door, peddling cheap imitations. I had sat with them in their opulent offices, proof, surely, that theirs was the only truth, and had heard them murmur of their competitors: 'I don't want to calumniate, but . . .' I had listened, while they had talked softly about their humility, their charity, their tolerance, their efficiency, their success, their exclusive hot-lines to heaven. I had spoken, too, with those who paid the telephone bill and I had seen the stars in their eyes as they gave. For months, indeed, I had lived in this world of power-driven sanctity, billion-dollar, supermarket salvation—buy now, pray later—and the time had come for me to seek out the amateurs, if, indeed, any of them still survived.

It was, perhaps, an extravagant ambition, but one well worth achieving, for it took me into a beautiful land, where there were no radios, no television sets, no glossy magazines, no telephones, no motor cars, no electricity, no computers, no commercials. It was the land of the Old Order Amish people, who had stepped gracefully, but with determination, off the time machine over two centuries earlier and had been living happily ever since without any of these man-made miracles.

Around 1740 they had sought and found refuge in America from religious persecution in Switzerland, the Palatinate and Alsace Lorraine. Today they are settled in nineteen States and across the border in Canada, living much as they did in the eighteenth century, minding their faith, dressing as their forebears dressed, scarcely touched by progress. Not only have they survived, but they have progressed. They are not clinging to the edge of a rapidly spinning world by the articles of their religion alone. They are expanding. Somehow they have managed to stand back from the gruel of civilization; and if the sight and the sound of it makes them sad, their sighs are gentle.

I met them in Pennsylvania-Dutch country, where they speak still their low German dialect and where, incidentally, the gruel gets thicker daily. I drove through a natural beauty that was being stained with motels and snak bars, olde-arte shoppes, antique boutiques, second-hand car lots and souvenir showplaces, garnished with red neon and brash chrome, all the ingredients of what an American friend calls International Ugly. Yet all the sludge of commerce could not drown the music of the place names—Blue Ball, Paradise, Bird-in-Hand, Fertility and Intercourse, the last so called because it is right in the centre of the area, a spot within horse-and-buggy distance of most Amish homes which use no horseless carriages.

The backroads, too, had survived the onslaught of the cash registers and there I met the Amish, refugees now from a different form of persecution, the tourists who hunt them with cameras, clicking and flashing and whooping: 'Gee . . . aren't they just like hippies?' They are more than an embarrassment to the Amish, who wear their hair and beards long. They are an occasion of sin, for these strict people regard photographs as un-Godly vanities, graven images.

Yet the tourists cannot be blamed for here is a phenomenon as remarkable as a moonshot. I drove from Intercourse to Paradise and, rounding a bend, I lost a couple of centuries, as I met a horse and heavily hooded buggy driven by a man who could have stepped right off the set of an historical film. He wore a stiff black hat with a rim at least three inches wide. His clothes were black and Dickensian. His face, grave above a vast black beard, was medieval. Beside him sat his wife, a traditional black apron over her black clothes, a white poke bonnet firmly on her head, demure, isolated, insulated against today. I slowed the car for the sake of the horse and the driver raised a hand in solemn acknowledgement. Memories of earlier perfidies have left the Amish suspicious of any stranger—*auslenner* they call him—but suspicion never corrodes their courtesy.

Why did they stop the world and step off? How do they survive? I asked no Amishman because to do so, I felt, would be to cross a line that they had drawn gently but firmly between themselves and others. I have no doubt that I would have been received politely, but I would have been invading a privacy that is being threatened from too many sides already.

Instead I took my curiosity to perhaps an even better source, to Daniel M. Glick, who had been an Amishman, but is now a Mennonite,

a member of a related sect that is relatively less severe, but still too
strict for most. He was verging on seventy years of age when we met,
small, but sprightly and brimming with happy tolerance. He had left
the Amish, but he had not lost his love for them.

When he told me of his reasons for leaving, however, I realized that
the tolerance of both Amish and Mennonite went hand in hand with an
uncompromising self-discipline. The opinions of others were respected
always, but never accepted without conviction; and the source of that
conviction was a literal interpretation of the Bible, from which Daniel
quoted constantly as we spoke.

'Our ways parted for a number of reasons,' he told me. 'One was the
practice of *meidung*. That means excommunication or, more literally,
shunning. It is a very severe punishment for those who break the rules
of the church consistently, do not confess publicly and do not repent.
The community, even the immediate family, will not speak with a
person who has been shunned, or eat with him, or have any relations
whatsoever with him. Religion embraces all aspects of life, social and
otherwise; and so *meidung* is hard to bear. The Amish, however,
believe that they are doing what the Bible teaches in I Corinthians, 5:11:
"If any man that is called a brother be a fornicator, or covetous, or an
idolater, or a railer, or a drunkard, or an extortioner; with such a one
not to eat." The Amish believe that means nobody must take a tangible
meal with him. We Mennonites say that Christ ate with publicans and
sinners in Galilee, but did not take communion with them. He shunned
them, excommunicated them in a spiritual way only.'

'Why do they turn away from progress?' I asked. 'Are there reasons
for that in the Bible, too?'

He smiled, nodded and quoted: '"Be not conformed to this world;
but be ye transformed by the renewing of your mind that you may
prove what is good and acceptable and the perfect will of God"—
Romans, 12:2. "Love not the world, neither the things that are in the
world. If any man love the world, the love of the Father is not in him".
That's I John, 2:15. The Amish put a premium on stability rather than
change, of course, because for so long they were persecuted.'

'And that applies to motor-cars and telephones, to radio and television?'

'They do not believe these signs of change are wicked in themselves,'
he explained. They feel, however, that the trend of life they bring will
break down the family unit and the basic structure of their community.

The young would hear and see new worlds on radio and television. With the automobile they could visit them. They could learn too much of these other lives and their faith could die. It is the same with their clothes. They dress as they have for centuries because they do not care to be changing all the time to styles designed to achieve more glamour and less modesty.

'We Mennonites believe that man should make use of all the science he has created for the good of men and the glory of God. We have automobiles and we have TV, though I must say that I do not quite approve of many of the programmes. So do the new Amish, a break-away group, who feel much as the Mennonites do. They are trying to promote Bible study among outsiders. The Old Order Amish frown upon that because they do not believe in proselytizing.'

'Do they never travel by car or use a telephone?'

'They will use an automobile if the journey is absolutely necessary and the distance is too far for a horse and buggy,' he said. 'But they will never own one and they will never drive one. Always they will get a non-Amish person to drive. In similar circumstances they will use a neighbour's telephone, but will not have one on their land or in their house. Sometimes you will see them using public telephones, but those are never on their property.

'Many of their views differ from those of the rest of the world. They believe, for instance, that no Amish child should go to school beyond eighth grade. That was as far as I got because my father was an Amishman and I did not part from them until I was twenty-three years of age. They hold to what I Corinthians, 3:19 teaches: "For the wisdom of this world is foolishness with God . . ." They say also, of course: "Who needs more schooling to go farming?" They have a point there because they are fine farmers. They know, too, that secular, outside influences could influence their young people and so most of their youngsters go to one-room schools, run by the Amish themselves. School always opens with readings from the German Bible, followed by the Lord's Prayer in German. First graders know little English, only Pennsylvanian Dutch, which has nothing to do with Holland, of course, but is a German dialect. Fourth graders right through eighth grade must be taught High German because their Bibles are not written in Pennsylvania-Dutch. I spoke no English until I went to school.

'Mennonites do not have such a strict view on education. We feel that we have a responsibility to this generation and that we cannot fulfil it without more education than our forebears. Though I left school early, I've been reading ever since. All my children have been to high school and all except the oldest daughter to college.'

The Amish, however, know nothing of compromise. When the authorities insisted that their children should have a twentieth-century education, they would not budge from their ways and went to jail for their principles. Impressed by their sincerity, the education officers relented and Daniel told me: 'From the eighth grade now, the boys work on the farm and the girls in the home. Reports on their work in these spheres are sent to the authorities.'

They were in trouble again with the Federal Government over their strict attitude to the question of insurance. They do not buy life insurance, for instance, saying: 'Who are we to gamble on the life-span Almighty God affords us?' They shun property insurance because their money would be integrated with that of non-Amish policy holders and the book of James says: 'Be ye not unequally yoked together with unbelievers . . .' They refuse to have lightning rods on their houses, regarding them as 'the efforts of little man to thwart the will of God'. For similar reasons they make no social welfare payments, which in the eyes of the law are compulsory. For a while the revenue authorities reacted to what they regarded as stubbornness by seizing Amish cattle. Then Congress passed a law absolving members of the sect from both social welfare payments and benefits.

They are staunch pacifists, signifying their belief in the principles of non-violence by using hooks and eyes instead of buttons which they regard as symbols of military uniform; and here again they base their ease upon the words of the Bible: 'For the weapons of our warfare are not carnal, but mighty through God to the milling down of strongholds.' To this they add the texts 'Be gentle unto all men' and 'Whosoever shall smite thee on thy right cheek, turn to him the other also'. Traditionally they have chosen to suffer loss or injury rather than protect themselves by physical force; and the authorities have accepted their stand. Amishmen are not liable for military service.

Taking an oath under any circumstances they regard to be contrary to the Scriptures, for the book of James teaches: 'But above all things, my brethren, swear not.' The book of Matthew adds weight to this with: 'Swear not at all.' If the Amish had any truck with the courts, this might cause minor difficulties, but such circumstances never arise. They never go to court to defend themselves, even when sued unjustly because I Corinthians, 6:7 states: 'Now therefore, there is utterly a fault among you because ye go to law one with another. Why do ye not rather take wrong? Why do ye not rather suffer yourselves to be defrauded?' Mennonites, too, hold this belief and Daniel Glick told me softly: 'I would not sue my brother.'

A Bible text and dignified tradition govern every Amish act. Pride and ostentation they regard as the worst of human faults, with laziness and frivolity not far behind, which is one reason why they retain their ancient mode of dress, most of which is home-made. The men wear full flowing trousers without the vanity of a crease. Their coats have no lapels and fasten up to the neck. They wear no ties and sometimes their shirts have no collars. They never wear gloves, not even in the depth of winter; but, when summer comes, they condescend to swap their big felt hats for broad-brimmed straw hats which their womenfolk weave and shape from rye grown on their farms. Occasionally they are decorated with a thin black band, but the main reason for the switch from felt to straw is utilitarian. Felt is too hot. They can work better with a lighter hat. Belts are never worn, pants being held up by broad home-made suspenders.*

The Amish women wear long dresses and always an apron, for Genesis says: '. . . and they sewed fig leaves together and made themselves aprons.' The apron is white for unmarried women and black after marriage. A *kapp*—prayer veil—must be worn at all times, for Corinthians says: 'Every woman who prayeth or prophesieth with her head uncovered dishonoureth her head.' They never cut their hair, for Corinthians again says: 'It is a shame for a woman to be shorn or shaven.' The books of both Peter and Timothy forbid them to wear jewellery of any kind. The sleeves of their dresses, needless to say, are always long. Broadly speaking, children wear similar clothes, though the rules with regard to the *kapp*, the prayer veil, vary according to age. It is white for girls until they are twelve. Once they become teenagers, it must be black. When they marry, it changes back to white again.

Their religious services are even less ornate than their clothes. Not only do they have no cathedrals, but no churches, meeting instead every second Sunday in a different Amish home. The ground floors of most homes are partitioned into rooms and the partitions are removed to allow the congregation—known as a *kair*—to gather. It is seldom more

* *Anglice:* braces.

than twenty-five families, for when it reaches that strength it divides, as space is limited. The service begins at nine o'clock in the morning—sometimes even earlier—and goes on until after noon, embracing two sermons, silent as well as spoken prayers and testimonies from ministers.

It may sound grim, but 'going to preaching' is, in fact, a friendly affair, an important part of the social fabric. When the service is over, the families sit down to a robust meal and a good long chat, for conversation remains an essential part of life in the absence of such pale substitutes as television. Generally, however, work and religion are the twin themes because the Amish draw no line between work and religion and life. It is almost mandatory that all teenagers seek full membership of the church and from April to October they are given religious instruction on church days. They are taught, also, personal deportment and the *regel und ordnung,* the rules and regulations which will be their guidelines. At a ceremony in the autumn, they pledge themselves formally to these laws and are baptized.

Amish homes could be described, I suppose, as spartan and wholesome. The food—all home-grown—is excellent and the helpings are large, for Amishmen say: 'We eat a lot, but then we burn up a lot.' It is regarded as fuel, rather than an indulgence. Furniture is rigid and heavy padding is discouraged. Musical instruments are banned, though the Amish sing a good deal. Toys and particularly dolls are home-made, for they frown on 'boughten dolls', perhaps because their smart clothes and pert faces would not fit an Amish household, perhaps because they are frivolities on which money should not be wasted. Certainly the Amish dolls I saw were solid and homely.

Children go to bed at half-past eight or nine o'clock and the family gets up with the sun. In the long winter evenings, the father reads aloud from the old German Bible, while the mother sews or braids rugs. Children play checkers or study. The family unit is strong, with three generations sometimes occupying the one building. New wings are built on to the main homestead—the Grossdawdy House—as the old folks retire and the sons marry.

Amish weddings bear little resemblance to those elsewhere. There is no wedding gown for the girls, for instance. With their Sunday best, however, they wear a pinafore in white organdie. After the wedding it is put away and never used again until death, when it becomes one of the burial garments. After the ceremony, which traditionally takes place in November when the harvest has been gathered, there is no honeymoon. The couple, indeed, do not set up house together until the following spring. Every weekend, however, they visit friends and relations to receive wedding presents—*haus dier*. Divorce is virtually unknown in Amish circles. On the other hand, no matter how devoted a couple may be, they must never show any outward sign of affection, for that would shock the prim, dignified Amish people. They have large families, sometimes as many as sixteen children.

In one respect there is a slight parallel between Amish and other lives. The young men may not have souped-up cars to impress their girl friends. When they reach the age of sixteen, however, they are given a fast, sporty buggy with a spirited thoroughbred horse. The wheels have no rubber tyres, for that would be leaning towards the soft life; but they spin fast enough along the country roads. The boys take their girls to church in their buggies and to the social festivals which from time to time brighten the otherwise austere lives of these people.

Steady courting has a ritual all of its own, according to a leaflet issued by the Pennsylvania Historical and Museum Commission. In it John A. Hostetler writes: 'The boy who has a steady girl will see her every week or two on Saturday nights. Before entering the home of his girl he makes sure that the old folks are in bed. When his flashlight focuses on her window, the girl knows that her lover has arrived. They spend several hours together in the "sitting-room", but they do not leave the home on such occasions.'

Saturday night is courting night presumably because these are an industrious people and every member of the family works. From an early age boys help their fathers on the farm, learning not only agriculture, but other skills, such as carpentry. Girls help in the house. Sometimes a boy will go out to work for a neighbouring farmer or as a carpenter's assistant. A girl may become a maid in a nearby house. 'They're much in demand,' Daniel told me, 'because they're hard workers and reliable.'

The extraordinary feature of these restricted lives—one which bewilders an *auslenner* like me—is that they glide along so smoothly without the oil of modern science. Amishmen will not own tractors. Their ploughs are drawn by a three-mule team. They use windmills and water wheels, but not electricity. A stationary steam engine is permitted to drive a belt for threshing, filling the silo, steaming tobacco beds to kill insects and to purify the ground before the seed is planted. Occasionally a farm will have a single-cylinder petrol engine which may be used for milk coolers, corn shelling, ice-cream and butter churns or to drive the domestic washing machine; but these are their only concessions to progress. If any agricultural technocrat were left with those tools to make a living, he would have the bailiffs on his land after the first harvest; but Amish farms invariably are the envy of the area. Ask an Amishman how he manages so well with little more than the sweat of his own brow and his know-how to help him and he will point to the Bible which is heavy with texts about what should be done with the land. The earth, it insists, must be replenished and subdued. He will quote, too, the Gospel According to St John, which states in chapter nine, verse four: 'I must work the works of Him that sent me, while it is day: the night cometh, when no man can work.' Verse twenty-three of the twelfth chapter of Leviticus has a profound affect on the Amish farmer. It reads: 'The land shall not be sold for ever: for the land is Mine: for ye are strangers and sojourners with me.' He accepts every word of that literally and therefore, while he may buy land for himself or his son, he will never sell it.

Amish farms and therefore Amish families are virtually self-supporting. They feed themselves with their own produce, canning, butchering and baking at home. Always there is a surplus, which is kept for church socials, hay-making and threshing festivities, weddings, or for unexpected emergencies—barn fires, floods and so on. When catastrophe destroys the property of one Amish, his fellows believe that he is bearing the wrath of God for the whole community. So they help him, practising what they hear preached—that they are their brother's keepers. They care for their own—the old, the sick, the infirm and the needy. Even their enemies have a fair chance, for verses twenty and twenty-one of chapter twelve in Romans read: 'If thine enemy hunger, feed him; if he thirst, give him drink: for in so doing thou shalt heap coals of fire on his head . . . Be not overcome of evil, but overcome evil with good.' The only people who merit no help from the Amish are the lazy, the feckless, for sloth is a deadly sin. No moment must be wasted, for it is governed surely by some *regel* or *ordnung* or text. Women, for instance, are taught that they 'must do good or read God's word in their spare time, instead of taking care of canaries, gold-fish or house flowers'.

It is better to wear out than rust out, of course, if I may squeeze a West of Ireland phrase into the profusion of Pennsylvania Dutch; and Daniel Glick bore me out. 'Yesterday I was talking to an Amish lady of ninety-four,' he told me, 'and she's still making rugs.' Then he took me to an Amish graveyard where the simple headstones—no marble angels, no Forest Lawn frolics there—told of many who died in their seventies, eighties and nineties. I would not say that many of them had been laid low by lightning or twentieth-century status symbols, like ulcers or thrombosis, but rather that they had been buoyed up by a peace of mind which Daniel paraphrased neatly and unconsciously as we walked among the graves.

'Life is sweet,' he said. 'I love life, but I have no fear of the transition.'

There walked a contented man. Were the younger generation like him? Were they deaf to the throb of the jukebox? As they sat on the hard furniture at home, were they never tempted by soft cinema seats? Working from dawn to dusk in the fields, did they never think of jacking it all in for an easy city job with big money? I said to Daniel: 'Amish curtains are thick. Do the youngsters never feel like cutting their way through them?'

'Of course they do,' he said. 'They "go gay", as the Amish say. Some buy cars and hide them in garages down town. I've heard that some even buy little transistor radio sets and hide them in their big hats. Some, of course, leave altogether and are shunned. As a matter of fact, more have left in the last twenty years than in the fifty years prior to that.'

'Doesn't that mean that the sect is dying?'

He shook his head. 'Amish people live long,' he said, 'and they have big families. There is another point. Family bonds are stronger than many youngsters think. They go, but they hanker after the old life after a while and so they come back. There was one young fellow who was shunned because he joined the Air Force, took up arms. He travelled all over the place, flying those supersonic jets, but he couldn't fly fast enough for the memories. There was a girl he remembered and there was more. There was a way of life. Loyalties lie deep and love for the old ways is real. When he left the Air Force, he came back, confessed to his Elders, repented and was received back into the faith again.'

'Where is he now?'

'He married his girl. He has settled down. He's driving a horse and buggy now instead of a supersonic plane, ploughing his land behind a team of mules. He's learned that happiness doesn't depend on travelling fast and far.'

'So you think that the Amish will survive, expand, perhaps?'

'I think so. Their life is simple, but it satisfies.'

I was glad to hear his verdict, for my respect for these people was growing fast. They were true to their principles and they forced their views on no one. The world might think them odd, might laugh at their ways; but they passed no judgement on the world. They knew the meaning and the value of love, but they asked for no love offerings. They practised what they preached, but they respected the right of the *auslenner* to live otherwise.

Yet I had found little sympathy for them on my journey, little understanding of their philosophy. 'The Amish are selfish,' the clerical jet-set had told me. 'If they believe that theirs is the only truth, they should shout it from the mountain tops. That is their duty. What good do they do, cutting themselves off from the world?'

Daniel Glick had an answer to that question, a number of answers, in fact. He told me: 'The Amish know the real meaning of charity. They care not only for their own, but for all who are in trouble. Like the Mennonites, they have a disaster service which operates throughout the United States and Canada. Whenever there is a catastrophe, they will hire a bus with a non-Amish driver, go to the area and help in a meaningful way. When hurricanes hit the Mississippi area, the Amish were there. When a tornado swept across Indiana, bus-loads of them set out from here immediately. They give all they can to the world in times of need and they give willingly. That is the meaning of love.'

I had one last question. I asked him: 'How do their ministers live? Are they paid well?'

'They are paid nothing,' he told me. 'They work at other jobs to support themselves and their families, but they ask no money for teaching the word of God.'

I thought of the vast, streamlined offices I had seen in the months immediately behind me, of the discreet, expensive suits, the smooth cars, the private executive jets, the art galleries, the museums, the universities, the electronic jungles, the voices with a million intimate, strident words, amplified a million times in so many languages, the collection plates that were never empty, yet never quite full enough for those who jingled them. The men who ran these empires were the professionals, who knew about the business of religion. Then I thought of the horse and buggy people, the amateurs who simply knew about religion. As I thanked Daniel and said good-bye, I could not help wondering what the businessmen would think of him. Would they listen? Would they understand? Would they learn?

What would they say, for instance, if he quoted to them, as he had done to me, a text from Corinthians which the Amish have woven into their lives? It is:

'Charity suffereth long and is kind; charity envieth not; charity vaunteth not itself and is not puffed up . . .'

ACKNOWLEDGEMENTS

Consciously, subconsciously and unconsciously, hundreds of people helped me with this book. Even those who felt that my cause was unworthy kept the boat moving by rocking it; and here I would like to thank them all, though I face the task with terror. My memory is uncouth and I can but beg the forgiveness of those whose names I may omit.

The religious organizations I visited I shall take in alphabetical order, leaving that of merit to greater, braver men. Thanks in the first place, therefore, to all in A. A. Allen Revivals, Inc., including the Rev. Dr Roy M. Gray and the Rev. Dale Moran in Miracle Valley, the ebullient Raymond G. Hoekstra who travelled from Dallas to Chicago to meet me and, of course, the Rev. A. A., himself, who saw me only briefly, handling me with care, as if I were a rusty, unexploded bomb from World War Two.

The aims of Christian Crusade were laid bare for me by the Rev. Dr Billy James Hargis and various kindly soldiers on his staff at Tulsa, Oklahoma. The next 'C' must be for Chicago, for there I found a number of groups, all working for a common cause, which was to give a fighting chance to so many who had been deprived of it for so long. There was the Rev. John Fry, for instance, whose courage has made him an honorary member of the ghetto, a high tribute. I am grateful, too, to my hosts in the Chicago Theological Seminary, particularly to Bob Meyners, Craig Rennebohm and Tim Liefer. A little later I was helped by the Rev. Clyde Miller and Don Rose of Project Equality. Just to demonstrate how ill-conceived was this alphabetical system of mine, I now must backtrack to New York to thank those of the Project's Eastern Division, the Rev. Herbert H. Mardis and Ken Daly, before returning to Lake Michigan to pay tribute to the staff of a somewhat similar group, Operation Breadbasket.

Next comes the Church of Latter-day Saints. Among the Salt Lake City Mormons who answered my naïve questions so patiently were Henry A. Smith, who entertained me to lunch in Brigham Young's old house, and Dr Whitney Young, who not only conducted me on a tour of Temple Square, but took me to his Chapel for service and his home for an excellent dinner, cooked by his wife, who turned out to be no mean theologian. In London, Dr W. Dean Belnap, President of the British Mission, and Elder David Hamilton guided my faltering feet.

Men and women of the Delta Ministry in Greenville, Mississippi, showed me a little-known world of hunger and oppression. I stayed in the relaxed home of the Rev. Henry A. Parker and his charming wife, Jean; and he fed me to his experts: Mrs Thelma Barnes, the Rev. Rims Barber, Joe Harris, Jake Ayers and James Hodges.

George M. Wilson of Minneapolis; Dr Walter Herbert Smythe and the Rev. Gil Stricklin of Atlanta; and the amiable Bill Brown of New York were my pathfinders in Billy Graham country. The Rev. Charles Duarte in Hollywood brought me up to date on the International Church of the Four Square Gospel, which may not hit so many headlines since the death of its colourful founder, Aimee Semple McPherson, but still packs a strong Pentecostal punch. The work of the Jehovah's Witnesses came to me through courtesy—and here it is an appropriate noun—of Ulysses V. Glass in Brooklyn, New York and, in London, of Andrew Heley and David Sibrey.

Bob Jones University I glimpsed under the cautious guidance of Robert Harrison, its Public Relations Director, who was allowed to show me the cloister, but not to grant me an interview. If the straitjacket chafed, he showed no pain and I recall only his politeness. Those at the Oral Roberts University in Tulsa were less shy, despite the fact that their founder had embarrassed some by switching from the Pentecostals to the Methodists, and there I was sated with facts, glossy literature and details of remarkable progress by Gerald Pope and Lee Braxton.

To the founder of the Universal Life Church in Modesto, California, the Rev. Kirby J. Hensley, I owe a special debt of gratitude because he brought a gale of laughter into what too often was a solemn enough journey. I soon learned, indeed, that many men of God take themselves very seriously, which is surprising in view of the amount of time they are supposed to spend pondering the infinite. The Rev. Kirby J. is much too wise to make such an elementary blunder, though here, of course, I am biased because he made me a Minister, which added tone to the proceedings.

My next stop, both alphabetically and geographically, was the World Wide Church of God in Pasadena, California. There the Rev. Dr Garner Ted Armstrong and anonymous members of his staff showed me an oasis of theological academy that would have scalded the hearts of the early Christian monks, who preferred to spend their lives in beehive huts; but the Church, I suppose, must move with the times, even unto executive jets and colour television.

Here endeth the list of religious organizations mentioned in this book.

I must add, however, that I have a sneaking suspicion that Don Rose and Ken Daly of Project Equality, and Bob Meyners of the Chicago Theological Seminary are Reverends, too, but I know that they will not sue me for failing to ask for their precise rank. In the fields where they work, titles carry little kudos. Results are more important and these they are getting.

To salute all those others who helped me, I switch from alphabetical to the geographical order of my journey. I began in New York which, as usual, failed miserably to live up to its reputation of being tough, rough and rude. I would like to thank Ed Fisk, Religion Editor of the *New York Times*, and his colleagues in another department of that fine journal, Pat Reynolds and Nat Goldstein; Peter Frieburg of United Press International; Moira and Jack Casey, together with their dog, Fionn MacCumhaill, who ate my brief-case in fun rather than in anger; Jonathan Ward of CBS; Adrienne Claiborne, who cast a fine-mesh net for me and hauled it in, busting at the knots with facts; Mike McCann, who is a neighbour of Rev. Ike, but not exactly his confidant; David Maysles, who with his brother, Albert, made a fine film, *The Salesmen*, about those who sell Bibles; Warren Marr II of the National Association for the Advancement of Colored People; David Michaels and his wife, who regaled me with many fine stories, both religious and otherwise; the Rev. Dr Wyatt Tee Walker, Pastor of Canaan Baptist Church of Christ on West 116th Street and Second Vice-President of the Southern Christian Leadership Conference; the Rev. Charles S. Spivey, Jnr., Executive Director of the National Council of Churches' Department of Social Justice; the staff of the Brooklyn Library, who dug deep into their shelves for me; the staff of Americans United for Separation of Church and State, who opened their files for me; and Morris Herman, a Brooklyn cab driver, who agreed to drive me through the Manhattan jungle even though he was off duty and then refused the fare because, he said, I was a visitor in town.

In Boston, George Collins, Religion Editor of the *Boston Globe*, marked my card early, accurately and without hesitation. His colleague, Brendan Malin, who, incidentally, once was a colleague of mine on the other side of the Atlantic when the world was young, helped vastly, too, as did his wife, Joan, who not only fed me and housed me, but washed my shirts. In Pennsylvania-Dutch country, Donald M. Derlinger and that fine old philosopher, Daniel M. Glick, introduced me to the lives of the shy Amish folk. In Chicago, Mark Benney, a hard-punching columnist in the *Hyde Park-Kenwood Voices* and an Englishman, if you don't mind, hacked some heavy rocks from my path before I moved on to Salt Lake City, where Jack Goodman of the *New York Times* organized my scattered life with an easy efficiency, bred from experience and tolerance. Many people in this city, indeed, came to my aid, particularly Hal Molitor of the New House Hotel; Jack Gallevan, publisher of the *Salt Lake Tribune*; Jerald and Sandra Tanner of the Modern Microfilm Company, which produces, among other journals and books, *The Salt Lake City Messenger*, a publication which tilts constantly at Mormonism and manages to survive in a spot which the Mormons virtually own; Dr C. H. Hardin Branch, Professor and Chairman of the Department of Psychiatry at the University of Utah College of Medicine; Sam Weller, who appropriately runs a bookshop, and his colleague, Wilfred Clark. I was helped, also, by some poly-gamous Mormons, but obviously I cannot mention their names here.

In San Francisco, graceful city that it is, Wallace Turner of the *New York Times* and author of *The Mormon Establishment*, gave me the bene-fit of his time and knowledge. In Los Angeles, Sally O'Quin of *Life* magazine gave me sane advice, as did her friend Solvega Gross. Had it not been for my old friend Bridget Parker, and her husband Leigh, however, I might be in Los Angeles yet, lost and sending up distress rockets. Bridget drove me with expertise and patience throughout the bewildering maze that city is and the pair of them put up with my erratic comings and goings in their Palos Verdes apartment. Ollie and Geoffrey Barr watched over me in Laguna Bay, aiming me in all the right directions; and as I moved South to Del Mar, this delicate, difficult task was taken over by Joyce and Shelley Hendler. It was Shelley, a research scientist at the University of California, who found in a scienti-fic journal the St Jerome quotation at the beginning of the book, a feat unique enough to earn him a doctorate, if he had not got one already. In Tulsa I was helped by Dr Gordon V. Drake, who—quite coinciden-tally, I promise—resigned from Billy James Hargis's Christian Crusade two days after my arrival; and by Gordon Fallis of the *Tulsa Daily World*.

Though the scene is set in the United States, much of the writing was done in Britain. I am grateful to Daphne and Grant Henke, who with extreme generosity gave me a temporary base; to Geoffrey Glassborrow who always was good for the nerves, and his wife, Aileen, who came up with the title; to the Rev. Raymond Lee of the Church of St Mary of

Bethany in Woking, who was willing to give me his advice no matter how often or at what hour I asked for it; to Esther Rantzen of the British Broadcasting Corporation, who put together a thought-provoking programme about the Jehovah's Witnesses; to the International Publishing Corporation's library staff at Endell Street, London; to David Ascoli of Cassell and Company, Limited, who should join my wife and my family in the College of Cardinals whenever there are vacancies; and to Mary Griffith, who—by chance, I swear!—went into hospital soon after she learned that she was to edit this book, but happily came out fighting as subtly and as effectively as ever in time to get a stranglehold on the manuscript.

Inevitably I milked shamelessly newspaper and magazine files on both sides of the Atlantic for background material. My thanks, therefore, go to *The Times,* the *Daily Mirror,* the *Sunday Mirror,* the *Daily Mail* and the *Daily Telegraph* in Britain; and in America, *The New York Times, Life* magazine, *Time* magazine, *Tempo, Playboy* magazine (for the words of the late Bishop James A. Pike), *Church and State,* official organ of Americans United, *Christianity Today, The Watchtower, The Brooklyn Heights Press, The Salt Lake Tribune, The Deseret News, The Rockford Morning Star, Concern* magazine, *Eternity* magazine, *The Nation* magazine, *Soul Force,* journal of the Southern Christian Leadership Conference and *The Greenville News*; and in Ireland, *Nusight* Magazine.

Among the books which I consulted were *No Man Knows My History* by Fawn Brodie (Alfred A. Knopf, New York); *The Lion of the Lord* by Stanley P. Hirshon (Alfred A. Knopf); *The Making of a Crusade* and *Those Who came Forward,* both by Curtis Mitchell, and both published by Chilton Books of Philadelphia and New York; *The Strange Tactics of Extremism* by Harry and Bonaro Overstreet (W. W. Norton and Co., Inc., New York), *The Story of My Life* by Aimee Semple McPherson (International Correspondents, Hollywood), *Crusading Preacher from the West* by Dr Fernando Penabaz (Christian Crusade, Tulsa); *Billy James Hargis Tells It Like It Is!* by Billy James Hargis (Christian Crusade); *Billy Graham* by John Pollock (Zondervan Publishing House, Grand Rapids, Michigan); *Evangelism, Inc.,* by G. W. Target (Allen Lane, The Penguin Press, London); *The Negro in Mormon Theology* and *The Mormon Kingdom,* both by Jerald and Sandra Tanner and published by Modern Microfilm Company, Salt Lake City; and *Celestial or Plural Marriage,* written and published by Joseph W. Muller, Salt Lake City.

INDEX